A

CHRONICLE

of

CANNINGTON

Originally

The Somerset Farm Institute

1921 - 2004

Hon. Editor: GAJ Loxton BA (Hons), NDA, NDD.

AD 2006

British Library Cataloguing in Publication Data
A catalogue record for this book is available from the British Library

Published by Snowdrop Publishing & Cannington Old Students Association
COSA
The Cottage at Rackley
Compton Bishop
Axbridge
Somerset
BS26 2HJ

Printed by the publisher

ISBN 0-9537458-4-8

Front Cover

Clockwise from top left

Cannington Court
Cannington College
A Shire type horse
Stan Acland B.E.M.
Ewes and lambs (1930s)
Dairy Shorthorn Herd (1930s)
Oats in stook (1930s)
Walled Gardens from Church Tower

Centre

Cheese display at Cannington
1954/5 Dairying Course with Miss Monie
(key, p.147)

Back Cover

Wheat field, June 1939

(Left to Right)
Captain D.M.Wills, Agricultural Committee Chairman
Mr G.Furse, Lecturer & NIAB Crop Recorder
Sir R. Dorman-Smith, Minister of Agriculture
W.D.Hay, Principal, Somerset Farm Institute

Dedication

This Chronicle is dedicated to Students, Former Students, Lecturing Staff and Farm and Domestic Staff of the Somerset Farm Institute, the Somerset College of Agriculture and Horticulture, and Cannington College.

Reminiscence

Could I but just return again,
And spend that year anew,
Now that I finally realise,
The happy year that flew.

The high stone wall, the gardens warm,
Where oft I used to roam,
The old church clock, with chiming voice,
The big hall with it's dome.

The trapdoor leading to the roof,
And Burnham now in sight,
The darkened quad, the Warden's voice
"Put out that 'something' light".

The comradeship and friendliness,
No atmosphere of strife,
Just really living for a space,
Before the whirl of life.

So thus I still recall and see,
With memory's tireless eye;
And oft and oft I've wished to be
Back at the S.F.I.

Brenda Underwood. 46/47D (Clarke)
(from 2004 COSA Magazine)

Editors Acknowledgement

The Editor expresses his gratitude to all those whose letters, articles, reports and photographs have been used in this Chronicle, including newspapers and periodicals, some now defunct. They provide the essential elements of this Chronicle.

MEMBERS OF THE COMMITTEE AND STAFF OF THE SOMERSET FARM INSTITUTE, CANNINGTON.
Back Row, left to right—Mr E. A. Austin (Member of Committee), Mr B. C. Brewer (County Poultry Instructor), Mr A. D. Turner (Horticultural Superintendent), Mr A. Daunton (Member of Poultry Committee), Mr J. W. Dallas (Assistant County Agricultural Organiser), Mr T. H. Golledge (Member of Dairy Committee), Mr P. S. Syme (Vice-Principal of the Somerset Farm Institute), Miss E. M.
Second Row left to right—Mrs E. J. Sage (Member of Dairy Committee), Mrs S. Brookes (Matron of the Somerset Farm Institute), Miss E. M. Monie (Head Instructress in Dairying), Mr J. H. White (Member of Dairy Committee), Mr J. H. Mackie (Member of Dairy Committee), Mr W. J. H. Porter (Member of Committees), Miss N. Collier (Poultry Instructress), Miss I. Welch (Assistant Dairying Instructress), Miss M. C. Taylor (County Dairying Superintendent).
First row, left to right—Mr W. D. Hay (Principal of the Somerset Farm Institute and County Agricultural Organiser), Mr James C. Morland (Chairman of the Horticultural Committee and Member of Dairy and Poultry Committees), Mr D. M. Wills (Deputy-Chairman of the Agricultural Instruction Sub-Committee and Chairman of the Poultry Committee), Capt. the Hon. T. H. Watson (Chairman of the County Agricultural Committee and Chairman of the Agricultural Instruction Sub-Committee), Mr J. H. Cann (Chairman of the Farm Committee), Colonel M. Locke Blake (Chairman of the Dairy Committee), and Mr A. F. Somerville (Member of Committee).

The Founders and Early Staff of Cannington

(From The Western Daily Press, Saturday, March 12th 1927)

iv

CANNINGTON
OLD STUDENTS
ASSOCIATION

COSA ACKNOWLEDGEMENTS

In thanking the contributors to this book we would mention in particular the following:

Nan Eaves, Norman (Benny) Goodman and Caroline Woolley for gathering information and supporting the Editor

To the 'grand old men' who spent happy hours reminiscing with us and giving inspiration : Jack King; John A Hebditch; Reg. Shattock and Ronald White.

To another group who talked to us about their 'good old days':
Our President, Ivor Crane; Cy Bartlett; Brian Thomas; Nina Heywood; Roger Lane and
Stanley Chedzoy

To Stuart Brookfield, our Patron, who wrote about so many past staff and students.

Also the many contributors that our Editor contacted personally, including Bob Webb, Keith Williamson-Jones, Michael Bell, particularly Annie Sherborne and Katriona King - and anyone else who has pointed us in the right direction.

Thank You All

We would also like to thank:
Alistair of Microbitz, Wells, for his patience and support with the computer files;
Nick of Mendip Vale, Horrington, Wells, for being so helpful with the binding of the Chronicle and
Sally of St. Andrew's Press, Wells for persuading us to 'not spoil t'ship for ha'pporth o' tar'

Last, but not least, we would like to give our heartfelt thanks to our Editor, Geoff Loxton.

Our thanks to Geoff are very special as he is neither a past student nor staff member. His patience and fortitude during the compilation of these pages has been exceptional and it has to be said that, were it not for him, this book would not exist.

OUR SPONSORS

When promoting a project of this sort it is always good to know that people believe in what you are doing and so it has been especially pleasing that the county of Somerset has had so much faith in our work.

We would like to thank to following organisations for their financial support.

The Royal Bath and West of England Society
Bridgwater Agricultural Society
Yeovil Agricultural Society
Frome & District Agricultural Society
Dunster Show Society
Mid Somerset Show Society
North Somerset Agricultural Show Society
Somerset County National Farmers Union
Somerset Federation of Young Farmers

Bridgwater College – Business Development Area
Bridgwater College – Head of Area, Cannington Centre

Somerset County Council
Sedgemoor District Council
West Somerset District Council
Taunton Deane Borough Council

The Levels and Moors Leader Plus Project

CONTENTS

Foreword

The County Agricultural Colleges, of which Cannington has been such an outstanding example, played a vital role in the agricultural revolution which took place during the second half of the twentieth century. By the time that the college was officially opened in 1921, farming had been in the doldrums - barring an all too brief revival during the First World War - for over half a century. The result was that techniques were old-fashioned and out-dated, morale was low, innovation almost non-existent and education neglected. The ignorance that Miss Saker and Miss Masters had to overcome in raising standards of milk hygiene in the early days of Cannington says all that needs to be said about the frankly backward attitudes that prevailed at the time.

But in Somerset at least, the 1920s proved to be the darkest hour before dawn. The creation of the Milk Marketing Board in 1931 - very largely at the instigation of farmers from Somerset, be it noted - paved the way for a revival in dairy farming, and by that time, the first crop of Cannington students were back on their farms, fully equipped to take advantage of the opportunities offered by better times.

Then came the Second World War, the threat of starvation and the Dig for Victory campaign. Cannington was given over to the Womens Land Army for the duration - thereby playing its own, very significant part in the war effort. But out on the farms, the knowledge passed on at the College during the previous decades was bearing fruit.

Not immediately, maybe. The farmers of Somerset clearly had not been listening carefully enough to what W.D. (Bonny) Hay had been telling them about the value of re-seeding worn out pastures and proved to be distinctly recalcitrant when it came to putting in the plough! But after a stern talking-to from the Minister of Agriculture, and under the determined leadership of the War Agricultural Executive Committee, they got the message, and for thirty years and more, the industry hardly looked back.

The 1940s and 50s were great days for farming, and great days for Cannington. The pursuit of self-sufficiency under the protection of guaranteed prices, gave the farming community a sense of purpose and a feeling of being valued that it had not known for many decades. It was a time of great excitement as well as of great self-confidence, as the advance of mechanisation and the development of new techniques led to a faster pace of change than farming had ever known before. Once again, Cannington was at the forefront, not just in teaching the new techniques but in giving its students the open minds and hunger for knowledge that meant that they could make the very most of all the exciting new opportunities.

But all good things come to an end, and by the time that I first came to know the College, in the early 1980s, doubts were already beginning to set in about how many young people would be needed in future in an industry that was becoming the victim of its own success as surpluses piled up, and concerns for the environment began to take precedence over concerns for the national food supply. As it turned out, it wasn't the problems of farming that posed the greatest threat to the College, so much as the problems of further education funding.

I was appointed Governor - to my intense pride - just after the Further Education Funding Council had taken over control from Somerset County Council. It proved to be a case, not so much of out of the frying pan into the fire, as out of a comfortable embrace, and into a stranglehold! At every meeting we seemed to be faced with the prospect of still deeper cuts in staff and investment to meet the demands of our financial masters. It was a truly depressing time, and it is enormously to the credit of the College, and to everyone working there at the time, that in spite of all the external pressures and internal upheavals, the quality of the teaching was maintained throughout.

Now the College is under new management, and the industry it serves is undergoing yet more turbulence and uncertainty. Yet on both counts I am optimistic. Our new adoptive parent, Bridgwater, is well managed and successful. Horticulture - which has always been one of Cannington's greatest strengths - has been identified as a priority and much-needed investment is being directed accordingly.

As for the future of farming, there are good grounds for believing that we may have turned the corner. As the balance of supply and demand for food gets tighter, and the demand for land for the production of energy crops grows apace, all the signs are that the productive capacity of British agriculture and horticulture will be needed - and valued - over the years ahead.

That does not necessarily mean that we will need huge numbers of extra people in the industry, but it will mean that those working in farming and its related industries will need to be trained to an even higher level than before, with commensurate rewards. Farming is a dynamic, modern industry. It needs dynamic, modern people.

"A Chronicle of Cannington" is a record of endeavour, dedication, educational excellence and great humour. It reminds us of how much agriculture and horticulture, in Somerset and beyond, owes to the College and to the people who made it what it was. But - as has ever been the case with Cannington - we must look forward, not back. That the future for Cannington and the industry it serves will be different and challenging, no one doubts. But that does not mean that it need be any less worthwhile or rewarding than the illustrious past that this splendid treasure trove of records, recollections and photographs so wonderfully evokes.

Anthony Gibson, NFU Regional Director (Cannington Governor, 1993-2001).

Introduction

This is a Chronicle rather than a History, although some people may prefer to see it more as a "Scrapbook" - into which it has seemed to develop as additional material has gradually arrived!

Fifteen chapters record names, facts and events connected with Cannington over the years, largely in chronological order, but with less explanation and analysis than a History would provide. Historical explanation is confined to the economic background, particularly about that forgotten period between the wars, when British farming was in a terribly depressed state, before the Milk Marketing Board came to the rescue, and before W.D.Hay ("Wild White" or "Bonnie" or "Boots" or "Tripod" Hay) and the Cannington staff in Somerset re-created a belief in the future. Some explanation of that period seems necessary: how many younger folk, even those few who have been taught British History at school, know that the price of farm produce (and land) halved between 1921 and 1924? Come to that, how many older folk know it? And how many realise that the Milk Marketing Board, which was abolished in recent years as an alleged monopoly, could have again united scattered milk producers in their unequal battle with milk monopolies, now in the new guise of supermarkets?

To the initial fifteen chapters is added a 'Pictorial Medley' of people and activities covering the whole period, comprised mostly of undated photographs which throw additional light on many aspects of Cannington life. There follows a 'Roving Miscellany' which adds items of general relevance which would have unbalanced the chronological chapters. (It includes the Editor's "Excuse, Explanation and Apology", which attempts to justify a non-Canningtonian editing the Chronicle). This is followed by official annual photographs of students and staff, although, sadly, some photos and most names are missing. Finally, there is an Appendix covering later years, not least Stuart Brookfield's 1952-1985 memories, added to by Caroline Woolley, Nan Eaves and Benny Goodman from COSA magazine reports.

The primary aim of the Chronicle is to commemorate the educational, advisory and experimental complex which Cannington was for the best part of a century, and it is written particularly for students, lecturers, farm and domestic staff, past, present and future. Most ex-Canningtonians are now scattered all around the country, indeed around the whole world, where, in pursuits associated with agriculture, horticulture and food generally, they have no doubt contributed in no small measure to the efficiency and well-being of farmers and gardeners world-wide, and thus helped the many malnourished people of the Third World to feed themselves.

So Cannington is internationally known. But its students have spread abroad not only geographically: they are also widely dispersed throughout associated professions. Farmers, farm managers, farm specialists (shepherds, herdsmen, horsemen and pigmen of both sexes), tutors and lecturers, advisory officers, research scientists, equine experts, veterinary specialists (with small, large and even exotic species) cheese-makers, dairy factory managers, scientific advisory staff, consultants, farming equipment makers, salespeople, nutrition scientists, hoteliers: Cannington has produced them all - and more. To these potential readers must be added many other people who have a regard for Cannington, including those who count themselves as unlucky for never having been students there in their youth, and to whom Cannington was a beacon for the future. The Editor is one of those, having been eager to go to Cannington at sixteen, although prevented from entry by a combination of brucellosis and Adolf Hitler.

The Chronicle attempts to convey the unique "family" flavour of Cannington student life, foreshadowed in Brenda Underwood's *"Reminiscence"* in the opening pages. Her verses reveal a happy community, and reading them may convince "modern" educational theorists that happiness does not depend on an absence of rules, and that simple structured learning, unsullied by modern psychological theory, will be remembered for a lifetime. A note in the obituary column of the 2005 COSA magazine says it all. Barbara, wife for fifty years of George Hale (46/47), market gardener and dairy farmer, wrote that they read Brenda Underwood's poem together only the day before he died.

Finally, the Chronicle records the tremendous contribution W.D.Hay, A.D.Turner and their staff made towards victory in the Second World War of 1939-45, by organising the successful "ploughing-up" and "dig for victory" campaigns among Somerset farmers and householders. These campaigns were major factors in greatly increasing British food production and thus scuttling the German U-boat offensive, which aimed to starve Britain into submission.   GAJL

Background

Cannington is fairly centrally placed in Somerset

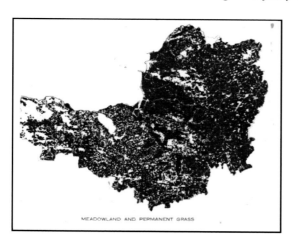

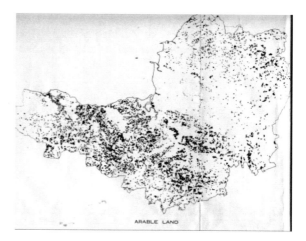

Grassland in Black

Arable Land in Black

(from the 1938 Land Utilisation Survey of Britain; Part 86: Somerset)

Sheeted Somerset Cows, owned by John Weir of West Camel, 1860.

(from Victorian Somerset, 1979 - by courtesy of 'Somerset Heritage Service')

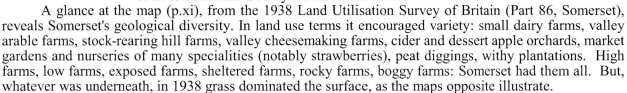

"Plough Permanent Grassland ?" - Madness!
(The Science of Husbandry Rejected)

A brief reference is made here to the complex geology of Somerset and the many forms of production this encouraged. The origin of the preponderance of permanent grassland and the lack of native breeds of livestock in the County are also considered.

A glance at the map (p.xi), from the 1938 Land Utilisation Survey of Britain (Part 86, Somerset), reveals Somerset's geological diversity. In land use terms it encouraged variety: small dairy farms, valley arable farms, stock-rearing hill farms, valley cheesemaking farms, cider and dessert apple orchards, market gardens and nurseries of many specialities (notably strawberries), peat diggings, withy plantations. High farms, low farms, exposed farms, sheltered farms, rocky farms, boggy farms: Somerset had them all. But, whatever was underneath, in 1938 grass dominated the surface, as the maps opposite illustrate.

But Somerset was not always largely permanent grassland. Before the Reformation much of the county had been held in extensive estates by the Crown and then the Church, and still had large acreages of arable land in medieval open fields. But at the Dissolution of the Monasteries in the 1530s much of Somerset came into the hands of lawyers and merchants who established small gentry estates and governed the county as JPs and sometimes Deputy Lord Lieutenants. Being businessmen with an eye to a bigger rent roll, they encouraged their copyholder tenants to exchange, consolidate and enclose their open field arable strips to provide more grassland for increasingly profitable cattle, sheep and horses (demanded by the growing urban population for food, clothing, footwear and transport). The resulting small fields suited livestock but not unwieldy six or eight-ox plough-teams, and corn went down as grass went up.

However, some of the new men were modernisers. In the 1630s, one of them, John Hippisley V, ploughed his Ston Easton demesne farm with four-ox teams, applied lime and marl, folded his Mendip sheep on cereals at night, cut out the fallow and introduced a rotation including legumes - peas and vetches. He recorded his methods and even noted his costs and stocking rate. If only John's son had published these notes as Edward Lisle's son did his father's jottings a century later in Hampshire! Lisle's *Observations in Husbandry*, with Jethro Tulls's *Horse-hoeing Husbandry* in Berkshire inspired mixed farming in those two counties, but in Somerset John Hippisley's unpublished methods were soon forgotten.

After John Hippisley's time, few Somerset landlords took any interest in "husbandry" and even penalised tenants who ploughed grassland. While East Anglia had 'Turnip' Townshend and Coke of Norfolk, and while Hampshire and Berkshire had Edward Lisle and Jethro Tull, who all encouraged mixed farming in their counties, Somerset had no populisers of the plough. Moreover, while Leicestershire had Bakewell and Yorkshire had Bates and the Collings brothers to encourage upgrading livestock, Somerset had no improving breeders. Farmers in the county were still guided by pastoral custom, passed from father to son, so permanent grass and scrub livestock prevailed. John Billingsley's 1794 forward-looking *General View of Agriculture of Somerset* was not popularised, as were such works in other counties, and if Somerset farmers heard of scientific husbandry, most ignored it scornfully as "mere book-learning". However, to "read, write and reckon" was thought essential (and respectable), and farmer's sons were made to take excessive pains over the "3Rs" (example overleaf). While Agricultural Societies and Shows encouraged improvement, there was no individual "leading light", of 'corn' or of 'horn'. Otherwise the native "Sheeted Somerset" (opp.) might have become a top dairy breed instead of disappearing altogether!

Even as late as between the wars (1918-39), many Somerset farmers were still guided by pastoral tradition. Cows were often milked outdoors in summer, an old custom encapsulated in the ancient name of Somerset. Most dairy farms were solely of permanent grass, with only a few hens and a pig or two as a gesture towards mixed farming. Grassland 'hained up' for mowing might be chain-harrowed and rolled in March, to level ruts and depress stones, but that was all the "cultivation" attempted. Few farms had enough ploughland to justify much expenditure on heavy horses or equipment, so arable cultivation remained backward. Candles and oil lamps lit farmhouses, while hurricane lanterns made deep shadows in the farm buildings they allegedly illuminated. Few farms had piped water or paved yards. There was no electricity.

Traditional Somerset livestock farming entailed hard work with long hours, seven days a week, 365 days of the year, leaving little time or energy for learning about modern methods, even if visits to "model" farms had been possible or suitable books easily available.

But help was at hand. Far-seeing members of Somerset County Council were to come to the aid of farming, and a major factor was the establishment of the Somerset Farm Institute at Cannington in 1921.

No Science or Husbandry in this 1850s school book *(Now in the County Record Office, Taunton)*
ONLY *"READING, WRITING AND RECKONING "* *(see previous page)*

The Application.

Master James Sexton
was born in the year of our Lord 1846. In what year will he be of age? — — — —

$$
\begin{array}{r}
1846 \\
21 \\
\hline
\end{array}
$$
Ans. = 1867

I took a farm on lease for 35 years, at the rent of £318. 7. 6. per annum — how much shall I have paid at the expiration of the lease

$$
\begin{array}{ccc}
£ & s & d \\
318 . & 7 . & 6 \\
\end{array}
$$
$7 \times 5 = 35$
$$
\begin{array}{ccc}
2228 . & 12 . & 6 \\
& 5 & \\
\hline
\end{array}
$$
Ans. £ 11143 . 2 . 6

I pay my servant 3s. 9d. per week — what do his wages amount to in a year? — — —

$$
\begin{array}{cc}
s & d \\
8 . & 9 \\
\end{array}
$$
$10 \times 5 + 2 = 52$
$$
\begin{array}{ccc}
4 . & 7 . & 6 \\
& 5 & \\
21 . & 17 . & 6 \\
. & 17 . & 6 \\
\hline
\end{array}
$$
Ans. £ 22 . 15 . 0

A privateer of 250 men took a prize which amounted to £125. 15. 6. to each man — what was the value of the prize? — — — —

$$
\begin{array}{ccc}
£ & s & d \\
125 . & 15 . & 6 \\
\end{array}
$$
$10 \times 5 \times 5 = 250$
$$
\begin{array}{ccc}
1257 . & 15 . & 0 \\
& 5 & \\
6288 . & 15 . & 0 \\
& 5 & \\
\hline
\end{array}
$$
Ans. £ 31443 . 15 . 0

Required the sum of the squares of 46 and 64

$$
\begin{array}{r}
46 \\
46 \\
\hline
276 \\
184 \\
\hline
2116 \\
\end{array}
\qquad
\begin{array}{r}
64 \\
64 \\
\hline
256 \\
384 \\
\hline
4096 \\
2116 \\
\hline
\end{array}
$$
Ans. 6212

343 Bushels of wheat at 6s. 3¼d. per bushel. — — —

$$
\begin{array}{cc}
s & d \\
6 . & 3\frac{1}{4} \\
\end{array}
$$
$7 \times 7 \times 7 = 343$
$$
\begin{array}{ccc}
2 . & 4 . & 0\frac{3}{4} \\
& 7 & \\
15 . & 8 . & 3\frac{1}{4} \\
& 7 & \\
\hline
\end{array}
$$
Ans. £ 107 . 18 . 0¼

A robbery being committed on the highway, an assessment was made in the neighbouring hundred for the sum of £386. 15. 6. of which four parishes paid each £37. 14. 2.; four hamlets £31. 4. each; and four townships £18. 12. 6. each — how much was the difference? — — — — —

$$
\begin{array}{ccc}
£ & s & d \\
37 . 14 . 2 \times 4 & = & 150 . 16 . 8 \\
31 . 4 . 2 \times 4 & = & 124 . 16 . 8 \\
18 . 12 . 6 \times 4 & = & 74 . 10 . 0 \\
\end{array}
$$

$$
\begin{array}{ccc}
£ & s & d \\
386 . & 15 . & 6 \\
350 . & 3 . & 4 \\
\hline
\end{array}
$$
Ans. £ 36 . 12 . 2

Finished February 2nd 1859.

Editor's Note: *These extracts from my grandfather's school book of the 1850s show great concern for the "3 Rs" but no evidence of any learning about farming - & no science either! James was at a Somerset boarding school for the sons of farmers, millers, etc. His family moved from Paradise (& Weavers) Farm, Emborough, to Rookery Farm, Chewton Mendip (ca.200 acres each) when he was three. Ten years later his father died, so he left school at 13 and farmed with the help of a nearby uncle . In 1887 he moved to Charlton Farm, Queen Charlton (300 acres). He died in 1924. His elder brother William farmed first at Grove Farm, Chewton Mendip, then at Cloford (Frome) for many years.*

GAJL

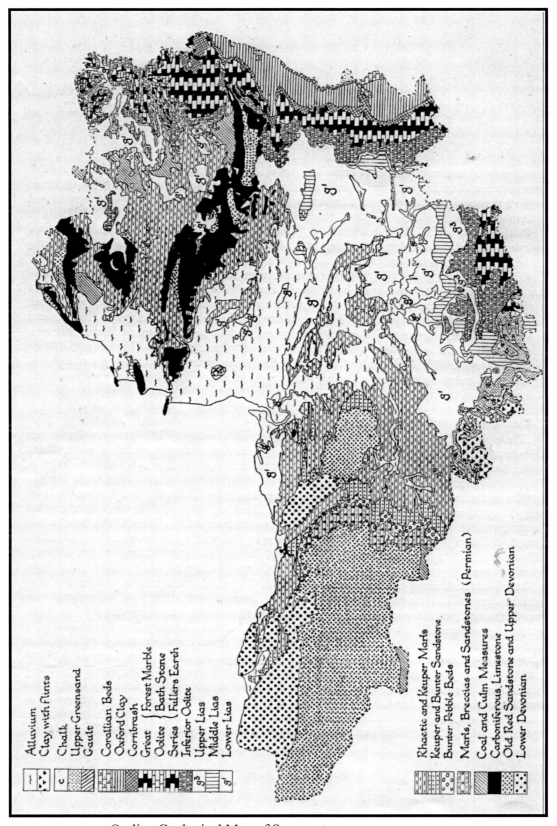

Outline Geological Map of Somerset

(The maps on pages viii, x, and xi are from the 1938 Land Utilisation Survey of Britain - Part 86)

Background

The Clifford Lease

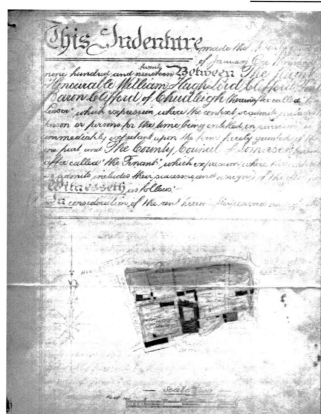

A Copy (reduced size) of part of the

Original 99 Year Lease of Cannington

(The shaded rectangle on the lower right of the plan represents the Burial Ground, to which access was reserved).

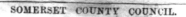

Perhaps the first open hint of the planned S.F.I.

(see opposite)

The Devon County

Dairy School

Iddesleigh, 1931
(see opposite)

Chapter 1. Beginnings

Following the Technical Education Act of 1889, Agricultural Education in Somerset became the responsibility of a Sub-Committee of the Education Committee of the County Council. There is no surviving specific evidence of activity in this sphere at that time, but 'G.E.S.' wrote in the Old Students Association 1929 magazine (No.2; p.19) that "It was in the year 1890 that a Cheddar Cheese School was opened at the Palace Farm, Wells, and for a number of years it was carried on by the Bath & West Society in conjunction with Somerset County Council, until it was taken over entirely by the County Council". There is no other record of such a school unless it is the students of this school who appear in the photograph on page 96. This photograph, contributed by Mr John Norton, is labelled "County Council Cheese School", and "about 1880".

Be that as it may, the Education Act of 1902 heralded change and resulted in Agricultural Education in the County coming under the aegis of the Agricultural Instruction Sub-Committee of the Agricultural Committee. Dairy, Horticultural and Poultry Sub-Committees were then established to lead the work in their respective spheres. In Dairying, for instance, Miss Dora Saker was appointed as early as 1914 as Itinerant Dairying Instructress - seven years before Cannington was founded - and carried out dairying advisory work throughout Somerset, arranging cheese-making schools in various centres around the county at co-operating cheese-making farms. Such dairy schools (see pp.2, 3) were not confined to Somerset, other counties, including Devon, were introducing similar forms of education in dairying. (see photo opposite).

But a big advance was on the way. In January 1919 an advertisement (see opposite) from the Agricultural Instruction Committee appeared in *The Times, The Farmer & Stockbreeder, The Scottish Farmer, The Livestock Journal* and *The Scotsman*. This is the first surviving public indication that a Farm Institute was being considered. It was a brave move in view of past failure. (*The Farmer's Express* of July 26th 1926 reported "Many years ago the County Council established an experimental farm which became notable for not how to do things, and in fact got to such a state that the Council sold out and searched around for more desirable agricultural educational methods." Further moves by the Council were recorded by Mr AD Turner, who was later for many years County Horticultural Superintendent:

In 1918 I was a temporary Civil Servant living at Taunton, having recently left the first Farm Institute established in Britain, situated in Caernarvenshire, North Wales. As I had helped to establish it from an overgrown estate with a castle mansion, it was expected that I might know, from experience, what was required to start a Farm Institute from, literally, "grass roots".

I was directed to go with the Agricultural Organiser to look over the Donyatt Estate near Ilminster, owned by the County Council, with a view to selecting a suitable site for the proposed Institute. I was to make an open report as a guide to senior officials who would make a detailed inspection. The County Organiser was careful not to express an opinion during our visit which might influence my report, but at the end of the day, when I said I would be making an adverse report, he said how relieved he was for he could not bear to think of working with that type of soil and without accommodation for students.

The County Council, ever in the forefront in agricultural education, was anxious to have a share in the grant available for the establishment of Farm Institutes. The local County Council member is said to have discovered Cannington Court, formerly a Nunnery and later a Catholic Remand School. The Councillor, Mr Cann, did not have to search far for his discovery, seeing that he fished for trout in the village stream. A farm of suitable size in the village of Cannington could be purchased by negotiation.

Again I was sent to view the situation and make a draft report, and although the farm was not in my province, I had the Cannington Court building and the gardens to examine. I had unwritten instructions to make a favourable report as this was regarded as the only possible site, although I knew of a site near Taunton which I would have preferred. There is a lot more to this early history of the Institute,

1. Beginnings

but it must be summed up by stating that my report was neutral and in due time the Council obtained a ninety-nine year lease on Cannington Court, and by change of appointment I was installed in Court House as Horticultural Superintendent in charge of Horticultural Education in Somerset..

(from the 1973/4 issue of the Old Students Magazine).

The first advertisement for County Organiser was followed in August of the same year by advertisements for the posts of Assistant County Organiser and Horticultural Instructor at £300 pa each, and in November for two posts of Dairy Instructress with NDD and practical experience of small cheese making at £150. There seems to have been indecision on the horticultural side because the post of Horticultural Superintendent was advertised in November 1919 at £350 (filled by Mr AD Turner) and at the end of 1920 the post of Horticultural Instructor (under the Superintendent) at £200 rising to £300. In April 1920 the Assistant Organiser's post was advertised again at £300 with rising increments.

Several of the advertisements state that preference would be given to those who had done military service although how recently demobilised men were expected to produce the required three recent testimonials is hard to say. In May 1921 a Dairy and Poultry Instructress was sought requiring NDD and practical experience for £150 rising by £10 increments to £220 and on October 21st the post of Matron was advertised, for a person between 35 and 45, who was able to teach elementary Domestic Science and manage the housekeeping and accounts. There is no surviving official record of appointments resulting from these advertisements, but Mr. JA Symon was named County Organiser in the tractor demonstration advertisement of March 1920 (p.3) and Miss Masters was clearly a dairying appointment (p.5).

Meantime initial educational activities in the farming sphere were already being prepared, presumably by Mr Symon. A first step, in October 1919, was the holding of a series of "Lectures in Agricultural Science", advertised as:

"A systematic course comprising Lectures in Agriculture, Agricultural Chemistry, Veterinary Hygiene and Fruit Growing will be conducted two nights a week throughout the coming winter at the following centres:

TAUNTON - Opening Lecture, Monday October 20th, at seven p.m.

HIGHBRIDGE - Opening Lecture, Tuesday October 21st, at seven p.m.

STOKE-UNDER-HAM - Opening Lecture, Wednesday October 22nd, at seven p.m.

YEOVIL - Opening Lecture, Thursday, October 23rd, at seven p.m.

The course is FREE and all interested are invited.

For further particulars apply to:-

THE COUNTY SECRETARY FOR AGRICULTURE,

5, Graham Road, Weston-s-Mare.".

Miss D. Saker

The next event, the last for 1919 - was a "SHOW OF SMALL CHEESES" made by the pupils of the West Somerset Cheese Schools, at Shire Hall, Taunton. It was to be held on Saturday November 22nd, "when PRIZES to the value of £10 will be offered", and "DEMONSTRATIONS in DAIRYING will be given" and "Miss D.G. Saker, late Instructress to the Somerset County Council will give an address on Dairying". (By this time Miss Saker had joined the Board of Agriculture). Admission was 1/- to non-exhibitors. Tea was also 1/- and the proceeds were to be devoted to the Taunton Hospital. The advertisement added: "All who are interested are cordially invited to attend".

A "Somerset Cheese School" along the lines of the "West Somerset Cheese Schools" was advertised on July 20th 1920: "There are at present vacancies for Students at the above School during the months of August, September and October. Fee for board, lodging and instruction £1/5/0 per week." Particulars obtainable from the "County Secretary for Agriculture, Cannington Court".

The obituary of Miss Dora Saker, sad though it is to read, throws fresh light on Somerset's itinerant or travelling cheese schools, and it also illuminates the background to the nascent Dairy world of those days. Miss Saker died suddenly in 1926 in Bridgwater Hospital after only a few day's illness, following an operation for an internal complaint. To the layman this sounds like appendicitis.

An obituary of Miss Saker stated, in part:

"Miss Saker first commenced training in Dairying subjects in 1904 when for two years she was at the East Anglian Institute of Agriculture, Essex, and one year at the Midland Agricultural College, followed by one year's practical work on the farm of the Hon. Alwyn Fellowes (then President of the Board of Agriculture). In 1909 Miss Saker was Assistant in Dairying at Lord Rayleigh's Dairies, Terling, Essex and later was appointed an Assistant Dairying Instructress at the East Anglian Institute, Chelmsford, Essex, where she remained upwards of three years. She subsequently took up an appointment under the Somerset County Council as Itinerant Dairying Instructress and from 1914-18 did a great deal of advisory work in the County and in connection with the County Cheese Schools.

In September 1918 Miss Saker resigned, having been offered a position as assistant Advisor in Dairying at the Board of Agriculture, in which capacity she remained until being re-appointed by the Somerset County Council Agricultural Instruction Sub-Committee as Superintendent in Dairying at the Somerset Farm Institute, Cannington, near Bridgwater, also arranging and supervising the work of the Dairying Instructresses in the county. Nominated by the Ministry of Agriculture and supported by the Somerset County Council Agricultural Instruction Committee, Miss Saker was appointed Delegate to the World's Dairy Congress in the U.S.A. in October 1923, and subsequently wrote an instructive report on the Milk Industry in the parts visited and lessons that might be learned from the methods employed there. Miss Saker contributed from time to time a great deal in the press on Dairying generally, and especially in connection with Cheese-making, and in the course of her work obtained an interesting series of figures on the analysis of milk. She was also the author of several books and pamphlets on Dairying subjects."

On Tuesday, March 23rd 1920, at 2 p.m. it was time to go out of doors, "weather permitting". The Agricultural Instruction Committee advertised a tractor and ploughing demonstration for that time at Huntspill Court Plough Field "by kind permission of Ford Tiley Esq." But presumably there was some uncertainty about weather conditions affecting the tractors' ability to plough - surely no one thought that Somerset farmers would be stopped by a bit of bad weather! The advertisement went out over the name of J.A. Symon, County Organiser, from Cannington Court, near Bridgwater, so by this time a chief had been appointed and his office at Cannington was in operation. Extra-mural activities continued:

Wrington - 16.6.20 - Lecture on the Improvement of Poor Pasture - By Mr T. J. Jenkin B.Sc.
of University College, Aberystwyth. (with the Wrington NFU).
Cheese School - Applications invited from farmers able to offer dairy facilities for the Cheese
School with accommodation for 5 or 6 students at a time "during the coming season".
County Cheese School - 1921: at Mr Tabor's Farm, East Pennard. Fee for instruction, board
and lodging 25/- per week.

At this time, in addition to widespread work throughout the county, a great deal of unrecorded pioneering work must have been done at Cannington by the County staff, old and new, planning and preparing the gardens, the student accommodation and the farm buildings - because the Farm Institute was opened officially on 25th October 1921, when the Principal was named as Mr. T. Limond.

Itinerant or travelling cheese schools continued to be a feature of the work of Cannington dairying staff even after the opening of the Farm Institute in 1921. Miss Saker's report of June 1922 listed "Travelling Cheese School" classes at Chew Stoke (13 students), 1st Winford (9), 2nd Winford (11) and Regil (10). All but one student at each centre received Certificates, a total of 39. Unlike in Sept 1919, the 1922 Small Cheese Show which displayed the work of these scattered cheese-making classes was held at Cannington, instead of Shire Hall, so that prospective students and other visitors would be able to see the modern facilities prepared there for student cheese-makers. Some of the students' cheeses would also be shown at the London Dairy Show, reported Miss Saker.

Scholarships for agricultural education at a higher level were now announced:
Eight Dairy Scholarships for 1920 at Lancashire Dairy School or Midland Dairy College, Derby.
Two Senior Agricultural Scholarships of two years at University College, Reading, or similar college.

The work of the County Council in the period leading up to the opening of the Somerset Farm Institute was described in the *Bridgwater Mercury* in its account of the event:

"The opening of the farm Institute marks the beginning of a new form of agricultural education in the county, which should prove most helpful to young men and women who intend taking up agriculture, horticulture or dairying as their future occupation. The Agricultural Instruction Committee of the County Council have for many years carried on a system of instruction in agriculture, horticulture and dairying, and for some time also in farriery and basket-making, but recently the latter forms of instruction were abandoned. By means of courses of lectures given during the winter evenings in rural centres, much useful information was conveyed to farmers and others regarding the principles underlying the practice of farming, gardening and dairying, the value of which has from time to time been fully acknowledged by the farming community. During the summer period practical instruction in cheese-making was given in the County Cheese School, at short courses given by itinerant cheese schools or in the farm dairies by visiting instructors, the value of which has been reflected in the improved quality and appearance of the cheese made in the county. Arrangements were also made to supply expert advice to farmers and others on any difficulty arising in the course of their work, and the advice given on soil treatments, manures, feeding-stuffs, seeds, insect pests and diseases of plants must have been helpful to many.

We are glad to know that these forms of instruction will be continued, and that every effort will be made to encourage farmers and others to take advantage of arrangements made to give them expert opinion and advice. Although such instruction has undoubtedly been a great service to farmers and gardeners throughout the county, the need for a more systematic form of instruction has been apparent to many. This, however, was only obtainable at universities and colleges, where the courses of instruction were often too long and of a much more technical nature than required by those who intended continuing farming on their own. Consequently instruction given in the universities and colleges, excellent as it is, has not been taken advantage of on a very intensive scale by practical farmers, and it is to meet the requirements of this class of pupil that farm institutes have been established. It was not until the end of the war, however, that funds became available for the establishment of such institutes, but at that time a substantial grant was placed at the disposal of the Board of Agriculture for the purpose of developing agricultural education and research throughout the country. County Councils were recommended to set up a comprehensive scheme of instruction for their area, and by providing farm institutes, where young men and women could obtain courses of instruction of a more elementary nature than is provided by colleges and universities, which would appeal more to the practical agriculturalist.

The Board of Agriculture agreed to pay three-quarters of the cost of establishing such institutes, and further to contribute two-thirds of the expenditure on the County Schemes of instruction, so that only a quarter of the capital expenditure on the institute and one-third of the cost of carrying out the scheme falls upon the county rates. It was left to the local authorities to prepare a scheme of instruction suitable for their own district, but in every case it was recommended that the instruction should be more or less of a practical nature, and that technical instruction should be limited to the explanation and demonstration of problems which arise in the course of farming practice.

In 1919 the Somerset County Council rented Cannington Court on a 99 years lease from Lord Clifford, and set about altering and adapting it to make it suitable for the purpose of a farm institute. (lease p.xii.). The history of Cannington Court dates back to the 12th century, and was at one time the home of the Cliffords. In more recent times, however, it has been used as a nunnery, and latterly as an industrial school. It has been entirely re-modelled, although the outside architectural features have been maintained, and it now provides accommodation for 10 women and 20 men pupils, besides the teaching and working staff. It is fitted throughout with modern conveniences, central heating and electric light having been installed. Each pupil will have a separate bedroom, and common rooms have been provided, and there is also ample class-room accommodation".

A dairy, fully equipped with modern appliances has been established, and will become the permanent dairy school for the county. The County Council have also rented on long lease Court Farm, which adjoins the Farm Institute, in order to provide facilities for instruction and demonstrations in the practical work. It may be described as a mixed arable farm, on which a small dairy herd is maintained. This will provide practical instruction in all branches of farming, and pupils attending the Farm Institute will be required to spend a portion of their time on the farm, where they will work under the direction of the staff, and receive constant instruction in the cultivation and management of crops and the care of various classes of live stock. The afternoons will generally be devoted to lectures and demonstrations in the classrooms and laboratories. These lectures will deal with agriculture in all its branches, dairying and horticulture, elementary science, land surveying, book-keeping, and veterinary hygiene.

Candidates for admission to the Farm Institute must not be less than 16 years of age, and preference will be given to applications from persons resident in the County of Somerset. Normally the school year will begin about the end of September, and consist of three terms of 14 weeks. Initially, owing to the buildings not being completed, it was impossible to open the institute before the 24th October this year, so the first term will be a short one. Three classes of instruction are provided as follows:

1. A full year's course in agriculture, which will include instruction in dairying and poultry-keeping, and a certain amount of instruction in horticulture.
2. A full year's course of instruction in horticulture for persons whose object is to take up market gardening or fruit culture.
3. A course of 14 weeks duration in dairying and poultry-keeping, running concurrently with the three terms of the agricultural course.

In addition to the above, however, it is proposed to have short courses in dairying from time to time as may be required, and also to provide instruction for short periods for the benefit of people who merely want to attend for short periods of instruction in practical dairy work."

For all the approval implicit in these press reports, the Agric. Instruction sub-committee was not without its critics. Some people opposed any government involvement in commercial spheres in peacetime and saw advisors as ever more civil servants interfering in their affairs; some may have remembered the past failure mentioned on page 1. Farmers had been shocked by massive price falls following the unexpected Repeal in 1921 of the Corn Production Act, which had guaranteed farm prices. Many were farming with inadequate, out-of-date farm fixtures and had no prospect of getting piped water even in their farm-houses in the foreseeable future, let alone electricity. In any case, electricity seemed a luxury in farm buildings: what was wrong with a hurricane lantern? Moreover, a considerable group of ratepayers objected to the extra charge on rates which they thought would result from the establishment of the S.F.I. Fortunately the Agricultural Instruction sub-Committee pressed on regardless, and Cannington Farm Institute was opened officially on October 25th 1921.

Chapter 2 - Teething Troubles ?

For nearly three years after the official opening of Cannington there was no settled leadership.

J.A.Symon, who was described as County Organiser in an advertisement of March 1920, did not become Principal of the new Somerset Farm Institute. The first Principal was named at the opening ceremony in October 1921 as Mr T. Limond, although he served only for the first term. John Clapham (21/22), provides the interesting snippet that the first telegraphic address of Cannington was "Limond, Cannington" (Letter in the COSA 1921-1971 "50 Golden Years" booklet). The Principal's post was re-advertised during the first term, with replies required before December 7th, 1921, the end of term, and James Mackie M.A., BSc.(Agr) was appointed as Principal on 1st February 1922, with W.D.Hay as his assistant, as the latter records in his item "Looking Back" in the same 1921-1971 "Fifty GoldenYears" booklet. (Miscellany, p.98). Mr Mackie, with W.D.Hay on his right and A.D.Turner on his left, is sitting in the front row of the photograph of the staff and students of 1921/2, on pages 128, 129, 130.

Quoting from the 1922-3 Prospectus, a full list of Farm Institute staff appeared in the *Fruit Grower*, among other publications, on 12th September 1923 (indicating the interest of the Horticultural as well as the Agricultural Press) together with a list of current livestock and details of some of the work being carried on at the Institute. There was accommodation for 25 students of each sex. A small herd of Dairy Shorthorn cows was kept, and a flying flock of ewes. Three breeds featured among the pigs: Gloucester Old Spots, Wessex Saddleback and Large Black. There were seven work horses, mostly Shires.

The Staff
Mr James Mackie M.A., B.Sc. - Principal
Mr W.D.Hay B.Sc. - Assistant Principal
Mr A.W.Aitken - Farm Bailiff
   (Agricultural Course)
Mr A.D. Turner N.D.H. - Horticultural Superintendant
   (Horticultural Course)
Miss D.G.Saker N.D.D., B.D.F.D. - Dairy & Poultry-keeping Superintendant)
Miss O.E.Masters N.D.D.
Miss A.M.Reid N.D.D.
   (Dairying and Poultry-keeping Courses)

However, by 17th August 1923 James Mackie was suffering from an un-named illness, which as WD Hay explains in "Looking Back" resulted from war wounds (see Miscellany, p.98) and WDH was himself signing correspondence as "Principal (Temp)" after that date. James Mackie's incapacity continued, and at an Agricultural Committee meeting of November 1923, he is recorded as having written to thank the Committee for its "kindly consideration" during his illness. (Somerset County Gazette, 1/12/23)

The illness of Mr Mackie left the Institute and County short of staff, and at the November 1923 meeting of the Agricultural Instruction Sub-Committee (mentioned above) the Chairman suggested that another Assistant Organiser be appointed. Mr Hay gave details of work being done and supported the Chairman's remarks, adding that in other counties two or three Agricultural Organisers found plenty to do without a Farm Institute to look after as well, and Mr Gough from the Ministry of Agriculture said that the Ministry approved of another appointment. There was opposition, however. Mr White pointed out that the shortage of staff was a natural result of the Principal's illness and was thus only temporary. He said he went about among farmers a great deal and the view expressed by some of them was that there will soon be more officials at the institute than pupils, while Mr Berry said that if they appointed another organiser he would be looking for work half the time. However, Mr Somerville hoped they would not be alarmed by "silly talk" by people who did not know about the work which was being done. It was finally agreed to postpone a decision until the March (1924) meeting. (Mr. J.W.Dallas did not join the staff as Asssistant Organiser until September 1924, so WDHay was largely unsupported for a full year - Ed.)

SOMERSET COUNTY COUNCIL.

County Agricultural Committee.

THE AGRICULTURAL INSTRUCTION SUB-COMMITTEE.

COUNTY AGRICULTURAL ORGANISER AND
PRINCIPAL OF THE FARM INSTITUTE:
JAMES MACKIE, M.A., B.SC. (AGR).

TELEPHONE: BRIDGWATER 170.

(All letters should be addressed to the Principal).

CANNINGTON COURT FARM INSTITUTE,

NR. BRIDGWATER.

18th. January 1923.

Dear Sir,

Will you please insert, in an appropriate coloumn, the following paragraph, in the next issue of your paper.

I should be obliged if you would send me a copy for filing purposes.

SENT TO:-
✓Chard & Ilminster News,
✓B'water Mercury,
County Gazette,
✓Western Gazette,
Frome Standard,
Williton Free Press
and
Western Daily Press.

Yours faithfully,

Jas Mackie.

Principal.

SOMERSET COUNTY COUNCIL.

COUNTY AGRICULTURAL COMMITTEE.

EGG AND CHICK DISTRIBUTION SCHEME.

The Agricultural Instruction Sub-Committee in conjunction with the Ministry of Agriculture has established a number of Stations for the distribution of Eggs and Day old Chicks to Small Holders, Cottagers and other rural residents in the county. Eggs 5/- per dozen and Chicks 10/- per dozen.

Full particulars may be had from:-

THE AGRICULTURAL ORGANISER,
Somerset Farm Institute,
Cannington,
Nr. Bridgwater.

As this letter from Mr Mackie shows, work in a very practical sense was already in hand, work which was beneficial to even the smallest farmers, and provided a reliable source of egg laying stock for poultry keepers throughout the county.

The Horticultural Department was also at work. At a Council meeting of 23/3/1922 Mr.A.D.Turner reported the continuation of the same 1921 Demonstration Plots as "the plot holders have become familiar with the scheme of soil working, manuring and cropping". These Plots were at Portishead, Wellington, Street, Midsomer Norton, Bridgwater and at the Farm Institute.

Mr Mackie died as a result of his war wounds during the first months of 1924 and by May 3rd of that year Cannington correspondence was being signed by W.D.Hay as Principal. W.D.Hay wrote of Mackie: "He was one of the finest men that I have ever known and his death was a great loss to the Institute and country" (p.98). As W.D.Hay had himself endured the same war, including the Battle of the Somme, and "was wounded three times and gassed once", this was no small compliment (1965-6 C.O.S Magazine, "Profile"; p. 21, "W.D.Hay").

One of the Dairying appointments made in 1919 was that of Miss Masters, and sadly history was to repeat itself at her death in 1931, which sounds so similar to that of Miss Saker in 1926 (page 2) that again the layman thinks of appendicitis. An obituary recorded:

"It was with great regret that on September 3rd we heard of the death of Miss O.E.Masters, following an operation at St. Thomas's Hospital, London. Miss Masters had been a member of the Dairy Staff of the Somerset County Council for twelve years. A daughter of a Somerset farmer, Miss Masters had early associations with Dairying, and after gaining practical experience in connection with Dairying, trained at the Lancashire County Council Dairy School, Hutton, Preston. Miss Masters took her N.D.D. in 1918 and was appointed as a member of the Dairy Staff in 1919, during which time she was an Instructress at the Somerset Farm Institute, and for the past six years her work was chiefly in connection with the Farm House Cheese-making Industry. Miss Master's conciencsious work and kindly helpful manner is an undoubted loss to the County and to the staff of the Somerset Farm Institute, but her name will live in honoured memory for work well and faithfully done."

The extra-mural work in agriculture being carried out in the county at this time, some of it recorded in Chapter 1, continued as before, but with the addition in 1922/23 - among other extra activities - of field crop trials. Field experiments in yields of Wheat, Oats, and Barley were carried out, and the results published, with records of soil, subsoil, seed treatment, seed rates, previous crops, manurial treatment, yield of grain and straw. Parallel experiments with Mangolds also featured. Inspection was invited and thanks were expressed to the firm which supplied artificial fertilisers "gratis".

So in spite of a few teething troubles - not least the unexpected deaths of members of staff - and some opposition - the 1920s saw the Institute firmly established. The enthusiastic support of many farmers is demonstrated by the *Western Daily Press* photograph below (dated July 19th 1924) which shows a crowd of 60 or so farmers about to walk around the farm on a very wet Open day. At the end of the year their enthusiasm was no doubt increased by the announcement by Mr J.H. Cann, Chairman of the Farm Committee, that in spite of the extra costs arising from experimental work, the farm had paid very well and had not cost the rate-payer a penny, so he could say with great satisfaction that the Committee's support "had been justified".

Farmers setting out in the rain to view the Institute farm (Western Daily Press, 19th July 1924)

INSTRUCTION IN THE COUNTY.

Instruction in the County comprises :—

(1) Lectures on Agriculture, Horticulture, Dairying, Poultry-management, Bee-keeping and Veterinary Science arranged at suitable centres. Long courses or short courses of lectures can be arranged as desired.

(2) Demonstrations can be arranged according to the subjects in either of the above.

(3) Farm Orcharding and Fruit Grading by means of demonstrations or visits.

(4) Field Experiments on farm and garden crops.

(5) Demonstrations in the production of Market Milk by the cleanest and simplest methods are held at farms where desired.

(6) An Itinerant Dairy School is held in villages where desired. This consists of ten lessons and is intended principally for those who can only leave their homes for a few hours daily.

(7) Itinerant instruction in cheese-making, where the Instructor spends from 3 to 7 days on individual farms giving practical instruction.

(8) Instruction and competitions in manual processes, such as Hedging and Ditching, Spar-making and Thatching and Orchard Pruning.

(9) Scholarships for promising boys and girls.

(10) Grants to Secondary Schools in aid of Rural Science work.

(11) Cheap Analysis of Fertilizers and Feeding Stuffs.

The services of the County Staff are available at all times for the giving of advice and information either by correspondence or by visits. Further particulars on the above matters will be given on application to the County Agricultural Organiser.

SOMERSET FARM INSTITUTE,

CANNINGTON,

NR. BRIDGWATER.

List of County Services provided by Cannington (1925/6 Prospectus)

Some of the hundreds of visitors to Cannington in 1926 (Western Daily Press - July 23rd)

Chapter 3. Extra-Mural or County Work in the 1920s.

During the 1920s, Cannington Open Days or Farm Days soon became well known throughout the farming community, but many people visited on other occasions also, encouraged by a standing invitation from W.D.Hay for personal visits "by appointment", based on his often stated principle that "Seeing is Believing". As a result, in 1926 W.D.Hay was able to announce that during 1925 over 1400 farmers and other country dwellers had visited Cannington. Mr. Hay also liked to get about to see for himself, and he soon became known to farmers around the county. In the Somerset County Gazette of 8/10/27 he was reported as having made 240 personal visits to farms all over the county in the previous two years.

No doubt the fact that the farm at Cannington paid its way persuaded many farmers that modern methods could not be as impractical as traditionalists believed they were, and that Cannington was worth a visit. In fact, in 1926 W.D.Hay was able to tell farmers that livestock had increased (to 75 cattle, 100 ewes and 11 horses - pigs remaining at 60) and in spite of this increase, milk yields had gone up from 570 to 800 gallons per cow per year, the farm supplying all the foodstuffs. However, one wonders if farmers listened to Hay's opinion on keeping records: "It is notorious that only a small percentage [of farmers] take the trouble to keep books in order to learn the branches which help and those which do not. The usual excuse made for not keeping books or for not recording milk [yield] is that the farmer gathers all the required knowledge by some mysterious process of intuiton - what miserable self-deception". *(Bristol Times and Mirror Feb. 1925).*

Cannington also made contact with farmers and other country dwellers by sending advisory staff out into the county to demonstrate a wide variety of farming operations, including those of a traditional nature. Demonstrations of Hedging and Ditching, held at Oakhill, Lamyatt, and East Pennard in January 1925 and at Oakhill, Ditcheat and West Cranmore in November 1926, were perhaps designed to appeal to those traditionalists who were still opposed to anything which looked like "impractical book-learning". Much of Somerset land is heavy or low-lying, with cattle and sheep everywhere, so good drains and fences are essential. In fact, on such land, hedges were usually originally planted on banks thrown up in the process of digging drainage ditches, so hedging and ditching were twin operations. Also on heavy land, a series of demonstrations of mole-draining were held in 1925, 1926 and 1927 at Ditcheat, Bishopsworth and Langport. This relatively new mechanical method of field draining could often take the place of the old earthenware tile drains of the nineteenth century, draining, just as they did, into field-side ditches. It was much cheaper, although it was not always open to use by a tenant farmer, unless the landlord would accept it as a tenant's improvement. These mole-draining demonstrations continued into the 1930s.

In 1926, following the success of re-seeded grass plots at the Institute, W.D.Hay demonstrated similar grass plots on farms in the Croydon Hill area, at over 700 feet elevation, sown in April 1925 on land earlier covered with gorse and bracken. Each plot had different manurial treatment, (basic slag providing phosphate) and was sown with different seeds mixtures. *(p.117 & W.Som. Free Press 19/6/26).*

More theoretical scientific education was also organised. There were visiting lecturers: Dr Charles Crowther, Principal of Harper Adams College, lectured on the feeding of pigs, while Mr Mackintosh came from the Dairy Institute at Reading and discussed feeding and rearing young cattle. Winter evening lectures by Cannington staff, on soils, manures and manuring, feeding-stuffs, grassland, milk production, milk recording and other farming subjects were held at convenient centres all over the County. Articles were written in local newspapers on the growing of vegetables, fruit and flowers in the farm garden, on bee-keeping, rearing of chicks from day-old, with and without a hen, feeding for eggs, the treatment of animal diseases and so on. "Stations" were also set up for the distribution of hatching eggs and day-old chicks, stock from trap-nested hens with a proven record of egg-laying, at competitive prices (pp.6, 48).

Rules for the production and sale of milk had been tightened up under the Milk and Dairies (Amendment) Act of 1922, so the greatest immediate need in the county was probably for an improvement in methods of milk handling. Milking methods were often archaic: the ubiquitous Somerset cow has to be milked twice a day and "wet-hand milking" was traditional. At the start, milk was squirted onto both hands so that they and the cow's teats were wet with milk, and as milking proceeded an occasional extra squirt of milk on hands and teats would keep them wet. It was said to be easier on the cow, which is questionable - what is certain is that it was very unhygienic. (The method no doubt arose from the ancient practice of milking while the calf sucked, when the teats were always wet from the calf sucking). A side-handled open-topped pail would be used (photo p.12) above which the milker's head in its greasy cap rested against the cow's flank, dislodging quantities of dust, dry dung particles and cow hair which then fell into the milk. Bearing in mind that the cows' teats were almost never washed, except by the milk with which the milker bathed them and which thence dripped into the milk pail, it is not surprising that milk often kept badly, or was tainted, having been well inoculated with coliform (faecal) and other bacteria.

If the milk was strained or filtered, it was through a piece of butter muslin stretched over the mouth of the churn into which the milk was tipped from the milking pail. After milking was over this milk-impregnated cloth was squeezed out into the churn by a milker's unwashed hands to ensure that no milk was wasted, further inoculating the bulk of the milk with harmful bacteria (photo, p.13). The "Grip-churn" milk strainer, introduced by Clares of Wells, was stronger and more efficient, but it was often still squeezed out by hand in the traditional way. It is true that the milk was then cooled down to near the temperature of the local water supply, but in fact this was not very low by modern standards, and probably rarely below 50° Fahrenheit (10°C). Conditions were worse when milking in the fields, when it might be an hour or so before the milk was cooled. Outdoor milking still went on - and at an Agricultural Committee meeting in 1926 Mr. Joyce said it was quite as important to teach young people how to milk out of doors as it was under cover. Clean Milk Demonstrations and advisory visits became central to the work of the Dairying staff, and Clean Milk Competitions were held, with medals and money prizes, the first being in 1924/5, with 66 competitors. There were two classes, one for herds of over twenty cows and one for herds of between 6 and 20 animals. Herds already producing "Grade A" milk were excluded.

Official reports to the Committee from the Dairying Superintendant (Miss Saker) show how comprehensive the work already was in the 1920s, covering all aspects of Dairying activity:

MISS SAKER'S REPORT FOR NOVEMBER 1925 (almost in full):

CLEAN MILK DEMONSTRATIONS
Miss M.C.Taylor

Centre	Attendance
Ilminster	10
Chard	25
Hinton St. George	15
Hambridge	27
East Lambrook	30

Further demonstrations have been arranged in the Wells, Street, Castle Cary, Wincanton and Templecombe districts.
[see photograph on page 12 - Ed.].

DEMONSTRATIONS AT SHOWS

At the Shepton Mallet Show and Yeovil Show a working Dairy was held where demonstrations were given in Cheddar, Caerphilly and Small-holder cheese-making, Butter-making and Milk Testing.

Clean milk demonstrations were also given in a separate shedding adjoining the Working Dairy at the Shepton Mallet Show.

It is felt that these demonstrations are of great help in getting in touch with a number of people who would never otherwise ask for help.

CHEESEMAKING DEMONSTRATIONS

The Itinerant Advisory Cheese Instructress's visits have been as follows:
(Visits of advice are being paid on the days in between the Clean Milk Demonstrations).

Miss M.C. Taylor

Centre	Cheese Variety	Length of visit (days)	Galls. of Milk	Farm Visits
Wraxall	Cheddar & Caerphilly	6	80	3
Wick	do do	4	69	3
Axbridge	Caerphilly	4	79	2
Bleadon	do	6	28	10
Ditcheat	Cheddar	4	112	6
Rooksbridge	Caerphilly	4	122	5
Clutton	do	5	35	4

Miss O.E. Masters

Centre	Cheese Variety	Length of visit (days)	Galls. of Milk	Farm Visits
Huntspill	Caerphilly	4	86	5
Christon	Cheddar	2	56	1
Catcott	Smallholder	2	25	1
Kewstoke	Cheddar	5	65	3
Compton Dundon	Caerphilly	4	35	3
Muchelney	do	3	16	2
Dunball	do	4	16	3
Lodmore	do	7	16	5
Doulting	Cheddar	7	80	5
West Pennard	Caerphilly	4	25	3
Bruton	do	7	45	4
North Perrott	do	3	-	-

TRAVELLING CHEESE SCHOOL

Miss E. Allsup

Centre	Students	Certificates	Galls. Milk	lbs. Cheese
Yarley Hill	8	8	102	117
Meare	6	5	153	164
Burtle	10	9	112	128
Chilton Polden	8 (Class still in progress)			

Number of one-day home instruction visits paid: 7
Number of visits paid to old students: 8

VISITS OF ADVICE

Visits of advice have been paid to five cheese-making farms.

JUDGING AT SHOWS

The Dairy Staff have judged at the following Shows:

The London Dairy Show	Westonzoyland	Wiveliscombe
The Yeovil Agricultural Society	The Mid-Somerset Agricultural Society	

DAIRY SCHOOL CANNINGTON

Fourteen dairy students are attending for the full twelve weeks' course and twelve have attended, and are attending, for periods varying from 1 to 8 weeks. This has kept the average number of students in the dairy throughout the term at 20.

This number requires the constant supervision of my assistant and myself if the proper amount of instruction is to be given and leaves no more than half an hour for meals with a full twelve hours on duty. I do not consider that it is advisable to take so many.

The special six weeks' course, arranged for the four students sent by the Devon County Council, finished on the 9th November. These students have done good work and made every use of the instruction given. They all obtained "passed" marks in the theoretical and practical examination.

GENERAL

(a) The Dairy Staff attended the London Dairy Show and all except one attended the Dairy Conference arranged by the Ministry. All wish to express their appreciation of the permission given them to attend. Much useful information was obtained.

(b) Applications for advisory cheese visits continue to come in. These visits have extended for two months longer than ever before.

(c) For the purpose of maintaining a complete list of the [farmhouse] Cheese-makers, the county has been divided into twenty districts. Up to the present 707 names have been recorded; of these only one third have yet been in touch with the Instructresses. All have been sent the circular offering "Advice to Cheese-makers".

(d) It will be necessary to buy extra milk throughout this term as the regular suppliers are only sending between 55 and 60 galls. per day.

(e) Three past students of the Dairy School have been successful in gaining the National Diploma in Dairying and the British Dairy Farmers' Diploma in Dairying.

(f) Applications are received each week for Dairymaids and cheese-makers. There is no difficulty in placing in posts all satisfactory students.

(g) Referring to the suggestion made in Committee that a report on refrigerating plant seen at the Dairy Show should be made, I visited all the exhibits and found that, up to the present time, there appears to be no small plant available, the lowest estimate being £175.

(h) The order for the installation of the piping and a radiator in the soft cheese room and butter room has been given to Messrs. Kelland, but delay in carrying out the order has been occasioned through non-delivery of the radiator.

(i) An estimate has been obtained for the loft storage over the ripening room and as soon as the services of the carpenter are available, this will be begun.   *[signed]*   **D.G.Saker**

CLEAN MILK DEMONSTRATIONS

MISS BRITTAIN DISCUSSING THE OLD AND THE NEW MILKING PAILS AT STOWEY

Newspaper Report of Points being Demonstrated

Miss Brittain explained that when the cows have been tied up in the cow-sheds ready for milking they should be cleaned : the flank of the cow, its tail and under its stomach should be brushed - long hairs should be clipped - the udder should be washed and thoroughly dried with clean cloths. Quite good milking outfits were obtainable: she liked a sort which would cover the milker's knees. The pail with the large open top was not to be recommended as there was so much space for dirt to get in. Lids with a small opening could easily be procured to fit on the tops of pails and these were preferable. The pail that the lecturer had had a handle about half way down at the back of the pail; this handle, she said, was convenient when emptying the pail, as with it there was no necessity to put the hand on the bottom of the pail, where there may be some dirt picked up from the ground. Milking stools should be kept scrupulously clean because they were the last things the milker's hands touched before milking the cows. As soon as the milk had been obtained it should be strained and cooled as soon as possible; it should not be left standing about in the cow-shed longer than was absolutely necessary. If, however, it had to be left in the cow-shed it should be put into pails with tightly fitting lids. When milk was cooled at once its keeping qualities were considerably added to, germs in it increased rapidly while it was warm. (p.40)

Miss Brittain went on to describe how utensils should be cleaned and sterilised. First they should be washed in cold water, then scrubbed with hot water. If soda was used it should afterwards be rinsed off with cold water. After this the utensils should be sterilised with steam, and Miss Brittain showed how this could be done easily and at little cost. Large utensils could be turned up over a boiling copper which had a hole in the cover to let out the steam. Small items could be put in a container with a perforated base which could also be put over the steaming copper.

In reply to a question Miss Brittain said she thought cows should be clipped two or three times a year and she had not known of a case where it was detrimental to cows to be clipped at this time of year.

(Wellington Weekly News, 8/10/1927)

(EDITOR'S NOTE). General Summary of Cannington Rules for Milkers

Milker to be dressed in a clean smock and cap. The cows' udder to be washed and dried. A partly covered pail similar to the one on the left of the photograph opposite (and on left below) was recommended. The cows' udders to be kept clipped. Hands to be washed and dried before each cow, and kept dry. The milker must not lean his head against the cow: this would dislodge cow hairs and dirt which might fall into the milk. The milking stool to be scrubbed after each milking; i.e: twice daily.

PROBLEMS

It was difficult for older milkers to adapt to these methods. Few farms had hot water, and washing hands and udders in cold water before milking each cow on a winter morning was not popular. Use of the partly covered pail after using an open pail for many years was awkward. A man with big hands who had been wet-hand milking all his life found it difficult to keep his hands dry, especially when milking a cow with short teats. Traditionally, milkers had leaned their head against the cow's flank, in front of her stifle joint. It was restful (and warm in winter) and the milker would get prior warning of a kick from a difficult cow because she would shift her weight to her off foot just prior to kicking, and the milker' head would first feel her stifle joint move! Washing milking stools was not popular, either. Once a day was the usual maximum. Who wanted to sit on a perpetually damp wooden stool?

It was only through strength of personality and constant repetition that Miss Taylor and her assistants won their battle for hygienic methods with the milkers of Somerset, and many would say that they bullied them into submission!

Miss O.E.Masters

(ca. 1914)   Old-fashioned method:
butter-muslin strainer being squeezed
by hand to ensure no milk was wasted.
(see page 10). Here the milker is wearing
an old type home-made "milking pinny".

"Covernee"

overall

on left

with modern

milking pail.

(COSA Magazine adverts)

Chapter 4. Student Life in the 1920s

The first student at Cannington was Ernest Hebditch from Over Stratton. Ernest was interviewed the day before the term started and having been accepted slept there overnight to avoid having to go home for just one night before starting term the next day.

The first four agricultural students to enrol in September 1921 were the afore-mentioned Ernest Hebditch, and Tom Parsons, H. Brooke-Wilkinson and John Clapham. As the year progressed other students joined. Tom Parsons remembers some of them: A Rawlings, Meade, Creighton, Bunny Bush, Walker, Mollie Mackie, Gwen Pitt, Mary Terell and Miss White.

Mr Limond was Principal for the first term, with Mr Basil Cameron as Vice-Principal, until they were replaced by Mr Mackie and W.D.Hay. Mr A.D.Turner was Head of Horticulture with Mr Maidment as deputy. Miss Saker and Miss Masters were the Dairying staff and Miss Lenegham was Matron. The caretaker and his wife were already Mr and Mrs Croaker.

"BUNCHIE" remembers

Once upon a time, long ago in October 1921, the Somerset Farm Institute was born, and lived happily ever after is how I feel I should begin my reflections. I well remember attending the official opening by the Minister of Agriculture, Sir Arthur Griffith-Boscowen. Only the boy's side was ready for students at the time, the girl's opened the following January. The whole scheme being a new venture by the County Council the first batch of students had to behave with decorum, but we gave the village people "food for talk". How different everything looks today (1952) with the five tennis courts and well cared for gardens. A far cry from the rubbish heap and allotment outside the dairy.

Dairy and poultry were run concurrently in the early days; our dairying instructress, Miss Saker, was given £10 by the Committee to start a poultry section, which consisted of two breeding pens in the garden by the Nuns' Cemetery, with home-made poultry houses and 12 Light Sussex and 12 White Leghorns. Another lot of laying hens, about 24, were kept down in the lower orchard with the sows. We had nothing in the way of equipment for games and so got up a concert including the village people and had quite a successful result which helped to purchase a type of heavy walking stick for hockey playing which we practised at the bottom of the drive leading to the Principal's house. A kindly person laid us a tennis court at the top of Rodway Hill next to what was then the cowman's cottage on the right hand side opposite the farm buildings.

No member of the staff possessed a car; the Principal, Mr Mackie, had a motor-bike, the two dairying instructresses, Miss Saker and Miss Masters rode push bikes as did the County Itinerant Instructress, Miss Taylor, and many winter nights they would cycle in pitch dark to outlying villages to give lectures.

I remember the advent of W.D.Hay in the spring of 1922: how on Sunday afternoons he would go for walks with any boys or girls who cared to join him to Charlwick, Combwich, etc., all the while giving helpful talks on this plant or that weed. During the winter months the girls had to be in by 8 p.m. and the boys 8.30 p.m. One night in protest the boys all climbed onto the flat roof over the cloakrooms and serenaded in hopes that Mr. Hay would come out to them, when they intended to deliver their ultimatum - extension time 'or else'. The Vice-Principal completely ignored them, and eventually, one by one, they shinned down the drainpipe and went indoors.. We girls had the last laugh! In May 1922 Joey the famous was born: what a thrill for the farm bailiff, Mr Aitken, old Jim Pridham and Tom Burge the carter. Joey proved a faithful servant for many years.

Mr Winewell, the popular village schoolmaster at the time, and Billy Bag, who ran a taxi service to and from Cannington and Bridgwater Station, both accomplished concert artists, often produced concerts and would borrow some of us to take part in them - and how we enjoyed ourselves.

I look back at my time at the Institute as some of the happiest in my life - remembering such names as Mollie Mackie, Bance Walker, Edith Masters, the Fookes brothers, Welky, Hely, Parsons, Cook, Clapham, Mead, to mention a few.

I am sure that all these would agree with me that in spite of no TV or wireless - those were the days.   *("Bunchie - 1958 COSA Magazine - .Mrs Pittard - see page 109))*

On September 6th 1924 the *Frome Standard* approvingly commented that while in 1921 Cannington had started with only four students, in 1923 it started with 45! Several early students recorded their memories in the COSA Magazine: one of the 45 of the 1923 intake wrote:

It was in 1923/24 that I started at the Somerset Farm Institute at Cannington at the age of 16. The staff at the time was:

Mr W.D.Hay - Principal	*Mr Turner - Horticulture*
Miss Saker - Head of Dairy Department	*Mr Hedderwick - Farming*
Miss Masters - Dairy	*Miss Taylor - County Supervisor, Dairying*
Miss Page - Poultry	

My aim was to become a cheese-maker and go out onto farms. However, I found I had to attend other subjects such as Poultry, Butter-making and Dairying in general.

At the time I arrived, Miss Saker was in America, and Miss Taylor had undertaken her duties, Miss Saker returned and Miss Taylor went back to the County. We were sorry to lose Miss Taylor, but we soon settled down with Miss Saker, finding her an excellent person in all ways. Lectures in all four subjects were taken at times between the practical courses. At the end of term were examinations. For relaxation we had dances in the hall with music by a student named Perry at the piano, enjoyed by all. Debates on many subjects in which the students took an active part. One in particular was 'Trial by Jury'. The 'Judge' in full robes and a wig, three 'Barristers' in wigs, two 'Secretaries' (I was one), two 'Policemen' and one 'Prisoner'. About twenty students in various attires. Fortunately the 'Prisoner' was found 'Not Guilty' (I cannot remember what the charge was).

I look back with very happy memories of my time at Cannington, my name was Sparks but I was soon called "Sparkie", unless when it was stern Sparks! I went to two farms cheese-making, but unfortunately the milk caused trouble with my hands and I had to give it up.

Mrs Marion Lynham (Sparks) 1923/24

Sixty Years Ago - a Student from 1924 (from COSA Magazine No. 9, 1986)

I was at Cannington 1924/5; at that time it was the only Institute in the West Country and students came from the four Western Counties, many on Ministry of Agriculture Scholarships. The only subjects were Agriculture, Horticulture and Dairying. The Dairy students outnumbered others as the only other Dairy Institute was at Usk.
There were 44 students, all housed in the old building. Some staff lived in the rooms on the right of the arch. In the dining room we ate at long tables. We filed in, girls from one end and boys from the other - the Head girl and boy sitting at the ends, dishing up.

No-one went out in the evenings; lights out at ten. We made our own entertainment. Wednesday there was always a debate and one was detailed to take part. Saturday was for dancing to records, and on other evenings there was music and games. As the evenings lightened badminton was played in the Quad. A cook was once very irate when a shuttlecock went through the kitchen window into the pancakes!

This photograph of 1924 students appeared in the Western Daily Press, July 1924

4. Student Life in the 1920s

Highbridge Cheese Market - ca. 1920

(by courtesy of Wessex Momentoes, Yate, South Glos.)

We walked many miles round the lanes, but were expected to be in for meals. We were allowed to go to Bridgwater Saturday afternoons, and there were a few trips; always in the cheese lorry, which was canvas topped and was probably used in the 1914-18 war. We were taken to Highbridge Market with the cheese, the only auction in the country for Caerphilly, as practically all of it was made in Somerset. I think we went twice to the pictures. The same vehicle transported a very scratch team to hockey matches. At home we played on the top field, behind the present blacksmiths, sharing the field with the hens. They were in the old-fashioned houses on wheels and often had to be moved before play could commence, leaving deep tramlines across the pitch. On one occasion someone hitched a lift inside and the bottom fell through leaving a pair of feet sticking out below and a delayed start to the game.

Most of the girls slept in the open-topped cubicles which have now been re-organised and turned into fewer rooms. One night the boys crept through the ceiling, tapping as they went. One or two gullible students were led to believe it was the ghosts of the nuns.

Most of the dairy students went on to be farm cheese-makers. We were so lucky in having Miss Saker as our instructress: she set an example to us all in a truly happy Christian spirit. Mr Hay also set a very high standard and everyone respected them. It was a happy time. Gladys Stephens (Butler) 1924/5

A Student Week in 1925 (From COSA Magazine No.1)

Although most students were awake, the rising bell rang at 6.30. We scampered down the stairs, some of us only partly dressed, to get to our various departments by 7 o'clock; some to the poultry, some to the dairy, some to the gardens. We worked hard until 7.45, and then back to the Institute for breakfast at 8 o'clock. Afterwards we went off to make our beds. The head boy now went to the Vice-Principal's office for the list of work arranged for the agricultural students for the morning; some would be attending to the sheep, some doing horse work, some helping the cowman; others hoeing, hay-making, etc.; depending on the time of the year. The other students went direct to their various departments.

Parsons, Maddever, Lovell - 1928

Left: Dairy hoeing party - 1928/29

At twelve o'clock the work stopped; off with dirty boots, and some would change their clothes, ready for dinner at 12.30. Dinner finished, we would go out in the courtyards for tennis or badminton. From 2 to 4 we had lectures, given by the Principal, Vice-Principal or some other lecturer, on book-keeping, chemistry, botany, management and feeding of stock, soils, dairy etc. After tea, at 4 o'clock, some of the students had outdoor work to do again: milking, feeding pigs, or counting stock on the marshes, whilst those who were free would go for a walk or stroll about until 7 o'clock, which was supper time. Supper finished, we worked alone until bedtime. Lights out at ten o'clock.

On Wednesday, which was half-holiday, in the wintertime we had a hockey match against a visiting team, which always caused excitement. Sometimes we went away and played return matches. Everyone, including the staff, looked forward to Wednesday evenings, when we had our debates. A debate was arranged beforehand: two students for the subject, two against, and a chairman, who introduced them and made a few remarks on the subject to be debated. After each speaker, questions would be asked by most of us, and I am afraid we used to get very excited and wild. At the end we voted for or against. Another evening greatly looked forward to by everyone was Friday, when we had a social, with dancing and games, the music supplied by the students' own band. Those nights we went to bed very happy, but rather tired. Saturday was a second half-holiday, with matches arranged; or we went to Bridgwater or Taunton. I think all old students would agree that they had a helpful and happy time at Cannington. We were well treated, well taught and well fed. (Author not identified).

From Christine Williams on behalf of her Aunt, Dorothy Keel (Derrick) 1924

Young women were on one side of the boarding section upstairs and the young men at the other end. Matron was very strict. The men had to be up early for the morning's milking. Students sat in the same place for each meal at tables that ran the whole length of the dining room. Men sat on one side of the room and women on the other. However, on Saturday afternoons there was mixed hockey. Some lectures were mixed, too, e.g. gardening and poultry keeping. All students were known by their surnames. Miss Saker was head of dairying; her junior was Miss Masters. On the Saturday before Monday's examinations Miss Saker said to her students "Don't you girls forget if you haven't done your revision it is too late now. Go for a good walk on Sunday afternoon to be ready for Monday". (COSA Magazine 2000).

Horticultural Life 1928/29

In those days there were only four of us. Mr A.D.Turner was then our Chief, Mr. Cramp the Instructor day by day, and Mr Forshaw looked in on us from time to time, especially for Farm Orcharding. The weather did a great deal of good in that we used to go tobogganing in Cannington Park, no better place in the world for such sport, and all students used to share the fun. We horti. people tracked down those who left marks in the snow leading to our garden frames in No. 4. We caught Nellie, J.Clarke, Taylor, Kathleen and others from the girl students' department pinching violets to adorn their rooms.

The wintry weather held up the planting of several thousand fruit trees and bushes (soft fruit) which had to be heeled in until the thaw. When Taws did thaw it became a veritable sea of mud, however there was no option, day by day and long after the usual tea hour of 4 p.m., Donald Harris, Harry Leeson, Lady Baring - now Lady Hills - and myself struggled on under the tutor's guidance to make sure we were in a straight line. The roots, too, had to be carefully spread to give all a chance to survive. I cannot remember but I don't think that we lost many, if any. Owing to such planting and a wonderful summer which followed, they all had to be mulched against the fearful heat and dry weather.

One episode, which must be mentioned, was the planting of some lettuce in No.5 garden under the peach trees. Two of us planted the lettuce while the other two students brought the plants to us. Time was short owing to the luncheon hour drawing near and as we were waiting for plants we went round to No.2 to see what was happening. To our amazement and amusement we found they each had a cut-worm which they were racing one against the other, and each backing their particular "'oss". The winner was presented with a piece of lettuce and its life was spared: Voe Victis! When this sporting event was over we got back to work and finished the job by lunchtime.

In those wintry days of 1929 we were able (indeed we had to) watch the stores of fruit, etc., in fact I once said to Mr. Cramp "Ought we to look at the apples?" "Very thoughtful of you, Keirle", says he, but I know that we had one all round each time we paid a visit. Then we used to peep into Miss Monie's cheese store, usually when she was testing, to get a little bit of lovely Cheddar to taste. I am quite sure that many of our present day students will also look back with similar warmest affection over their days at Cannington. (1929, 1960 &1962/3 COSA Magazines - Percy Keirle. H/1928/9)

4. Student Life in the 1920s

A Second Horticultural View

There were only four regular Hortis, and I was the only girl. At that time most students were known by their surnames, which may seem odd to the present generation. Harry Leeson was the oldest of our party, and because he had reached the advanced age of 25 we called him Mr. Leeson in all seriousness. Mr. England was automatically Mr. as he was Senior Student.

We planted up the whole of Taws Field with experimental plots of apples and blackcurrants. How well I remember their perfect alignment, and the cold wind that blew across the field in that icy winter. We trudged back in the late afternoons with weary satisfaction at the end of a hard day's work.

Classroom work started at 7 a.m. in the winter, but when it was daylight we had an hour's digging, which made us enjoy breakfast.

In my dormitory I happened to have the first cubicle, which by its position was the easiest one for Matron to show to prospective parents. She complained to me because the first thing that confronted them was my list headed "MICE caught under my bed". I thought it exciting, and so refused to discard my wall decoration, but it resulted in her having to mysteriously pass my door and open the next.

I can't remember why I didn't buy a trap, but arranged brown paper stretched across a bowl of water, with cheese hanging from the bed spring which the mice couldn't reach without sliding through a trap door in the middle of the paper. I then had to get up to drown them mercifully. Sometimes I had two in a night, and still treasure the list which totalled 30 in under two months.

There was of course no heating upstairs (probably the same now), and my cubicle was extra cold because the cord of the sash wndow was broken and the top wouldn't go right up during the whole of my time there. I suppose none of us had any clothes beyond our uniform, so not having a coat I always wore my thick Jaeger dressing gown if working upstairs.

We took turns at week-ends in stoking of the small greenhouse and I still clearly remember the acrid coke fumes.

We thoroughly enjoyed mixed hockey. Red-haired Miss Kaye Maddever ran like the wind and terrified the defenders.

We usually worked hard in the gardens, but I remember one day when we were digging we all turned up some big and lively cutworms so we decided to make them have a race. Before the winning post was reached, Mr Cramp, our popular Instructor appeared, which was disappointing.

1921-1981 COSA Diamond Jubilee Magazine - Lady Rosemary Hills (nee Baring) 1928/29H

Percy Keirle, Miss le Fevre, Lady Rosemary Hills

A Third Horticultural View

In what was to be the happiest year of my life, I entered the Institute in 1928. The students numbered fifty or as the Prospectus elegantly put it, twenty-five males and twenty-five females. In those days things were pretty rough; the dining room very dingy, only radiators for heating and drying clothes.

The discipline was very strict. If the boys arrived at the farm three minutes late, they lost their free afternoon. Mr A.D.Turner was Horticultural Superintendant (what a title) - there were only four of us Horti students. Mr Cramp was Head Gardener and John Forshaw completed the trio. Joe Fling worked in the fruit section.

The year was an important one for Horti students as we were to plant out Taws with apples, for a nutrition trial. Unfortunately the land proved too strong, so the idea was a flop. Of course in those days we only had horses, and when Taws was ploughed the mess on the headlands was terrible after rain. Never before and never again was I to experience such mud. The second term it snowed on and off for six weeks. One of my pals had a car, an Austin I think, and four of us used to go out on some Sunday afternoons. I know one morning the thing was frozen solid and Jim H. with the starting handle swore he lifted the front wheels off the ground. When we did get it to go we went off to Combwich and there found the sea frozen over. They must have made cars in those days! When the snow went the rain came and of course the whole place went down with 'flu!

When the weather did clear we were very late with our planting - besides Taws we had another field to plant with currants and gooseberries, the latter in flower but they lived all right. We worked hard for weeks but they let us off lightly for the exams.

Memories: Donald S. from the Scilly Isles laughing as he tried to shovel frozen ashes: he had never seen a frost before - Mr Hay telling us the farm had made a profit of £500 - the debates and dances we had. When a vote of censure was carried on self and J. (richly deserved too) we made a dignified exit. A lady student next day said how sorry she had been. I told her she had been laughing and clapping. "I know I was, but I was awfully sorry for you". It seemed a bit thin to me. Then the competition among the girls as to who could wear the shortest skirt, handsomely won by little Miss - The serious looking young man who joined us the last term, who organised a very efficient cider smuggling syndicate his first night - I had a financial stake but did not run the blockade - Mr Hay telling us we were a cut above the usual student: we were pleased but not surprised; and it was forty years before it occurred to me he might have said that to each batch! So much for memories; but we worked hard and played hard, we got on well with each other and although conditions were crude, we enjoyed ourselves. Yes, indeed, definitely the happiest year of my life. *(1921-1981 Jubilee Number COSA Magazine - H. Leeson, 1928 H.)*

Dairying and Agricultural Mishaps

Does any reader remember when the late Miss Britton, who was going to give a 'Clean Milk' demonstration up at the farm one afternoon, received a bucket of water completely over herself? The dairy students had to put the cheese away before going up to the farm with the agricultural students. The agric students were causing quite a nuisance round the door of the dairy, when the writer of this incident decided that the only way to get rid of the cause of the trouble was to wash it away! So with a bucket of water in hand, all went quiet and on hearing footsteps the culprit flung the water - and poor Miss Britton caught the lot! After her shock the culprit was asked to meet her in the dairy after tea, when she proceeded to count all the open drains and suggested that, if one of these had been used, it would not have been necessary to use the open doorway. The incident closed with a good laugh!

Does any reader remember when a certain Head Boy, who was 'doing' cows at the time, mistook the time of 11.30 p.m. for 5.55 a.m. He got up, waking all the students of the lower dormitory, and arrived at the farm to hear the clock strike midnight. Checking his watch he discovered he had made a mistake in the time. On his return to the dormitory he woke all those who had just fallen asleep and then at 5.30 a.m. we were all woken up again when he got up at the correct time! The student in question was John Perham, who now lives at Ilminster.

Do you remember the paper chase when the hares followed by the hounds went down across the farm and over the River Parrett? The writer of this incident, a hound at the time, jumped in the river, tried to swim across, but was caught in the current and had to be pulled out. The hares crossed the river and came back but no one got the paper bags. In the evening, Mr Porteous, one of the hares, brought the other hare a drink. When he had finished it he was told it was strong Epsom Salts, because where the hares had crossed the river there was a sewage outlet pipe!

(1921-1981 Jubilee Number COSA Magazine - Arthur Chamings, 1927/28)

4. Student Life in the 1920s

Agricultural and Poultry Students

Clarke and John (Pip) Soane

Higgs, Hooper, Venn, with
W.J. England

(Showing the old type open milking pail and the new part-covered type)

AGRICULTURAL STUDENTS - 1930

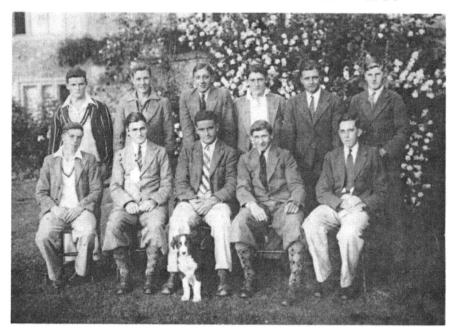

1930 Somerset Farm Institute/Bridgwater, Agricultural students.
Top (left to right): Peter Leach (Nether Stowey), R. Bowden (Felstead), Jim Jelley (Swindon), Richard Henderson (Queen Council),
B. Nursaw (Bristol), Philip Blacker (Clutton). Bottom (left to right): B. Sillman (Bristol), John Girling (Cowley, Cheltenham), G. G.
Gregory, vice principal and Taunton/Bristol Rugby Club and England (D), International England Rugby Player, now deceased. I
understand relations in farming at Taunton to the present time. Roger Vowles (Flax Bourton), Bob Tanner and dog "Midge". Not
included, Richard Rewbridge, absent (Nether Stowey).

Photograph from John Girling [1930/31] in the 1983 Magazine.

(Editor's Note: "Queen Council" must surely be a misprint: more likely to be Queen Camel)

<u>Personalities in Verse</u>

Clarke, Soane, Higgs and Venn, pictured opposite, are also immortalised in rhyme.
(from the December 1929 [No.2] student magazine):

There was once a student called Clarke,
Who thought he would have a great lark,
  So avoiding all scandal
  He turned the cube handle
And stood on his head in the dark.   (Machinery mishap?)
(Miss Maddever writes overleaf that Clarke was the most popular student of her year)

Derick and Pip were two so benighted,
They never knew when they were slighted,
  They went to a party
  And ate just as hearty
As if they'd been really invited. ('gate crashing' or 'free-loading' already in vogue?).

Poor Higgo, who never did hustle,
Was charged with wearing a bustle:
  Said he, "It's a lie
  Which I flatly deny,
It's merely my natural muscle" (Obesity in a hard working student of those days?).

Venn thought his food should be balanced some way
So he feasted on haddock and hay
  And then, for dessert,
  Had dough-nuts and dirt
Concluding with claret and clay. (What a dedicated omnivore!).

A DREAM OF DELIGHT OF E.J.D.H. (presumably Derick Higgs - Ed.).

Dainty Derek, full of greed,
Of the V.P.'s warnings took no heed.
At the last night supper he did eat
Till all proclaimed it a wondrous feat.
Cakes and jellies, fruit and pies,
Each were placed before his eyes;
Nevertheless he ate them all
Never had helpings seemed so small;
And all the while, his corporation distending
As if its limits knew no ending.
When suddenly with a rush and roar,
Poor old Higgo dashed to the door,
Funny noises buzzed in his head.
    Derek sat up and found himself in bed. (by H.G.West)
        (VP - Vice Principal)

<u>Editor's Note</u>: Derick Higgs appears to have been the Billy Bunter of his year. If this is so, it seems likely that in the photograph opposite he is the central figure of the three students arrayed in milking smocks, rather than the more meagre left-hand one - in spite of the note on the back of the original photo. (The rather scatty way that many Cannington photos are labelled casts doubt on the reliability of much of the labelling, so this view is quite reasonable - Ed.).

In the following piece from Miss Maddever, "Pip" Soane is "the fearsome hockey player", and Clegg is "the well-dressed". She refers also to the "laughing" Ivy Taylor, and Foot, the "pernicious thrower of wet dishcloths". The first named no doubt earned his mention: Miss Maddever was herself a fearsome hockey player: "she ran like the wind and terrified the defenders" (p.18).

4. Student Life in the 1920s

DIGGING UP THE PAST - by Miss K.D. Maddever

The first students came to Cannington in 1921, yet when I managed to arrive there in October 1928, I had the feeling that the place had been "like that" for years and years, and that the staff, too, had all been there for ages and ages!

At that time we had, I honestly believe, the finest staff in action that any Farm Institute could ever hope to employ, and of course they must needs have (appropriately?) nicknames! First Mr Hay (Boots) in a plus four suit and heavy footwear. He was too energetic for some of the students, always arriving at the unexpected point at the not too convenient moment: suffering no fools gladly and setting a hectic pace for everybody (and heaven help you if you were late for a meal). Then Mr Turner (ADT) the famous horticulturist , whose students respected him so heartily for his wide knowledge and stern discipline. The late Mr Porteous ("Porky"), a Vice-Principal whom we all liked because he stood no nonsense, and yet had a lively sense of humour. We always believed that his best fun in life was teasing "Faith" (Duncan), the then Matron. Incidentally she made her biggest mistake on the day when she decided to teach the girls some domestic science in the Institute kitchen. Then, too, Miss Collier ("Nippy") the cool, calculating one of the poultry section. Mr Furse ("Roots"), well named to rhyme with "Boots" and the fact that he did crop recording for N.I.A.B. He was a wonderful hockey player and therefore a positive hero of the day. Needless to say the students took a deep interest in the budding romance between him and our beloved "Furnella" (Miss Furnell - Miss Monie's assistant at the time). Last, but by no means least, the two outstanding ladies who ruled our department - the late Miss M.C. Taylor and Miss Monie. We were schooled and drilled in splendid fashion, and nobody queried whether it was necessary to polish things twice or thrice - it was done and 24 (or was it 28) of us were kept busy and happy. It wasn't until I arrived later at the University of Reading that I realised how much happier one was while being organised efficiently throughout the day and how much basic knowledge we had acquired almost unwittingly.

The girls were a bouncing cheerful lot. Le Feuvre, the French lass, who was afraid of the dark and mice! Carrie Clark, who crawled around after dark just to scare her. Parsons, who knew a lot about cheese making already, and with a pained expression said on my first day "That cheese is *fast*", and I couldn't see that there was anything to worry about: I'd never seen a cheese made before and anyway the sickly smell put me off! Then there was Nellie Whitmore, one of the poultry girls, who strangely enough really like hens. On horticulture we had Mr Leeson, Percy Keirle and Lady Rosemary Baring. She was a great sport, and the late Dick Clark (the most popular of students) and I were thrilled to be invited as guests to her wedding when the reception was held at Dunster Castle. I remember also Ivy Taylor, who laughed whatever befell, and by contrast the serious-minded Tuck and Hardwicke.

From Devon came some short course students - E.L.Heywood, later an assistant matron, Clegg the well dressed, and Ginger Baker.

Of the Agri. boys, the ones I remember best were "Pip" Soane the fearsome hockey player, Jim Hooper, Jack England, David Venn, Cousins, West, Judd who owned a car, the Perrott brothers Bill and Tom, and last but not least, Foot (a dairy student from Dorset), a pernicious thrower of wet dishcloths! In those days we cleaned aluminium buckets with "Zum". In haste one day Miss Monie said, "Foot, Foot [get the Scottish pronunciation right!] fetch the Zum". He turned to me with an agonised expression and said "Zum what, did her say?". [You also need Zumerzet - or Darzet - pronunciation and grammar here! - Ed.].

Now to those who have not been or may not be privileged to return to Cannington as a member of staff, as I was fortunate to do, I would like to give a bit of inside information. All the dairy students are "written up" in a marvellous book maintained by Miss Monie, where one's character and ability are assessed with revealing clarity and accuracy - so here is a warning to future students of the next generation who may read this: if you don't wish to be called "an escapist" or one with "more brawn than brain" get down to it and get on with it - or you won't look good in the annals of the dairy department.

(extract from the 1958 COSA Magazine)

22

Chapter 5. Extra-mural or County Work in the 1930s

In the 1930s British farming was in the doldrums. The world recession showed little sign of lifting and the unexpected and unprecedented Wall Street crash in 1929 seemed to end all hope of recovery. To politicians, farming was small fry compared with industry, and the country was flooded with cheap imported food (which helped to keep down industrial wages). Apart from a subsidy for Agricultural Education and Sugar-beet, help with a cereal scheme and the proposed creation of Marketing Boards, farming had received little encouragement from Government.

Not many people know that already before the 1914-1918 war many landowners had lost confidence in the future of agriculture and had been selling land so that they could invest in industry or the Empire (or anywhere abroad) and this continued in the post-war period. (High Death Duties following early wartime deaths were an added factor). In the years 1914-1927 landowners sold a full quarter of English land, often to tenants on mortgage. This was almost unprecedented: such a large proportion had only been sold once before - 400 years earlier - at the Tudor Dissolution of the Monasteries.

At first land prices remained steady. Longleat estate in Wiltshire sold 8,600 acres of land in 1919-1921 at prices of £40 per acre, not too unreasonable at the time. (Chap. XII, "Eclipse - 1914-1939"; *English Landed Society in the Nineteenth Century*, FML Thompson, 1971). But in 1921 the Repeal of the Corn Production Act halved farm prices, which the Act had guaranteed. Wheat went from 19/- to 10/- per cwt in 1920-1923 - see Ralph Whitlock's *Agricultural Records*, 1978, p.236 (and *Farmers Weekly* of 30-10-1936, p.34, for equivalent figures from 1920 of 90s to 50s per qtr.). At the risk of labouring the point, in 1919 the Editor's father, just out of the wartime army, took on the family farm at Queen Charlton at a £6,000 valuation in partnership with a brother, only to find the valuation of the same joint tenancy and stock down to £2,400 in 1924 (same valuer) when his brother wanted to be bought out to leave and get married. (The younger city brother, with his £3,000 inheritance still in cash, was thus able to buy in to the partnership cheaply - Ed.). Prices continued downwards. Land prices dropped dramatically and after 1921 much less land was sold, but even in 1929 the Savernake estate (Marlborough) still sold some land, but for as little as £11 per acre (FMLThompson again). Horse breeders suffered doubly: lorries and cars rapidly replaced horses, and the urban market for young broken-in work horses - heavy or light - disappeared.

Fortunately for Somerset farmers, nearly all of whom kept a number of dairy cows, under the 1931 Agricultural Marketing Act the Government allowed producers to set up Marketing Boards, subject to a poll of all producers. The most successful, the late lamented Milk Marketing Board, formed in 1933 after a vote in favour by a majority of all milk producers, helped farmers get a fair price for their milk (See Appendix, p.100). But in Somerset farmers had Cannington Farm Institute, the creation of a far-seeing County Council, which had taken advantage of a Government subsidy for agricultural education in setting it up. Moreover, they were either very wise or very fortunate in finally appointing W.D Hay as County Organiser and Principal of their Farm Institute, although originally they had appointed him only as deputy. The advice and encouragement emanating from Cannington, in addition to the Institute's invaluable student educational work, must have been a significant factor in leading farmers out of the depression.

County work during the 1920s is recorded in Chapters 2 & 3, but in the 1930s it expanded further. As before, "Systematic" Weekly Evening Classes on agricultural subjects "especially for Farmers Sons and Daughters" continued, covering the Feeding of Livestock, Manures and Manuring, Diseases of Animals, Poultry Management etc. Milk Recording was particularly emphasised. Classes would last eight to twelve weeks and in 1937, for example, were held in places as county-wide as the following:

The Golden Lion, Wrington - 11th October	The Auction Room, Farrington Gurney - 9th November
Red Lion Hotel, Crewkerne - 29th October	Reading Room, Constitutional Club, Clevedon -16th Nov
The Bear and Swan, Chew Magna - 1st November	The Bell Inn, Evercreech - 18th November
Langport Arms Hotel, Langport - 3rd November	The Council School, Wiveliscombe - 22nd November
The Schoolroom, Wheddon Cross - 5th November	National Farmers Union Office, Taunton - 23rd November
The Lion Hotel, Wiveliscombe - 8th November	St. John's School, Highbridge - 24th November

Over the winter the total number of this type of meeting must have been in the region of 120, at a minimum, but there were many other individual evening classes as well during that winter, held on particular subjects at the request of branches of the Young Farmers Clubs, NFU branches, Womens' Institutes and other rural organisations. There were 22 Young Farmers' Clubs in Somerset in 1937, with a total membership of 842, and Cannington led the way in encouraging their formation. (Appendix, p.69). A well publicised example occurred in May 1938 when both W.D.Hay, and Sir Archibald Langman for the N.F.U. spoke at the inaugural meeting of Wells Y.F.C.

The encouragement of grassland improvement by ploughing and reseeding had been a major aim of W.D.Hay and the Cannington staff from the beginning (p.9). There had been a long period during which farmers generally had been led to believe that the only way to improve permanent pasture was by renovation - heavy chain-harrowing and perhaps the application of lime or basic slag (a phosphatic by-product of steel smelting) without ploughing. This followed the traditional view that "to break a pasture would make a man, but to make a pasture would break a man". This old theory held that ploughed pasture produced heavy crops of grain and large profits, but when replacing the pasture from seed the cost and loss of production would be so great that it would lead to a farmers' bankruptcy. Consequently for centuries Somerset landlords had imposed heavy penalties on tenants who ploughed grassland - they believed it would ruin their farms.

Farmers who had visited other counties where alternate husbandry (alternating arable crops with grass) was practised knew that it was a workable system. But in Somerset most farmers were tenants, and were bound by their tenancy agreement and could not plough. Being a Scot with experience of alternate husbandry, W.D.Hay was aware that remaking grassland from seed was a matter of routine for a competent arable farmer and was determined to improve Somerset grassland by this method. He ploughed and directly re-seeded grassland at Cannington, without taking an arable crop, to demonstrate the method, and encouraged farmers to do the same, emphasising the need for phosphate.

In 22/9/34 he is quoted thus in the County Herald:

> **BACK TO THE PLOUGH.**
> Mr. W. D. Hay, the agricultural organiser for the county, referred to the success attending grass seed mixture trials, which, he said, showed plainly the great improvements which small alterations in a seeds mixture could produce. The results had led to an extraordinary amount of waste land being ploughed up in the West Country, including as much as 40 acres in one place. Some of the land had been derelict 50 and 60 years.

Since 1926, a number of farmers had ploughed old and "worn-out" grassland and re-seeded directly, under Hay's guidance, having learned of its wisdom by the success of re-seeding at Cannington (p.117). As a result, during May and June 1938 Cannington staff were able to show the good results of ploughing and direct re-seeding on farms in twenty places around the county: Moreover, Hay assured farmers that in no case had a landlord refused to rescind the ploughing ban!

SOMERSET COUNTY COUNCIL,

COUNTY AGRICULTURAL COMMITTEE.

AGRICULTURAL INSTRUCTION SUB-COMMITTEE.

DEMONSTRATION

OF

GRASS SEEDS MIXTURES

AND THE

IMPROVEMENT OF OLD PASTURES BY PLOUGHING and RE-SEEDING

will be given by members of the County Agricultural Staff at the following centres, by kind permission of those concerned, at the dates and times given:—

MONDAY, 30TH MAY. 1938
- 10.30 a.m. Messrs. F. THOMAS & SONS, Higher Rodhuish, Washford.
- 2.30 p.m. R. CLATWORTHY, Esq., Upcott, Winsford.
- 10.30 a.m. Captain D. M. WILLS, Barley Wood, Wrington.
- 12 noon Mr. FRANKS, Churchill.
- 2.30 p.m. Messrs. WATTS BROS., Weston Lodge Farm, Weston-in-Gordano.

TUESDAY, 31ST MAY.
- 10.30 a.m. F. J. WINZER, Esq., Wellshead, Exford.
- 2.30 p.m. Messrs. WESTCOTT BROS., Eastcott and Birchanger, Porlock.

WEDNESDAY, 1ST JUNE.
- 11.30 a.m. Mr. HAYES, Nicholls Farm, Kingsbrompton.
- 2. 0 p.m. Messrs. HAYES & SONS, Redcross Farm, Kingsbrompton.
- 4. 0 p.m. R. STEPHENS, Luckyard, Wheddon Cross.

THURSDAY, 2ND JUNE.
- 11. 0 a.m. Mr. WEBBER, Henlade, Taunton.
- 2.30 p.m. W. STOWELL, Esq., Glebe Farm, Churchstanton.
- 10.30 a.m. J. STOATE, Esq., Parsonage Farm, Watchet.
- 12 noon W. A. KING, Esq., Sandhills, Washford.
- 3. 0 p.m. J. MELHUISH, Esq., Blagdon Farm, Wheddon Cross.

FRIDAY, 3RD JUNE.
- 11. 0 a.m. Messrs. NORMAN BROS., Gupworthy, Wheddon Cross.
- 2.30 p.m. J. VELLACOTT, Esq., Withycombe Farm, Winsford.
- 11. 0 a.m. T. MERCHANT, Esq., Tuxwell, Spaxton.
- 2.30 p.m. Somerset Farm Institute, Cannington.

TUESDAY, 7TH JUNE.
- 11. 0 a.m. H. BURROUGH, Esq., Oath, Othery.
- 2.30 p.m. J. LANG, Esq., The Elms, Curry Rivel.
- 4. 0 p.m. A. R. SCAMMELL, Esq., Stapleton Farm, Martock.
- 11.30 a.m. F. H. STEER, Esq., Kingsbrompton.
- 2. 0 p.m. W. A. LEACH, Esq., Leigh Farm, Kingsbrompton.

All interested in the establishment and improvement of grassland are cordially invited to attend these demonstrations.

W. D. HAY,
County Agricultural Organiser, Somerset Farm Institute, Cannington, near Bridgwater.

164725

The twenty places were:

Othery	Spaxton	Wrington	Churchill
Weston in Gordano	Pawlett	Priddy	Oakhill
Washford	Exford	Porlock	Taunton outskirts
Churchstanton	Kingsbrompton	Watchet	Martock
Whaddon Cross	Winsford	Curry Rivel	Cannington (SFI)

Following these successes, in a letter to *The Times* in June 1938, W.D.Hay wrote:

"I hope you will allow me to criticise some of the statements which appeared in *The Times* of May 30th which may prove misleading to many farmers in this county. We in Somerset have not passed through the phase of renovation of old pastures and we have never advocated "no permanent pastures at all", but we certainly have done a considerable amount of work in connexion with the breaking up and re-reeding of old and worn-out grass land with very striking and beneficial results. This is not a new phase with us. Some twelve years ago on a number of farms in the county we sowed down good "permanent" seeds mixtures (with slight alterations to keep pace with our more recent findings) and have done so annually ever since. The results from the start were so striking that the work was extended to embrace a large number of other farms all over the county and in all cases excellent pastures have been the result, much to the benefit of the farmers, who have been pleased to acknowledge the obvious advantages of these 'new' pastures over their old ones, especially in a time of drought such as we have recently passed through".

Hay went on to point out that success depended "almost entirely" on three factors:
i.Good cultivations   ii.Good seeds   iii.An ample supply of available phosphates (as high grade basic slag)

In addition to demonstrations publicising examples of successful reseeding, there were also open days during which hundreds of farmers visited at Cannington and learned about the methods being used there. However, not everyone liked "scientific farming", Cannington or W.D.Hay, and it took some years of campaigning to break down the opposition.

The movement was not helped by a famous speech at Kettering in 1938 by Mr.Neville Chamberlain (the Prime Minister). He said Britain ought not to try to grow more food. We were a manufacturing country and could only sell our wares if our customers could earn sterling by selling us food - and it was cheap food. (Cheap food kept wages down, benefiting industry! - Ed) But fortunately, in that year of 'Munich', public opinion forced the belated recognition by the government of the danger from Hitler Germany and in the following year this resulted in a £2 per acre subsidy for ploughing up old grassland - announced by the Minister of Agriculture, Sir Reginald Dorman-Smith, in June 1939.

There were always dyed-in-the-wool traditionalists who thought W.D.Hay's drive to plough was wrong, and who almost worshipped permanent pastures. Typical adverse comment followed a remark by a writer in a NFU journal that while driving through Somerset although "it is a very pretty sight to see these fields covered with buttercups, it is not good first-class farming, and unfortunately buttercups are not the only weeds present". A letter from Stogumber in the West Somerset Free Press of 24th June 1939, replied: "Surely, sir, most fields covered with buttercups are the best grazing land" and suggested that ploughing up such pasture was mad. The writer went on to make an impolite comment that W.D.Hay's salary was not covered by Cannington farm profits, and concluded: "To a lot of agriculturists the Cannington Institute does not warrant the ever-increasing expenses, and I have yet to learn from an economic point of view of its usefulness to the majority of farmers". This sort of denigration was supported by those who held the doctrinaire view that no Government expenditure in the commercial sphere was ever justified: it stifled initiative and always resulted in an increase in civil servants, regulations and form-filling. Some people also fondly believed that "Herr Hitler" wanted peace, that there was no war danger, and some even thought that to increase farm production was a form of warmongering!

There was also the even more longstanding theory which still lingered on, that there was no place for science in agriculture, that farming was learned only by experience, not by "book learning". Cheese, for instance, was made only by expert use of the senses of smell, feel and taste, acquired by families over many generations, and transmitted "by inheritance". There was opposition to modern cheese-making methods as taught at Cannington, exemplified by an article from the well known Somerset farming journalist *Man o' Mendip* on page 28 of the *Farmers Weekly* on Oct 30th 1936. He reported on the success of Mr S.T. White and his wife, of Sock Dennis, Ilchester, who had won many prizes for Cheddar cheese, including at the Dairy Show, cheese largely made by Mrs White. Man o' Mendip wrote:

"In Somerset, most of the principal cheese-makers are related either by blood or marriage. The result is a vast body of inherited knowledge, which can produce the best cheese by the old methods. The sense of observation, taste and smell is so developed in these skilled makers that they need no aids such as acidometers, and they have the strongest prejudices in favour of the old ways to which their bank pass books are probably a good reference."

5. County Work in the 1930s

Asked how he retained the rich nutty flavour for which Cheddar Cheese was famous Mr White replied "I never use a 'starter' to ripen the milk, I ripen it naturally overnight in the old-fashioned way. Neither Mrs White nor myself has been to a farm institute or college, but we are satisfied with results, despite modern teachings, much as we respect our agricultural instructors."

Man o' Mendip went on: "Mr White took me to his thatched dairy where there was no steam-jacketed vat etc., but one of the old round copper tubs, a boiler and two presses. That was all - simplicity, scrupulous cleanliness, and hereditary knowledge"

We also learn that when Mr White was 14 years old his father sent him to learn Cheddar cheese-making from George Lester, and by the time he was 16 he had won first prize for Cheddar at Frome Show. From 1925 to 1927 he made the champion Cheddar at the Dairy Show and won supreme honours at this show five times in all. Undoubtedly the Whites, like so many other traditionalists, were extremely good cheese-makers, but the fact is that good results, and consistent results, are also obtained by a more modern approach. Moreover, modern methods are more easily taught and do not take half a lifetime to learn. But the average farmer reading *Man o' Mendip's* article would be led to think that Cannington methods were only second best, and not as good as was claimed. This sort of news report did not openly criticise Cannington, or modern methods, but criticism was implied, and represented the suspicious attitude to "book-learning" which was so prevalent at the time in farming circles, particularly among the older generation.

It was by constant meetings, lectures, demonstrations, competitions, farm visits and articles in local newspapers, together with support for Young Farmers Clubs, that W.D.Hay and the Cannington staff gradually persuaded the Somerset farming community to accept modern scientific methods. However, an additional and vitally important factor was the effect of Cannington on farmers' sons and daughters as students of the Institute, who accepted scientific ideas gladly, having in many cases been frustrated at home on the farm by what they considered to be the "stick-in-the-mud" attitudes of their fathers. However, a point in Cannington's favour with the older generation was no doubt Mr England's principle of "Work hard, play hard" and his claim that he would develop their muscles as well as their knowledge!

Cheese-making in an old round copper cheese-tub.

But Cannington had other roles too, apart from spreading knowledge and developing muscles. It also housed a weather station, with G.E.Furse as 'Observer', with records published regularly, and also hosted the National Institute of Agricultural Botany wheat variety trials, also under Mr Furse.

At the same time the Horticultural Department was becoming well known as a centre of excellence, and - apart from its educational achievements - became famous for its experimental collection of early dwarf pyramid apple trees, planted in the 1920s, which compared the new M2 and M9 rootstocks from East Malling.

Moreover, the Poultry Department, in developing the work recorded on page 6, organised Accredited Breeding Stations and Accredited Hatcheries under a Ministry of Agriculture scheme which encouraged the production of blood-tested and trap-nested stock, which were made available to poultry producers in the county and elsewhere (p.48). Egg-laying trials were part of the scheme and poultry breeders could enter standard pens of their hens for them to be trap-nested at Cannington under controlled conditions, and their results officially registered. People could then buy hatching eggs or chicks with a Cannington "seal" knowing that not only were they healthy, but also that they were from proven good egg laying strains. (pp.48,55).

Cannington was coming to be accepted as the agricultural and horticultural centre of the County by producers in both spheres.

The 'cheddaring' process in a

modern steam-jacketed vat

Chapter 6. Student Life in the 1930s

As good an introduction as any to the life of a student of the 1930s can be found in the Prospectus for 1935-1936   Not only does it detail the Syllabus for each of the Cannington departments, recorded in the Miscellany (p.118), it also lists the rules of conduct and the clothing needed by each type of student (p.39). The Prospectus also describes in some detail the farm, gardens and livestock and the facilities available to students. It also lists the Staff; the only survivors of the original staff being W.D.Hay and A.D. Turner.

THE STAFF 1935-36

Principal -W.D.Hay
AGRICULTURE
The Principal
Vice-Principal - W.J.England
HORTICULTURE
Superintendant - A.D.Turner
Instructor at Institute - R.A.Engledow
DAIRYING
County Superintendant - Miss M.C.Taylor N.D.D.
Head Instructress at Institute - Miss E.M.Monie N.D.D.(Hons) C.D.D.
Asst. Instructress at Institute - Miss L. Tomlinson N.D.D,
POULTRY HUSBANDRY
Chief County Instructor - H.H.Duckett N.D.P., L.D.A.
Instructress at Institute - Miss M.L.Mann N.D.P.

GENERAL INFORMATION

OBJECTS

The primary object of this Institute is to provide instruction in the science and practice of Agriculture, Horticulture, Dairying and Poultry-Husbandry to young men and women who intend taking up one or other of these industries as their future occupation, or who may desire to take a Farm Institute course as a preliminary to more advanced instruction in a College or University. The instruction is of a practical nature, the whole aim being to make it of immediate utility and application.

THE INSTITUTE

There is hostel accommodation for 25 women and 25 men students. The premises are fitted with modern conveniences, central heating and electric light throughout. Each student has a good bedroom, and there is ample classroom accommodation. Separate common rooms are provided for men and women students.

A Library of standard works on Agriculture, Horticulture, Dairying, Poultry Husbandry, and other subjects is provided, to which students have free access.

During the winter months there is a weekly debate which helps greatly in bringing out backward students. There is also a social evening arranged weekly which was attended by the staff and students. Recreation is provided for in the form of lawn tennis, table tennis, hockey, cricket and football.

THE FARM

Court Farm, which adjoins the Farm Institute, has been purchased by the County Council and provides facilities for instruction and demonstration on practical farm work. It extends to 175 acres and contains about 50 acres of arable land and 3 acres of orchards, the remainder being pasture and meadow land. The arable land lies on red sandstone formation and may be described as a silty loam, but much of the meadow land is typical of the heavy alluvial soils adjoining the River Parret.

A special feature of the farm is the grassland which has been systematically close grazed and manured, the whole grassland being treated as a crop.

The arable land has been reduced to 50 acres as a temporary measure. About a quarter of this area is under roots: mangolds, swedes, sugar beet, potatoes, kale etc. The remainder includes winter wheat and oats and spring barley with as many catch crops as possible.

EXPERIMENTS AND DEMONSTRATIONS

Different methods of cultivation and manuring are tested. Manurial and variety trials of practically all the common farm crops are undertaken.

A special feature of the farm is the National Institute of Agricultural Botany Crop Testing Station where variety trials of Wheat (spring and winter), Oats (spring and winter), Barley, Mangolds, Swedes, Potatoes and Sugar Beet are carried out, providing a most interesting feature of the farm. Trials of various [grass] seeds mixtures are also showing striking results and are well worth a visit.

LIVESTOCK

Livestock is well represented on the farm. There is a really good herd of Dairy Shorthorns, and by the use of first class sires there is being built up a milking strain with strong constitution. (Half of the herd is milked by machine, and half by hand).

A flying flock consisting mostly of Dorset Down ewes crossed with Southdown rams produce early lambs for the Easter fat lamb trade.

A pure bred Large White herd together with representatives of other breeds including Large Blacks and Wessex Saddlebacks are used to demonstrate the type of pig suitable for the bacon trade under the newly inaugurated Pig Marketing Scheme. Experimental work on feeding and management also take a prominent part in this department. A new model pig fattening house has been erected incorporating the most up-to-date methods of management, feeding and weighing of pigs.

The work horses are a very good type of Percheron breed.

The farm buildings have been remodelled so as to effect economy in the housing and feeding of livestock. Gravitation water has been laid into the premises and electric light installed. The machinery and implements are of modern types and include all those commonly used on a mixed arable and grass farm.

THE DAIRY

The Dairy attached to the Institute is fitted up in the most up-to-date manner for the practical handling of large quantities of milk. It is fully equipped with modern appliances for the treatment of milk and the making of butter and various types of cheeses. One of the features of the course is the number of students who have found posts after completion of the necessary training.

HORTICULTURAL DEPARTMENT

This comprises about 18 acres of land specially arranged to provide facilities for giving instruction to students in all the chief branches of horticultural practice and to provide demonstrations on methods of management, cultural details and comparative tests of varieties.
a) Gardens attached to the Farm Institute
b) Fruit Plantation, Market Garden and Nursery.
Cultivation machinery and power sprayer are in use.

THE POULTRY DEPARTMENT

All aspects of the Poultry Industry are catered for in this Section. Breeds now kept are: White Leghorns, Rhode Island Reds, White Wyandottes, Light Sussex and Buff Rocks. Ducks are represented by *the Aylesbury, Pekin, Rouen, Khaki Campbell and Indian Runner. Small flocks of Turkeys include Austrian White and American Mammoth Bronze. Embden, Toulouse, Roman and Chinese Geese each have their place in this section. The department keeps up-to-date with the rapid strides which the industry is making in intensive and extensive work. Incubating and brooding by electricity are now being undertaken, as well as battery brooding.* (Extracts from the 1935-1936 Prospectus).

PERSONAL MEMORIES

Various students have from time to time recorded their memories of those early days in the COSA Magazine, and some of these have been reproduced here.

From a Dairying Student of 1932/33

I started the dairy course at the Farm Institute in the Autumn of 1932 under a delusion: after leaving school in July we sought advice from the Devon County Council as I wanted to take a horticultural course. I did botany as a subject at School Certificate and always enjoyed gardening and growing plants but I was told that there was no opening for girls in those days and got conned into dairying, being assured it would be an open air occupation! I soon discovered that it was quite the opposite after finishing at Cannington.

However, I duly arrived at the Farm Institute and next day, decked out in our apple green cotton dresses, white collars, aprons and caps we reported at the dairy at 7 a.m. to be greeted by Miss Monie, whose accent gave us a little difficulty at first, especially when the steam boiler was going 'full blast' in the scullery. We were allotted our dairy duties, a week in each - the cheese room, butter room and scullery. Breakfast at 8 a.m., then back to the dairy for a morning's practical work. Miss Tomlinson (later Mrs J.Morris) was the butter making instructress, there were six churns and butter-workers which produced ½ lb of recognisable butter eventually; sometimes a student forgot to clamp the lid on the churn or put the bung in the churn when washing the butter grains, with disastrous results. We also did soft and cream cheese-making and milk testing.

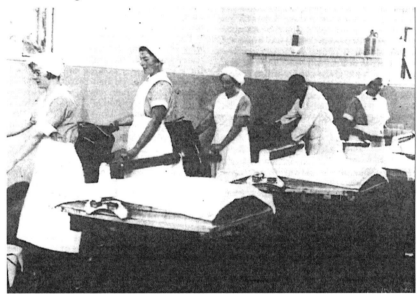

Butter-making : Left to Right: Coker (Devon), Connett, James, Kelloway, Marsh (COSA Magazine No.13)

Milk for the dairy was received from four local farms by horse and milk float (a two-wheeled cart):
1. The Farm Institute had a Shorthorn herd, and the milk was delivered in 10 gallon churns by Laurie White, a jovial soul.
2. Mr Wilkie of Blackmore Lane had a Friesian herd, this milk came in 17 gallon churns, not popular as they were so heavy to handle.
3. Mr Tatchell of Rodway Farm (a farm no longer), this was brought by a dear 'old boy', white whiskered and one of the old school.
4. Mr Berry of Park Lane, usually the last to arrive.

The total gallonage of milk was 100-120 gallons. This came in at the scullery platform (removed now by SWEB) the churns of milk manhandled off the floats and rolled over to the tipping tank, strained and then descended to cheese vats by chute as needed to join the evening's milk already in the vats.

The scullery students had been on duty at 5 p.m. to receive the evening's milk and wash up and steam the churns, ready to be taken back the next day, plus anything else you could dump in the scullery to get out of washing up. Cheese making started after breakfast, when Miss Monie had added her magic dose of starter (lactic acid yogurt), according to the acidity of the milk. Cannington had a very good reputation for Cheddar Cheese making and ex-students making cheese at farmhouses and small factories were supervised by Miss Taylor and her assistant. Miss Maddever carried on the tradition. The cheese in the dairy was always finished in time for lectures at 2 p.m. - 4 p.m. then the cheese room/scullery students had to go to the dairy again to turn the cheeses in the press and the scullery students to take in the evening's milk; as you may have gathered the butter room duties were more popular than cheese and scullery duties as you finished at lunch time. How many students remember scrubbing the Caerphilly room stairs, cleaning brass window catches and the copper and windows! The ripening room was a means of retreat for a while, turning the cheese on the shelves daily. Did anyone turn the turning dales the wrong way and all the newly made cheese shot out on the floor, sometimes with disastrous results?

The highlight of the week was two Agricultural students coming into the dairy for a week at a time, we had extra muscle power and usually some minor accidents! In the spring term we had short course students who were to make cheese in farmhouse dairies, often farmers' daughters, and six Devon students for a butter-making course.

After supper we had private study, which had to be done in the lecture room, sexes segregated: sometimes under the supervision of a lecturer - this was for an hour. We had no television, only the radio and radiogram in the hall (Clifford) for dancing, no mixing of the sexes except on Wednesdays and Saturdays, lights out at 10 p.m. We were all addressed by our surnames, it saved confusion if more than one person had the same Christian name; all the lecturers were addressed as Mr. or Miss, etc.

On Wednesday afternoons there were games, football or mixed hockey and in the evenings usually a speaker on a subject of general interest or else a debate amongst the students on a variety of subjects. Saturday afternoons we had football or hockey, if the games were at home the visiting teams stayed on and joined us for a dance in the main hall to the radiogram, these took place every Saturday. Dancing was the partnered era,

Miss EM Monie when you held your partner and danced in some sort of order. The staff used to attend as well, as seven of the staff were resident in those days. They were:

Agriculture - Mr W.D.Hay, Principal (he lived at Court Farm House); Mr G.G.Gregory, Vice-Principal; Mr Murchie (Assistant County Advisor), Mr G. Furse, NIAB Crop Recorder.

Dairy - Miss M.Taylor, County Advisor; Miss E.M.Monie, Cheese; Miss J.Tomlinson (later Mrs Morris), Butter Instructress; Miss M.Britten, Assistant County Advisor.

Horticulture - Mr A.D.Turner (Court House); Mr Ingledon, Head of Gardens; Mr Forshaw, County Advisor: mainly orchards.

Poultry - Mr Duckett, County Advisor; Mr F. Warburton, Assistant County Advisor; Miss M.Mann, Head of Poultry Section (opposite the cemetery); Mr Moses, Egg Laying Trials.

Matron - Miss F.Ferguson.

Ted Croaker was caretaker/boilerman, he used to get up steam in the dairy boiler for sterilising and heating the milk. He had two more boilers on the right of the quad entrance for hot water for the students, central heating and kitchen use, these all had to be stoked by hand, a young fellow used to help him with odd jobs. Ted also collected and sorted the post, he lived with his wife in the cottage by the first walled garden, they were like a couple out of "Pickwick Papers". Ted, tall and lean, cap dead centre and his wife, 'Granny Croaker' (as she was affectionately known) was round and comfortable, she liked you to admire her 'Ginneraniums' and during holiday time, when the curd settled mid-morning on a Sunday we had a rock cake and cup of tea in Granny's kitchen with a shining glowing range and dresser with treasured china.

Adjoining the Croakers' cottage was the laundry - in charge Mrs Bowering, her daughter Mrs Capel and one other (whose name escapes me), all great village characters. They did the laundry for the students, staff and domestic staff. No washing machines, spin driers or tumble driers, all done by hand in large troughs and put through a large wooden-rollered mangle (hard on buttons) no drip-dry material, all cotton and starched aprons, etc. They had their own boiler and dried the clothes on long lines above the boiler, if you were lucky you could use the iron in the dinner hour or on Saturday to press a few things.

The offices were on the right and left of the entrance to the quad, on the right of Mr Hay's, the. Vice-Principal's office, the second room the accountant's office - Mr Ball. On the left, the general office, Miss Santler was Mr Hay's secretary. Beyond that Matron's office and the staff dining room, the staff corridor above it.

There were four or five resident domestic staff who were responsible for the cleaning, helping in the kitchen peeling vegetables, (no potato peelers) and washing up, (no dish washers) and waiting at table for meals. No Priory Lodge or labs, just a long stone wall.

We enjoyed our courses and made our own fun, only allowed out at the week-end to be in by 10p.m., and one week-end at home a term, public houses out of bounds. We had a good social life as everybody lived in and around the buildings, although it sounds rather limited there were possible ways round a lot of the rules and all enjoyed it. I came back to the dairy staff in 1936 after hard labour on the cheese circuit, but that's another story! *From the 1990/91 COSA Magazine:No. 13. - from D.Lovell (Connett) 1932/33 D.* (who later joined the Dairying staff and afterwards was a Governor of SFI 1965-81, Ed).

From a Dairying Student of 1932/33

It was in 1933 that I packed my bags and trunk and returned home to Durborough Farm, Nether Stowey, having finished a very successful Dairying course at what was then the Somerset Farm Institute. I remember those days as having given me a lot of satisfaction and achievement due to the guidance of Miss Monie, Miss Taylor and Miss Maddever. Happy times! We worked hard and indeed had lots of fun in a very simple way. I still hear the echo of Miss Monie's Scots accent - "Snook, you must not go to the farm with the boys"

No sign of rigid segregation

of the sexes in this photograph

There were no 'mod cons' in the dairy. After the production of butter or cheese came the scrubbing of all wooden working tops and polishing of brass taps and cheese vat surrounds; not forgetting the copper boiler which was installed inside the main dairy entrance - no half measures - we must see our reflection clearly.

How nice it would be to reminisce with my old colleagues and chat about our more adventurous moments - the dances in the main hall with the last dance to the tune of 'Good night, Sweetheart", everyone trying to be hidden by one of those huge pillars. Our Saturday evening to the cinema in 'ye olde coach' run by Metford Day was also an event.   (from Joan Pope [Snook] 1932/33 - Mag.No.7: `1984)

They look demure enough here.

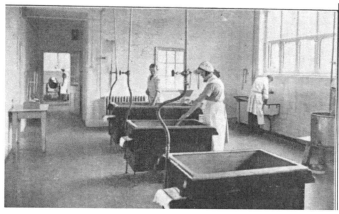

The Dairy in 1935. The Cheesemaking Room with a view of the Buttermaking Room at the far left. (from the 1935/36 Prospectus).

From a Dairying Student of 1935/6

"I went to Cannington as a Dairy student in 1935/36 when I was 16 in the days of W.D.Hay, Miss Monie, Miss Maddever and Jackie England and well remember the 'loose boxes' looking out over the quad, the women's common room with the gramophone blaring out. 'Red Sails in the Sunset' seemed to be our favourite record. Having to be in by 7pm, a supervised study period, cocoa and cheese at 9.00, lights out by 10.00!

The uniform for dairy students was white cap and apron worn over a short sleeved apple green cotton dress with voluminous knickers to match, presumably to hide the layers of "thermals" as they are called today, we needed to wear underneath - it was jolly cold in the dairy when we started off in the morning but trousers and wellingtons were not approved for women at that time. The training was tough but superb as was the follow-up by Miss Taylor and the County staff that we received while working as cheesemakers in the County afterwards." *from Mary Dench (Loxton). COSA Magazine 2004.*

The 1935/36 Dairying Course
(left to right): Unknown; Jean Derret ; Miss Taylor; Unknown; Bill Dredge; Kingwell;
Mary Dench (Loxton); Miss Maddever; Miss Mann?

From a Horticultural Student of 1935/1936 (COSA Magazine - 1998)

Muriel Loveridge wrote that there were three girls and 10 boys in her group in that year. The girls "were warned that Mr A.D.Turner was not keen on girls", but Muriel feels "they went some way towards his acceptance of females when they all worked well and did well in their exams". Muriel went from fruit farming to market gardening, then on joining the Women's Land Army helped to grow vegetables for a Sanatorium and finally ended as a gardener at a "Stately Home". She was disappointed when she came back to visit Cannington in the late 1990s to find that vegetables had been replaced by "useless exotic flowers". (*Photograph on left from Muriel Loveridge*).

Left: Two Horticultural students, Loveday Grenfell and Honor Henslow in March 1936

(See Honor Henslow's memories - p.102)

Below: The 1932/33 Annual Visit to Long Ashton Research Station by the Governors and HorticulturaL students (COSA Magazine 1999).

(photo from A. F. R . Fisher)

Disbudding Chrysanthemums - 1932/33
L:R: Bastable, Fisher, 'Chub' Pyne, Graham, Miss Shoobridge, Ridler-Rowe, Whittuck, Miss?, Mr Englefield, Sims.

1935/36 - Somerset Farm Institute - Horti Students
Left to right. CRJ Badman, ML Tickell, RWD Osmond, EJ Edney, AHM Brown, RJ Dorey, DW Eyles
PC Gammon, KG Nelmes, Miss M Loveridge, Miss L Grenfell, WG Baskerville, Miss H Henslow
sent in by Miss Loveridge.

Said to be 'Chub' Pyne digging - 1933

Left: Bill Heyward and staff - 1933

PART OF THE POULTRY TRAINING CENTRE, SHOWING BROODER HOUSE ON THE LEFT, BATTERY BROODER ON THE RIGHT, AND THE FOOD STORE AND INCUBATOR HOUSE IN THE BACKGROUND.

The poultry department was very active in the 1930s, but during the 1920s had suffered from cramped accommodation and needed more land for its required expansion. Fortunately a small field adjoining the farm came on the market and was acquired by the quick thinking of Mr D.M. Wills, Chairman of the Agricultural Instruction Committee. A local press item of 1931 gives the details:

"At a meeting of the County Agricultural Committee the Agricultural Instruction Committee reported a proposed acquisition of land for the use of Cannington Poultry Department.

It had been brought to the notice of their Chairman (Mr D.M.Wills) that a field at Cannington near the Institute, comprising about 6½ acres, was being sold early in September, and as the vendor was not prepared to keep the land unsold until after the meeting of the County Council, their Chairman himself made an offer of £600 for the purchase of the land, which was accepted. The committee recommended the County Council to adopt the purchase of this land for £600, subject to the approval of the Ministry of Agriculture. The Chairman, (Captain Watson) said the land available had been quite insufficient and unsuitable, and for several years Mr Hay and the committee had been looking round for suitable land on which to carry on the instruction on proper lines. This field was on the main road, just beyond the entrance to Cannington, and had been valued at £600 by the District Valuer."

There were objections, as was usual in such cases, and it was generally agreed that the price was higher than the normal agricultural price, and one committee member opined that the price might have been lower if it had gone to auction. However, it was pointed out that there was already an offer for the land of £550, and if they wanted it they had to pay more. The land provided a frontage suitable for building purposes and it was considered good value for money because now the whole of the [poultry] work could be centralised. The recommendation was approved.

A moveable poultry ark for use on a general farm to fold over grassland. They improved the grass and minimised the spread of disease

35

Members of the 1936/37 Poultry Course
At the back: Bowley, Soper; Middle two: Pearce, Tocer; Front: Mabb, Taylor, Hazell

FARM INSTITUTE SCHOLARSHIPS.

The Scholarships Committee recommended the awarding of the following scholarships and studentships at the Farm Institute:— Senior agricultural scholarship, value £120, for a further year, Wilfred Henry G. Blacker, aged 19, of Lower North End Farm, Clutton, near Bristol. Agricultural scholarships for three terms—Thomas Leonard Hunter (16), Wilcox Farm, Hatch Beauchamp; William Stanley Shattock (16), Branchflower Farm, North Petherton; George Jarrett (18), Byron Villa, Clevedon; Reginald Frank Tucker (16), Blagdon Hill, near Taunton. Horticultural scholarships for a further three terms—Richard Chivers Lamb (18), 24, Station-road, Taunton; John Edwin Fear (17), Fender House, Combwich. Dairying scholarships for one year— Marjorie Rosewell (20), Devonia, Crewkerne-road, Chard; Gladys Margaret Owens (16), Shepstones Farm, Langford, near Bristol; Cecil Trump (21), Laurel House, Alhampton, Ditcheat; Trevor Hillier (16), Rode, near Bath; Frederick John Cottle (16), Chilkwell Farm, Glastonbury; Leslie James Drew (18), Royal Hotel, Templecombe. Poultry scholarships for three terms—Joseph William Wall (16), High-street, Street; Kathleen Joan Cottle (16), West-street, Somerton; and Edith Joan Fear (18), Land's End Farm, Heath House, Wedmore.

The recommendations were approved.

Those were the days!
Notably George Jarrett & Wm Shattock!
(Som.County Herald 22/9/34)

George Jarrett in later years
(COSA magazine 1983)

1936/37 Agricultural Students
Back Three: Green, Cross, Lawrence; With pipe: Davidson;
Front: J.L.Braithwaite, Peares, Timstone, Jack Whittle, Russell

MEMORIES OF AGRICULTURE

Extracts from George Jarrett's 1935 Farm Diary. *(Photo opposite)*

Monday January 14th. Up at 4.45 a.m. to go over to Highbridge bacon factory, today they killed 95 pigs. From the time of killing to weighing it takes 20 minutes. To remove the hairs they pass through a burner operating at great heat. The pigs are first stunned by being electrocuted lasting about 10 seconds and then stuck. Arrived back at 8a.m. Lectures later at 9.30 - 10.30. Mr Hay discusssed our visit and 11-12 Botany with Mr Furze. In the afternoon visited Butcher Ellicott's slaughterhouse in Bridgwater, saw one bullock and 5 sheep killed. On pigs after tea with Tucker. Weather rather cold and damp.

Wednesday January 16th On pigs. Had a sow farrow 13, now 10 living. Went down to Wadlands with Bill White and did a bit of wall repairing where the pigs had been rooting about. In the afternoon rolled down the stone road leading from the piggeries out to the sows' run in Hockey field. Later feeding the trial pigs. Wrote to Uncle George enclosing the draft copy on cabbage growing. Wrote home. Germany had won back the Saar with an overwhelming majority of over 90%. *[Disputed border area which had voted under 1st.W.War Peace Treaty terms - Ed.]*. Had debate in evening. Mild and overcast.

Wednesday January 30th Butter making in dairy with Bosker. Made butter on our own. In the afternoon drawing timber in the Downs until 3. The West Gloster Hockey team, after this match today, were entertained to a dance in the evening after losing 4-1. They had a big amplifier fixed for the dance and we had a very good time 6-10pm. I announced one dance over the microphone which is the first time I have ever spoken into one. Cold.

Sunday February 24th On Poultry until 10.30am. After dinner 8 of us went for a cycle ride up through Nether Stowey and towards the Quantocks but got caught in heavy rain. Trump, Wyatt, Napper, Richardson, Stokes, Cottle, Box and myself. Wrote to Mother. Frost, heavy rain from 2.30 onwards.

From COSA Magazines 1992 &2005 (cont'd overleaf)

Students Ploughing and Harrowing (from the 1932/33 Prospectus)

<u>May 8th 1935</u>   (George Jarrett's diary - cont'd)
On cows till 11 a.m. when I went off with Mr England in the lorry up around Wells, Glastonbury, Radstock, Midsomer Norton, Midford etc., after examples of rocks for the Bath and West. Mr Ling and Mr Murchie went on in front in their car. Had some lunch on top of the Mendips and tea at Mrs Whites*, Church Farm, Clutton, where Mr England used to be. Got back at 7.30 after an interesting day. Fresh!
Mr England did his practical year here with Marjorie Hartley's (Withers) Grandparents.
<u>May 30th 1935</u>
Went down to the Bath and West Show at Taunton. Very good show indeed. Saw one of W.J. King's Gyrotillers and also a Combine Harvester. Very good entry of 61 Devons, 98 Guernseys and 90 Jerseys. H.M. the King took first with his bull *Bastridge Gentleman*. V. close
(From COSA Magazines 1992 &2005)

Men and teams at

the Farm entrance

(From the 1932/33

Prospectus)

<u>L to R</u> :   *Walt Quartly, Bill White and Tom Burge.`*

1934. *On the load: Maurice Heywood, Jack King; Walking: Tom Burge*
Two Percheron mares: Sabobile and Joyce
(The mechanical hayloader behind the wagon delivered continuous large rolls of hay - very difficult to handle - Ed.).

FROM THE 1934/35 PROSPECTUS

28

CLOTHING AND EQUIPMENT.

In addition to their ordinary clothing, students are required to provide themselves with the following:—

AGRICULTURE.

MEN.—
One three-quarter length khaki cotton coat—for poultry work.
Two three-quarter length white drill coats—for milking.
Two white cotton caps—for milking.
Two khaki shirts.

WOMEN.—
Two khaki coats.
Two pairs khaki breeches.
Two khaki handkerchiefs for head wear.
Two khaki smock overalls—for summer wear.
Two three-quarter length white drill coats—for milking.
Two white cotton caps—for milking.

HORTICULTURE.

MEN.—
Two khaki shirts.

WOMEN.—
Two khaki coats.
Two pairs khaki breeches.
Two khaki handkerchiefs for head wear.
Two khaki smock overalls—for summer wear.

POULTRY HUSBANDRY.

MEN.—
Two three-quarter length khaki cotton coats.
One three-quarter length white drill coat.
One white bib apron.
One coarse hessian bib apron.
Two khaki shirts.

WOMEN.—
Two khaki coats.
Two pairs khaki breeches.
Two khaki handkerchiefs for head wear.
Two khaki smock overalls—for summer wear.
One three-quarter length white drill coat.
One white bib apron.
One coarse hessian bib apron.
One brown beret for wet weather.

NOTE.—All the above equipment must be obtained from D. Philipps & Co., 15, Fore Street, Bridgwater.

DAIRYING.

MEN.—
Three white coats.
Six white aprons.
One coarse hessian bib apron.

WOMEN.—
Two apple green overalls (Length: 4 inches below knee).
Three white collars.
Six white aprons.
One coarse hessian bib apron.
Three white caps.
Two pairs apple green knickers.
One khaki handkerchief for head wear—poultry work.
Apple green jersey (optional).

NOTE.—The above equipment for the Dairying students must be obtained from W. & A. Chapman, Ltd., 20 to 26, North Street, Taunton.

ALL STUDENTS should also supply themselves with:—
Strong boots or shoes. Wellington rubber boots. Laundry bag and book. Note books and text books for lectures (obtainable at the Institute).

GENERAL REGULATIONS.

The Vice-Principal and the Matron are together responsible for the order and discipline at the Institute, the health and comfort of all students being the Matron's special responsibility.

1. Students must be punctual in their attendance at meals, practical work and lectures. They must be orderly in their work and assist in maintaining the discipline of the Institute.

2. Students must not absent themselves from meals nor during working hours without permission from the Vice-Principal.

3. Leave of absence will only be granted in exceptional circumstances. Such leave must be applied for on the proper form (obtainable from the Head Student) at least 24 hours previous to such leave being granted. This form must be countersigned by the Chief of the department concerned and handed to the Vice-Principal by the Head Student.

4. Students (or their parents or guardians) will be held liable for all damage to Institute property caused by them. In addition to the fees there shall be paid in respect of each student the sum of £1 as Caution Money at the beginning of the student's course to pay for damage to property or breakages (if any.)

   The Principal shall have an absolute discretion as to the application of this money and his decision as to the responsibility for damage shall be final and binding upon the parents or guardians and students.

   The money, or any balance not forfeited in this way, will be refunded at the end of the student's course. Breakages and damage must be reported at once.

5. Students are required to keep their quarters neat and orderly. All boots must be cleaned in the boot-room.

6. Students are forbidden to smoke in the bedrooms and in farm buildings.

7. Students are not allowed to have candles in their bedrooms.

8. During the winter and spring terms, students are not allowed out after supper without permission.

9. All Public Houses are out of bounds.

10. Head Students will be elected at the commencement of each term.

11. The use of cycles or motor-cycles before 4.30 p.m. on Mondays, Tuesdays, Thursdays and Fridays and 1 p.m. on Wednesdays and Saturdays is strictly forbidden. Motor-cycles must on no account be used during working hours without special permission.

12. Head Students will report any infringement of the above rules.

The Dairy Shorthorn Milking Herd

Traditional type
milk cooler

The Prince of Wales Cup YFC Stock-Judging - 1937   *(although cooling was*

Reg Shattock, R.G.Withers, R.C.Bird with Mr Congdon   *by water it was often*

(from Reg Shattock Branchflower Farm, North Petherton).   *called a "refrigerator")*

Chapter 7. County Work in Wartime.

The Horticultural Department

At the beginning of the war in 1939 the Ministry of Agriculture issued a series of Bulletins to encourage food production. The first, "Grower No.1, Food from Gardening" aimed to help gardeners and holders of allotments, particularly novices, in the production of food for their families, to relieve the demand for imported food, and to arouse interest in food growing in gardens and allotments generally. Demonstration Plots were to be established around the country in places where the public had easy access, particularly in Parks or Public Gardens, but also on allotments, to encourage and educate people in the art of food growing. This was the start of the ultimately very successful 'Dig for Victory' Campaign.

At the Meeting of the Agricultural Instruction sub-Committe of 7.12.39, the Horticultural Superintendant reported that a scheme had been arranged for Demonstration Allotments in co-operation with local councils and Allotment Societies, as centres for lectures and demonstations in 10 or 12 urban areas, cropped to a plan advised by the Ministry of Agriculture in a war-time bulletin; that these plots would be 30 square rods in area, worked by a person appointed by the council or society, the seeds and manures being provided by and the rent paid by this sub-Committee; and that each plot would cost about 45/- to 50/- to establish and maintain for a year. The sub-Committee approved of these arrangements.

The response in Somerset thus initiated by Cannington, was organised at first by Mr G. Powell with the later aid of Miss E.M. Cope, under the direction of Mr A.D.Turner, the Superintendant. As already mentioned on page 6, as early as 1921 A.D.Turner had established Demonstration Plots at six centres around the County, so he was not new to the game!

Twelve centres were chosen and in each of these places plots of 90 feet by 30 feet were established, each in the charge of a competent gardener. The centres selected were:

Minehead	Street	Glastonbury
Wells	Shepton Mallet	Wellington
Portishead	Midsomer Norton	Ilchester
Bridgwater No.1	Bridgwater No.2	Cannington (SFI)

Later plots were established also at Taunton, Radstock,Yeovil, Chard, Langport and Weston super Mare, and the final number was 23 plots.

Most of the plots were on allotment fields, but three were in public parks or gardens, and later four more were moved to public areas by agreement with the local authority. Only one plot had to be discontinued, and that was only because of the continued illness of the plot holder.

Plot holders in the scheme had to keep a diary and note down seeds sown, fertilisers and Farmyard Manure or compost applied, with dates. Each plot was supplied with 20 lbs Sulphate of Ammonia, 30 lbs Superphosphate and 20 lbs Sulphate of Potash. Plot holders recorded the weights of the crops and the date when they harvested them, as well as making a note of the hours they spent working on their plot.

At all of these plots, apart from regular supervisory visits, literally hundreds of lectures and demonstrations were given by either Mr Powell or Miss Cope, with a great response from the local population, in spite of the fact that many were new to vegetable gardening. The plots were watched carefully by the public who used them as guides to their own gardening, and were able to ask for advice from Mr Powell and Miss Cope while they were making routine visits. (See advertisement: p.44)

As a result of this scheme the name of Cannington became known among the general public as well as the farming community.

The Agricultural Department

The ploughing-up movement of the 1930s laid the basis for the more intensive wartime campaign which was immediately under way as soon as the war started. However, by harvest-time of 1940 it was clear that some farmers' crops on newly ploughed grassland had not all been successful, and that an educational campaign was needed to ensure that farmers became more capable of producing good crops in

SOMERSET WAR AGRICULTURAL EXECUTIVE COMMITTEE,

in co-operation with the

NATIONAL FARMERS' UNION

and the

SOMERSET COUNTY FEDERATION OF YOUNG FARMERS' CLUBS,

will Hold

MASS MEETINGS

of Vital Importance to Farmers and the Nation at

RED LION HOTEL, AXBRIDGE, 12th August, at 7.30 p.m. punctually. Chairman, Mr. E. T. TILLEY.

COUNCIL CHAMBER, GLASTONBURY, 16th August, at 7.30 p.m. punctually. Chairman, Mr. E. A. AUSTIN.

ROYAL CLARENCE HOTEL, BRIDGWATER, 20th August, at 7.30 p.m. punctually. Chairman, Mr. C. D. WAINWRIGHT.

AGRICULTURAL HALL, SPARKFORD, 17th August, at 7.30 p.m. punctually. Chairman, Mr. A. POWLETT.

BOYS' COUNCIL SCHOOL, WATERLOO-ROAD, SHEPTON MALLET, 19th August, at 7.30 p.m. punctually. Chairman, Mr. A. POWLETT.

LANGPORT ARMS HOTEL, LANGPORT, 21st August, at 7.30 p.m. punctually. Chairman, Capt. V. LEAN.

BLAKE MEMORIAL HALL, SOUTH PETHERTON, 22nd August, at 7.30 p.m. punctually. Chairman, Capt. V. LEAN.

CORN EXCHANGE, CHARD, 23rd August, at 7.30 p.m. punctually. Chairman, Capt. V. LEAN.

VICTORIA ROOMS, MILVERTON, 27th August, at 7.30 p.m. punctually. Chairman, Mr. E. A. RICHARDS.

THE GEORGE HOTEL, TAUNTON, 31st August, at 6.30 p.m. punctually. Chairman, Mr. J. C. BADCOCK.

TOWN HALL, DULVERTON, 26th August, at 6.30 p.m. punctually. Chairman, Mr. J. H. TURNER.

WHEDDON CROSS MEMORIAL HALL, 28th August, at 6.30 p.m. punctually. Chairman, Mr. B. HOSEGOOD.

WILLITON CHURCH ROOM, WILLITON, 29th August, at 7.30 p.m. punctually. Chairman, Mr. T. L. WHITE.

The Meetings are so arranged that those coming from a distance may get home before dark.

To Discuss:

(1) Crop failures, and how to avert them for the 1940-41 harvest.

(2) Treatment of grass land—re-seeding, etc.

(3) What is expected of the all-grass dairy farmer.

(4) Any other subject dealing with maximum food production.

Mr. W. D. HAY, County Agricultural Organiser, will address each meeting.

I am aware that harvest will be in full swing, but the production of food for the 1941 harvest is much more important than the farmer's absence for one evening to attend such a meeting.

D. M. WILLS, Chairman, Somerset War Agricultural Executive Committee.

1941. A series of "Mass Meetings" was arranged for August 1940 in many centres throughout the County to bolster the effect of an "open week" held at Cannington during July. The term "Mass Meeting" was not usually associated with the farming community, however the meetings were held successfully and must have made an appreciable impact on farmers.

The thinking behind these meetings was stated by W.D.Hay in letters to the local press, exemplified by the following one of 9/8/40.

"Sir - I wish to draw attention of your readers to the very important mass meetings of farmers which are advertised in this issue of your paper. I do so because of the importance of food production, especially for the 1941 harvest.

You may know that we held an "open week" at this Institute during the week commencing July 15th when we had large parties of farmers here to discuss crop failures and how to avert them for the 1941 harvest, followed by inspection of crops at this Institute.

I was astounded at the interest created during that week when we had well over a thousand farmers from Somerset and some forty to fifty from Gloucester and Wiltshire, but many more should have been here.

Since these meetings I have had a large number of enthusiastic letters from farmers and also from others who were disappointed that they did not come over to hear our views on the best way to ensure a full crop.

I am, therefore, very pleased to say that the War Agricultural Executive Committee have instructed me to speak at a large number of mass meetings of farmers covering the whole of the county. These meetings are convened in co-operation with the national Farmers' Union and the Somerset Federation of Young Farmers' Clubs.

It is to be hoped that every farmer (and especially those who know little or nothing about arable or grass farming) will attend these meetings and help to raise the standard of farming in the county, as it is most important that the maximum amount of food should be produced for the 1941 harvest.

W.D.Hay
Somerset Farm Institute, Cannington,
       Bridgwater".

A report of one of the mass meetings published in the Western Gazette on 16th August 1940 showed that farmers were being told to "pull up their socks":

WHAT THEIR WAR EFFORT MUST BE

COUNTY ORGANISER "TAKES THE GLOVES OFF"

A series of meetings arranged by the Somerset War Agricultural Executive Committee, in co-operation with the National Farmers' Union and Young Farmers' Clubs, with the object of ensuring maximum food production in the county, was opened on Monday. Mr W.D.Hay (County Agricultural Organiser) addressed a meeting of farmers at Farrington Gurney on Wednesday evening when Major C.M. Roberts presided.

Major Roberts said the industry had to be self-supporting and that was all there was to it. What they did not produce on their own farms they ran the gravest risk of having to do without. He knew in that particular district there was a large number of grass farms occupied by men who for generations had had a traditional dislike or fear of arable land and Mr Hay would tell them how they could get away from that tradition, and why they should do so. [see p.ix].

The County Executive had been given vast powers and if they were met with defiance or by obstruction those powers would be used to the fullest extent. The man who would not do his job must make room for somebody else who could and would.

Mr Hay, opening his address by remarking that he was going to "take the gloves off" and speak "absolutely straight", said farmers had got to see that there was some food in the country not only for human beings but for stock. There was no quota this time, but everybody had to grow as much as they possibly could. What was wanted in the main was milk, wheat, potatoes, sugar-beet, and vegetables. As an example of what was expected of the grass dairy farmers Mr Hay said for the 1941 year a dairy farm of 150 acres was expected to grow say 10 to 15 acres of spring oats, a reasonable acreage of beans - if in a suitable district - a few acres of kale and mangels, 10 to 15 acres of wheat and one to four acres of potatoes.

FAILURES PREVENTABLE

Mr Hay went on to say that 90 per cent of all the failures of crops of wheat, oats, and everything else he had seen during the last winter and spring were preventable. The speaker proceeded to deal with causes of failure, and said that in a large number of failures if everything had been done at the right time there would have been a crop instead of a failure or partial failure. The speaker also dealt with silage and drainage, and concluded by remarking "It is up to everybody to go home and think out how they can help the country - and, of course, themselves.

A number of questions were asked, and farmers present urged by the Chairman to "Go home and go to it".

CAUSE WAS NOT OFTEN WIREWORM

At further meetings at Wheddon Cross and Williton, Mr Hay said he had gone over some hundreds of acres of wheat crop failures in this county and in almost every case the farmer concerned had informed him that the failure was caused by wireworm. "I have yet to see, however" added Mr Hay,"one acre in this county where there has been a failure in which the primary cause was wireworm". There were five reasons why wheat might fail: too late ploughing, not putting enough work into the ground, no phosphates, sowing the wrong variety at the wrong time, and wireworms were to blame after that. "Then a farmer has the neck to tell me he is unlucky. There is very little luck in farming, but there is a lot in hard work and good management".

This was certainly giving it to farmers "straight from the shoulder". Not only were they being lectured by W.D. Hay, which they must have been getting used to by this time, but they were also being told by a revered member of the county farming establishment that if they didn't "Go home and go to it" there were "vast" powers available to turn them out of their farms in the last resort, and have the job done by others. It has been said that some farmers considered these powers to be overly draconian, but in fact most of them understood that the whole population had to make sacrifices to save the country and that they were lucky in that at least they were not being asked for the supreme sacrifice (of their lives) as were men who were not in a "reserved occupation".

As time went on, constant routine contact with farmers was continued by the simple expedient of stationing advisors at livestock markets, and issuing press announcements to let farmers know when advisors would be at each market (left). Many farmers attended markets regularly, often every week, to sell stock or produce, pay bills and keep in touch with price trends. For many farmers, and often their wives, this was also the one social and shopping occasion of the week. It was usually an ideal time for an informal chat: some farmers would be somewhat "mellow" after a post-sale drink, and few were in a hurry to get home. Early arrivals for payment at auctioneers offices would often be paid in cash (for small items like a calf) and this would finance a tax-free day out with the wife!

Advisory officers would be available to all who wanted to consult them, although the officers would, themselves, have to confine themselves to a cup of tea and a bun!

Western Gazette. 25/7/41.

SOMERSET WAR AGRICULTURAL EXECUTIVE COMMITTEE

ADVISORY SERVICE AT MARKETS

AN ADVISORY OFFICER WILL ATTEND AT:—

Market	From	To	Commencing On
SPARKFORD	11.30 a.m.	12.30 p.m.	Monday, 28th July, 1941
LANGPORT	11.30 a.m.	12.30 p.m.	Tuesday, 29th July, 1941
WINFORD	12.30 p.m.	1.30 p.m.	Tuesday, 29th July, 1941
FROME	12 noon	2. 0 p.m.	Wednesday, 30th July, 1941
WINCANTON	11.30 a.m.	12.30 p.m.	Wednesday, 30th July, 1941
WEST SHEPTON, Shepton Mallet	11.30 a.m.	12.30 p.m.	Friday, 1st August, 1941
YEOVIL	11.30 a.m.	12.30 p.m.	Friday, 1st August, 1941
TAUNTON	11.30 a.m.	12.30 p.m.	Saturday, 2nd August, 1941
FARRINGTON GURNEY	11.30 a.m.	1. 0 p.m.	Monday, 4th August, 1941
HIGHBRIDGE	11.30 a.m.	12.30 p.m.	Monday, 4th August, 1941
GLASTONBURY	11.30 a.m.	12.30 p.m.	Tuesday, 5th August, 1941
WELLINGTON	11.30 a.m.	12.30 p.m.	Tuesday, 5th August, 1941
ILMINSTER	11.30 a.m.	12.30 p.m.	Tuesday, 5th August, 1941
WASHFORD	11.30 a.m.	12.30 p.m.	Monday, 11th August, 1941

for the purpose of dealing with ANY PROBLEM IN CONNECTION WITH THE PLOUGHING-UP POLICY, particularly:—

CROPPING.
GRASS SEEDS MIXTURES.
SILAGE MAKING.
PROVISION OF FOOD FOR LIVESTOCK.
MANURING.
CULTIVATING.
INSECT PESTS, &c.

W. D. HAY,
Somerset Farm Institute, Cannington, near Bridgwater.

52621]

Not only were advisors available regularly at livestock markets to answer any question which a farmer chose to ask him, there were also from time to time meetings and demonstrations at these markets which dealt with specific subjects, and these events were advertised in the local press. However, while W.D.Hay and his assistants could thus informally keep important current topics well to the fore in the minds of farmers, more formal activities continued as before, as examples of local press advertisements shown below illustrate, encompassing horticultural advice from A.D.Turner's staff as well.

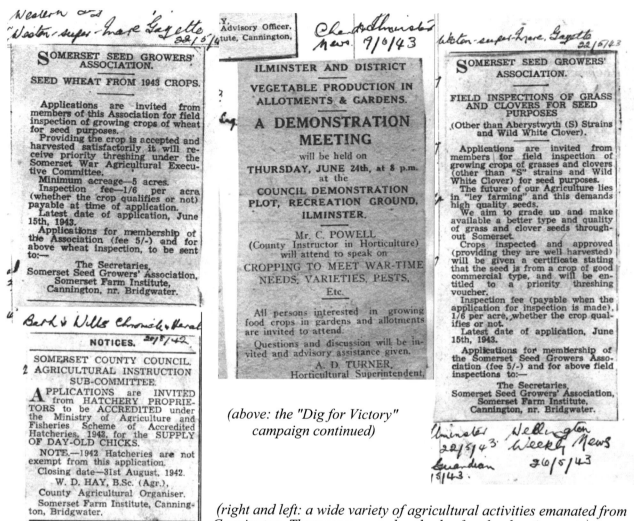

(above: the "Dig for Victory" campaign continued)

(right and left: a wide variety of agricultural activities emanated from Cannington. There were many hundreds of such advertisements).

The advertisements included here are only a minute fraction of those which went out to the press from Cannington during those war years. They had the effect of mobilising Somerset farmers behind the war effort to the degree which would have been impossible to imagine before the war. Somerset dairy farmers who had never dreamed of ploughing old grassland, and wouldn't have been allowed to by their landlords even if they had so dreamed (and anyway wouldn't have known how) were now mixed farmers, and growing wheat again. Most of them were operating some sort of system of alternate husbandry, although, it must be admitted, they were often still dependent on the advice of Cannington when a problem cropped up.

W.D. Hay and his Cannington staff had at last provided the "leading light" which Somerset had lacked for centuries. Back in Tudor times it had been impossible technically always to be sure of profitable use of the plough on heavy land in a high rainfall area, and this contributed to dependence on permanent grass (p.ix). A combination of W.D.Hay, a bit of Scottish science, plus tractor power, absence of competition from prairie wheat, a nearly successful U-boat offensive and the commonsense and drive of the Somerset farmer, together modernised Somerset farming.

Keen supporters of the "leading light" were the hundreds of Somerset farmers' sons and daughters who came away from Cannington inspired by the new farming they had learned as students there.

Chapter 8 - Cannington in the 1940s

Mr Bartlett remembers working as a boy at the SFI in 1940

As the chimes sounded for 2 o'clock I was straightway 13 again, in my summer job at Cannington in 1940, at the beginning of a long afternoon. The time was only measured by the chimes and the endless rows of tomatoes to be side shooted and tied in.

I'd started in July when my father had suggested a holiday job, less common then than now; but the war was on and labour shortages already evident. Cannington Institute had started me on the farm with an early harvest in a huge field, at least it seemed such to me, over the ridge to the north of the village. My job was to go well before the reaper-binder and collect the heads of wild oats. - sowing them was to be several years later! The main labour was Land Army girls whom I remember hand and knee weeding endless rows of seedlings, but I was too shy to talk to them. In 1940 plantings were severely practical though I can clearly remember strips of marigolds intersown with rows of carrots, onions and beans. Some things such as kohlrabi were new to me.

There were some compensations for working there. Nectarines could be bought for a penny each, and runner beans for a shilling a bag of 40 lbs weight, this to be wheeled home on my bicycle, for salting down for the winter ahead. The days were long, for I cycled from Bridgwater for an eight o'clock start, and there was an hour for dinner and a finish at five. This was for the sum of £1-13-9d a week as I remember it, a substantial amount for those days. (Editor's Note: Yes, only three years earlier, aged 14, the Editor for three months worked a 7 day week of 65 hours for 14/6d, and was glad to get back to school!).

Someone must have had sympathy with my lonely side-shooting, weed pulling existence and I was sent down to the orchard. Work was varied, digging up old blackcurrant bushes, picking and shifting early apples, clearing long grass from around the trees and a dozen other tasks. The summer prunings from each tree were weighed and entered in a note book, but no-one could tell me why. At 12.30 the three men went off to dinner and I had the place to myself. I soon learnt where the best fruit was and became very fond of the gages in particular. That's one reason why in my Devon garden I have Early Transparent, Cambridge and Coe's Golden Drop. Though they occasionally fruit and the taste is good they'll never be as good as those I filched on sunny afternoons fifty-one years ago.*(COSA Magazine 1992.)*

The Womens' Land Army - by Edna Liddle
(see photographs - pages 48-51)

In 1940 my job had finished - owing to the war we all had to help in war work. I was sent to a munitions factory, which did not suit me, neither did taking bus fares [as conductress - Ed] , so I became a Land Army Girl. I had no experience of the work but I knew that I wanted to be in the open air.

I put my bicycle, suitcase and myself on the train at Paddington and later that day arrived at Wiveliscombe station. The farmer met me with his horse and very dirty putt and, in due course, we arrived at Tolland. The farmhouse was small and I had no luxury of a bedroom but slept at the top of the stairs for the next three and a half years. Water for washing had to be fetched from the stream and all drinking water was drawn from a well some 200 yards from the house.

I soon found out that being a Land Girl was far removed from being a certified flower maker and shop assistant at Marshall and Snelgrove of Oxford Street. (Did you know that the Snelgrove family originally came from Somerset - they once had the paper mill at Wookey Hole - Ed.). Land Army girls were expected to do a man's work. Hedging, ditching and shearing were some of the jobs and if the farmer could make a fool of you he often would and get a good laugh out of it.

The most painful job was learning to help milk 30-40 cows by hand and this played havoc with the sinews and tendons of my hands and arms. My first job was daunting. I was shown a ten acre field covered with heaps of dung, given a fork, and told to get on with spreading - this to be done in my new white Land Army mac.

I got on very well working with horses - we spent many hours 'dragging', harrowing, ploughing and hauling. The animals seemed to know I was 'green' and I'm sure that they helped me. As time went on I found the work easier and my love of the countryside increased. Whilst cutting kale one morning a hunted fox came right up beside me and hid from the hounds.

I enjoyed cutting binds [or bonds - Ed] but when we were threshing barley it could be quite uncomfortable with the pieces sticking everywhere. Haymaking and harvesting were such hard work as all the moving of hay and straw was done by hand. Just for a moment consider the labour involved in haymaking in the 1940s. Two horses pulling a mowing machine, hay left for two days, then turned with horse drawn machinery. When dry, two rows turned into one then loaded manually onto a wagon, unloaded and put either into a barn or rick (the latter having to be thatched). Feeding the hay meant cutting out slabs with a hay knife and carting to the stock - a far cry from today's methods.

After nine years I received a long service badge but I loved the farm life so much that I continued the work for another ten. During these years I attended Cannington Farm Institute and successfully completed courses in Dairy work and Milking and my first savings were accumulated when a farmer gave me one bull and one heifer calf instead of overtime money and they bred many Shorthorn calves.

My Land Army years were happy ones and in 1950 I married a fellow farm worker but still continued farming until I became a Mum. The war certainly altered the course of many lives but in my experience it was for the better - a good way of life. (from COSA Magazine - 1995).

John Symes remembers the late 1940s

During the war Cannington was a training farm for the [Womens'] Land Army. (See WLA photographs, pp. 48-51 - Ed.). We were the first post-war intake of students proper. There were about 25 girls who did the Dairy course, cheese and butter making were the most important subjects, with some elementary milk testing. At that time there were far more farmhouse cheese makers.

Three or four lads did the Horticultural course. I am afraid they were considered a lower order than the Agris., of whom there were twenty-one or two.

The staff consisted of the Principal, W.J.England, who lectured and managed the farm. Mr. Furze, who lectured and was the N.I.A.B. trials officer, Mr. Mann was Warden and lectured on accountancy and bee-keeping.

Miss Monie was in charge of the Dairy course, and how! The farm staff were: foreman, Stan Acland, Walt Quartly who had been carter when all the work was done by horses, and had progressed to tractor driver, and Bill White, who had been pig-man, but with the shortage and rationing of all livestock feeds, the pigs had gone, as they had from most farms. There was also a cowman, Frank Wilkins.

Their efforts were supplemented by four Land Army 'girls' who had stayed on. Liz Bates worked mostly with the cows, Jill Barnes was Stan's right hand man, Betty Vaux and Cherry Clarke were in the Horticultural Department.

At the A.G.M. (COSA - Ed) Muriel Hucker (nee' Chinn) remarked on our naivety in those days, and in retrospect it really was astonishing. Many of us had barely left school and I think most of us fell in love with these sophisticated and worldly wise ladies. It would be "telling" to relate all the things they taught us, but dancing was high on the list, Waltz, Quickstep, Valeta, Polka. Such prowess as we later developed all started with an arm round the waist of one of these paragons. The dances were held in Clifford Hall, and the music came from a wind-up gramophone.

Priory Lodge had been built some years before, and my interview for a place took place there, though I never recall ever having been in there since. We were all housed in the old building. Looking at the front aspect, my room was the one on the extreme left, with the oval window. Not a room really, cubicle is a better description. Most of the lectures for the Agricultural students took place in Clifford Hall. The sexes were strictly segregated after 7.30 p.m., and only the very brave or foolhardy ventured into forbidden territory, though I believe Maurice Chick did put his foot through a ceiling while on a nocturnal foray.

I have mentioned that feeding-stuffs for livestock were rationed as they were for the human population, in fact rationing went on until the 1950s. (1953 - Ed) On each table in the dining-room were set out the appropriate number of glass screw-top jars, into which was put our 3oz. per week of sugar. The other 5oz. was used in the kitchen. Since September 1944 I've never taken sugar in tea. We spent our coupons for soap and tooth-paste in Mrs Burt's shop, now THE SHOP. Even waterproofs and wellington boots were rationed. When someone said that, of course, being Cannington, there would be potato harvesting machines, Mick Norman said "Yes, 25 of them". I believe we grew about 14 acres of Majestic, dug out with a spinner and all labouriously hand-picked into bags. The N.I.A.B. trials of cereals, in replicated plots of ¼ acre or so, were cut with the binder, and carefully kept separate for threshing and weighing. I am still suffering from hours spent singling mangolds and sugar-beet, all lifted, topped and loaded by hand, usually in freezing cold or pouring rain.

There was a flock of Dorset Down breeding ewes, about which I remember very little, except that on one cold, wet Saturday afternoon it was my turn to do the 'look'. I decided that the fields down by the river were no place for me, and walked in one gate and out the other, only to find three old ladies in a ditch, with just their heads above water. If you have ever tried to rescue a very wet sheep that doesn't want to be rescued, you will know why I have never since neglected to do a proper inspection of stock.

Mixed Dorset Down and Dorset Horn ewe flock with their Southdown-cross lambs.

I'll try to describe the Court Farm buildings. There was one Dutch Barn on the Downs. The entrance to the farm was what is now the entrance to the Brian Galloway building, which stands approximately on the site of a typical local barn. We carried sacks of wheat (252 lbs) and beans (264 lbs) up the outside steps for storage on the upper floor. Down below was a cake cracker, a root slicer and a chaff cutter. A mixture of cake, sliced mangolds or swedes, molasses, beet pulp and anything else available, was mixed on the floor and carried through the doorway into the cowshed adjoining. This cowshed held about 25 cows in one row, out through the door in the centre to the right were a couple of loose boxes; to the left of the yard, a single-row shed for 10, next a double-row shed for 18 or 20.

That is three sides of the yard, on the fourth side was the dairy, from which the churns of milk were taken by milk-float and cob to the cheese-making dairy at the old buildings, which is now the Floral Art Department. Between the milk room and the loose boxes was the midden, a large covered area lower than the yard, into which wheel-barrow loads of cowshed dung were tipped. On the western side, a ramp enabled the three Percheron horses to pull putt-loads of F.Y.M. (farmyard manure) to the fields.

The traditional herd in Somerset had always been Dairy Shorthorn on which the Cheddar cheese industry was founded. W.D. (Bonny) Hay, himself a Scot, and Jack England's predecessor, introduced some Ayrshires. With the setting-up of the accredited herds scheme and tuberculosis eradication, the Ayrshires, due to their good health record, became more and more popular.

The Court Farm cows were milked by means of three or four Gasgoigne buckets, which used the very early Stuart pulsators. In addition to the three Percheron horses and a cob, there were two Standard Fordson tractors. They were started by cranking a handle, using petrol then switched to paraffin, or more correctly Tractor Vapourising Oil (see page 86). One tractor had to be started by getting into reverse gear with much gnashing and grinding of teeth, the combination clutch and brake pedal depressed, then it would proceed backwards three or four times around the yard, before the heavy gear oil warmed sufficiently to allow a gear change. There was no protection for the driver, so we soon learned to hang a length of chain on the steering wheel, get off and walk to keep warm. Safety Officers would have a fit!

47

There was a very strong feeling of belonging to a family, among staff and students. We had a highly developed 'work ethic' and I think we all felt privileged to have the chance to get into the first stage of an academic agricultural education. Any thought of squandering it on booze or birds never entered our heads. Well, if you believe that I guess you'll believe anything. Robin Grant and Liz Rogers became 'friendly', married and lived happily ever after.

The amount of labour involved in running a farm in 1944 was enormous. Hoeing, haymaking, harvesting of all crops took countless hours of sheer physical force. Every forkful of dung was loaded by hand and spread by hand. Even the tiny tonnage of silage was forked onto carts and forked into the round concrete silos. Cannington pioneered the ammonia treatment of straw, only then it was long straw soaked in a solution of caustic soda, drained and washed.

At the western end of the village where the Scout hall is now, was the Poultry Department. I seem to remember a field of perhaps five acres divided into pens by six-foot high wire netting. In each pen were twenty hens and a cock, each hen with a numbered leg ring and the individual nest boxes had trap doors. Each egg was numbered and recorded - the same idea as milk recording - to breed from the best. (See photo below right - Ed).

Right: A Light Sussex breeding pen, opposite the cemetery, (1946/47)

Land Girls picking fruit

Above: *Land Army Girls transferring a trap-nested hen's number from her leg ring to her egg, so that a record of the number of eggs she has laid could be kept.* (ca.1940)

Shortages dictated our practices. Not least in the feeding of poultry (and pigs). In order to supplement the meagre cereal/protein ration farms took delivery of dustbin sized tubs of Tottenham Pudding: household waste, collections from schools and hospitals etc., cooked and reduced to a horrible glutinous mass was mixed with the meal. I really don't remember ever having such agonisingly cold hands as in the winter of 1944/45. The divine stupidity that decided that we couldn't use a shovel is beyond comprehension particularly as the odd bit of glass or a kitchen knife was sometimes hiding in the revolting gunge.

As in everything else, the changes in agriculture in the past 50 years will soon be as remote as the age of the dinosaur. I hope that what I have written has been of interest to someone.

From John Symes 1944/45 (in 1990/91 COSA Magazine)

(Editor's Note: John Symes is from Stogursey, where one of my family was hanged in 1685 for fighting on the wrong [Protestant] side in the Monmouth Rebellion. I'm still cross about it!).

WLA:Early winter morning, not yet light, no shelter from the wind, picking cold wet Brussels Sprouts

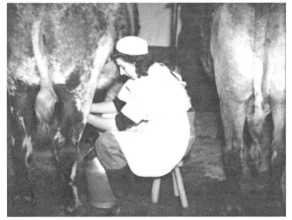

WLA: early morning, some warmth from the cow, but hand muscles protesting "How much longer!"

WLA: Cutting out a "flap" of hay with that old hay knife, then ease the flap onto one's head and carry it down the ladder to the cowstall.(then half a dozen more). Making a girl to do all that?

("Nearly breakfast time, thank the Lord!")

WLA Breakfast Time *All former students said they were fed well at Cannington, so no doubt the Womens' Land Army girls were also well fed - they seem to have earned it.*

"HMS Pinafore" - 1948/49

The Cast

(The post-war student intake

kept up standards)

WLA: It's called muck-carting in some parts, but in most of Somerset it's called dung-hauling.

WLA: A Standard Fordson and a two-furrow trailed plough.

Demonstration? Or are they clearing a blockage? There's enough straw or strawy dung on the surface to cause one.

They've probably been forking that straw into the last furrow to clear the ground for the next two furrows.

(This is not ploughing for beginners!).

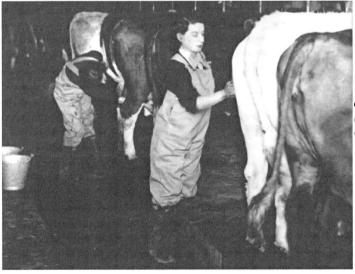

WLA: A quiet job before afternoon milking: clipping, grooming and washing the cows. (Everything must be done by the book at Cannington)

Left: Nan Hebditch (later Eaves) 45/46D after milking; at the cowstall at Court Farm, Cannington, and John Pearce.

Nan was one of the six charming daughters of Harold Hebditch of Stoke-under-Ham. It was from HH that the Editor acquired 75% of his farm management ability while living with the family and working on the farm in the early war years.

Right: A page of Nan's rough notes taken during Miss Monie's lectures on cheese-making. (reduced). After her studentship, Nan stayed on and was in charge of the dairy.

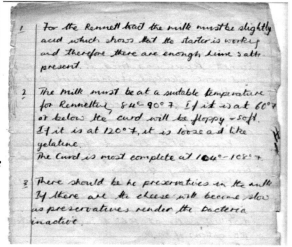

The End of the 1940s (1949-50)

It took a good man to get to sleep on the boy's "Bottom Corridor" during the 1949-50 year; only one had the art, old Mike Davey! Technically speaking, everyone should have been in bed, and half asleep, by 10.0 p.m. - practice proved different.

The first thing to be decided was whether the dreaded "top Corridor" was going to raid us after "lights out" (used as a smoke-screen for battle!). Having found that the inmates upstairs were quiet (a description of an attack will never be printed), it was felt safe to undress. Halfway through this rather lengthy process the familiar striking of the church clock warned that lights should go out. Arthur Lawrence, leading this gallant move, would proceed to undress in darkness yet cussing everyone in general for not following his example.

By 10.10 p.m. most of us were floundering in the inky dark bathroom. Trouble started when one, returning to his cubicle, found that his bed and bedding had vanished. While the bedless victim was hunting the airing-cupboard for his treasured belongings, the rest of his mates grumbled at him for keeping them awake.

Eventually quietness came, but not for long, this time it was the upstairs crew stirring the peace. Now in Room 1 lived the Institutes head boy, Benny Goodman; it was his thankless task to plod upstairs to plead for quietness. When he was again comfortable in between the sheets - then listen - at this stage it was not unusual for Jack Palmer to start reading aloud one of his girls' daily letters. It was usually Hugh Hammond who objected to Brian Hack visiting Room II to have a chat, and often a wrestling practice, with "Blockhead" (my usual nickname).

Graham Dawes, the comedian of the corridor, usually rolled in long after the rest were quiet, it is still a mystery where he came from. Several sleepy voices would ask him to start his one-man band imitation, if Graham obliged (which was seldom) we would soon fall asleep to the music of the Salvation Army Band.

Bill Buffrey always concluded the day by wishing Hugh, Brian, Jack, Graham, Arthur, Mike, Benny and David a "Good-Good-Night". *David J. Gwilliam. 49/50 (1952 COSA Magazine)*

Chapter 9 - Cannington in the 1950s

High Jinks for dairy students! <u>Shirley Moore</u> (nee Daniels) tells her stories.

I remember being in the Dairy one day when Miss Monie was expecting a group of people to show them how we made butter. Just before they appeared, while most of us were merrily churning, one student, who was patting butter into shape, suddenly tossed it in the air and it rocketed up to the ceiling, and simply stuck there! Hoots of laughter were followed swiftly by gasps of dismay when another student forgot to latch down the lid of the churn, and we stared in horror as all the buttermilk contents flooded the floor. However, everyone rallied round, grabbing all our precious buckets of specially chilled water beside our churns, and sloshed the floor clean, then frantically swept and squeegeed the excess water down the gully, so no one was any the wiser - we hoped - when Miss Monie sweetly made her entrance. The pat of butter was later scraped off the ceiling!

Another day, the Agri students were going out all day, maybe it was a visit to BOCM. In the D/P lecture room someone hatched up the idea of wrecking the boys bedrooms while they were gone! All seemed to be quiet when three of us, I think, slipped off our shoes, lined them up neatly outside the door, then raced silently along dark corridors and up flights of stairs. Our aim was the West Wing, and we had no idea where to go exactly. The room we targeted for making it thoroughly untidy belonged to Pat Pile, John Fisher and Jimmy Gore, and we wrote on the mirror with someone's shaving stick "Guess who?" They must have been absolutely livid when they returned and saw what we had done, and we, of course, had to pretend innocence. However, they had their revenge, and when we passed under the arch from the quadrangle, they were ready with buckets of water, to chuck out of their windows and thoroughly soak us!

The Agricultural student <u>Michael Bell (49/50)</u> relates three unplanned events:

<u>No.1</u>. I was on milking duty one morning about January 1950. It was a bucket plant with a cooling stand with four churns with rubber pipe connections and one churn underneath the cooler. The water pipe was connected to the cooler and the water flowed out in a pipe to the outside water tank out of the window (photo p.40). I went by and the outside pipe had fallen out of the tank because it was not quite long enough. I pulled the pipe to put it back in the tank and in the dairy the whole cooling system collapsed, all the four connected churns went over, flooding the floor and wasting about 20 gallons of milk, and the overhead tank above the cooler lost about another 8 gallons. I did apologise, that it was my fault, but I was forgiven. The staff then said that they would be about 30 gallons short of milk for the college dairy butter or cheese course. I will not mention the way they intended to get over the problem!

<u>No.2</u>. In the spring of 1950 I discovered that I had some spots in the lower part of my body. These started to grow and I decided to see the Matron, Miss Hobbs, who was a mature lady to sort out the problem with little embarrassment. I went to her office twice a day for three or four days, and luckily you could see into the office through the window because each time the assistant matron who was only just older than I was was there. I was too embarassed to see her, but all the time the spots were growing. After about the fourth day Miss Hobbs was back and I plucked up courage and went in. "What's the matter?" she asked. I said I had trouble with spots. She looked at my face and said "Don't worry, all teenagers get trouble with spots." I said that they were not on my face, but between my legs, and for the first time in my life a female told me to drop my trousers. She immediately said it was ringworm, which I had never seen before. Two or three lots of iodine and they were gone. Near enough the most embarrassing time of my young life.

<u>No.3</u>. Probably it was in June 1950 that we were at Rodway Farm seeing a pick-up baler for the first time. There were about 10 agri. students and some dairy students. This was I think a Case baler with the needles tying from the back of the pick-up reel side-on. I was standing behind when the needles tied the bale and they tore my trousers down to the knees. I had to walk back to the college with the other students including several females holding my ripped trousers to try to save another embarrassing time. Half an inch closer and my own person would have been involved and I might not be a family man today!

<u>C.H. (Tim) Nicholls 52/53</u>

When I left Cannington I went to Seale-Hayne Agricultural College for two years. There I obtained my National Diploma in Agriculture and went on to become a Livestock Officer attached to the then Northern Rhodesian Government. But this was in 1960 after I had served for two years National Service in the Army, mostly in Cyprus, and vain attempts to rent a holding to farm on my own account.

Perhaps foreign travel during my Army service gave me the inclination to work abroad when it became apparent that I was not going to be granted the rental of a Council Farm, because I had no hesitation when the chance in Northern Rhodesia turned up. I enjoyed the work in Africa, mostly I was endeavouring to control Notifiable Diseases, for example rabies, and there are a number of people around today who can thank the work that my department carried out in saving their lives. Anyway, during the time I was there the country obtained its independence from the British Crown and I felt it was time to return to my homeland. Eventually I was able to obtain, in conjunction with my brother, a mixed agricultural and horticultural holding which is where I am today.

I remember my time at Cannington with much affection. It was certainly a formative year of my life, as it was in countless others, I expect. Definitely a highlight, and I can remember far more about Cannington than I ever could about Seale-Hayne, perhaps this was because it was the first time I had left home and everything was very different from home. Some of the experiences that I had during that year are with me still. Mostly I remember the social times we had; who likes to remember work! We had formal dances in the Hall, having been coached by the caretaker in the arts of Old Tyme dancing. Music was supplied by Mrs. Burt's Band. The girls were mostly unrecognisable in their posh frocks. After all, if you had been milking at Rodway that morning you could be forgiven in mistaking the lovely young thing in your arms as being the same girl that raced you down Rodway Hill at 5.29 a.m. In the musical line there was also lots of singing round the Baby Grand piano and I seem to remember a record player of some sort, it was 78s in those days, of course.

Oh yes, the quiet and we hoped, unsuspected trips through the churchyard to the Blue Anchor public house. Conveniently situated and with rough cider at 6d a pint! That's about 2p now, I suppose. Of course, it was strictly against College Rules to nip out for a pint, but fruit is sweeter if it is forbidden, don't you think? We raided the larder for chocolate marshmallows, of which I was particularly fond, we let off crow-scarers from bedroom window sills and there was an accident with lighter fuel over which I shall throw a veil!

One thing, though, is that I reckon that we lads had a stronger sense of romance in those days, the obvious was never pointed out perhaps, things were still a bit of a mystery. Although it seems topics of conversation amongst lads of today are not any different, it is still farming and girls. And not necessarily in that order of course.

Rationing was still the order of the day and we all had our own portions of sugar, butter and jam. Plenty of cheese, though! I certainly do not remember being hungry. Miss Monie took us all through the intricacies of cheese-making but we boys must have been a bit of a nuisance as we didn't always take things as seriously as we might have done.

Some practical work, like hoeing sugar-beet, I did not like because I felt I was being used as cheap labour, but the job had to be done by someone and we all had a turn. Grafting apple trees was a different matter though, because Mr Brookfield's instruction has lasted through the years. Court Farm had its Shorthorns and Rodway its Ayrshires and we also took turns in the piggery, the poultry unit and the carpenter's shop. With lectures, private study, practical work making up our days at Cannington I must admit I'm left wondering how we ever had the time for larking around, but in common with today's young people we had a lot of fun. It was certainly a year to remember. (from COSA magazine - 1982)

Kathleen Rogers (nee Prowse) 54/55 P

Should she live in? Or travel to the College daily? My Mother asked Mr Ballardie in the Spring of 1954. "She will miss out on so much College life if she does not live in", came the reply. That was my introduction to the Principal of Somerset Farm Institute and a decision was made at that interview for which I shall always be grateful. As one of only two on the poultry Course I joined the twelve girls and forty eight boys who enrolled as students on 27th September.

On arrival Mr Ballardie introduced us to a member of staff and this part of our initial welcome has always remained vividly in my memory. "You will be treated as adults and it will be entirely up to you how hard you work and by implication, what results you gain at the end of the year. No one will make you attend lectures or do 'Private Study'; it is entirely up to you".

We were then introduced to Bob Wright (Warden) who immediately began listing the rules of the establishment by which the adult/children must abide.

1) Lights out by 10p.m., (11p.m. on Sundays).   2)
No Motor Bikes or Cars.
3) No boys in girls quarters - which were guarded by Matron (Miss Hobbs) as everyone
   had to pass her bedroom to gain access to our 'horse boxes'; and vice versa.

4) No Communal Common Room

5) Sign out and in if you want to go home for the weekend.

6) Boys were not allowed to invite girls from the village to dances.

7) No visiting local hostelries.

Our two boys, both later students, said "whatever did you do, Mum?" Well we became a 'Community' for ten months, making our own fun. Local speakers were invited to talk and give film shows, Mr Harmer, the caretaker, taught us old time dancing once a week. We would cycle to the cinema in Bridgwater on Saturday nights. There were darts and table tennis matches, long walks and a discussion group, which spent a fair amount of time discussing how to get round some of the rules.

The upstairs room at the back of Clifford Hall became the unofficial communal Common Room. Midnight feasts were enjoyed by both boys and girls with some degree of ingenuity. The Poultry section was housed at the west side of Cannington, opposite the cemetery, where various pedigree breeds were housed and penned, the hens were rung and trap nested so that progeny had their own family tree (p.48).

Agri students had a week each term on the Poultry section which they hated and they did everything except learn much about the hens, ducks, geese which were kept - it was considered the week for all kinds of high jinks like locking people in chicken houses and soaking poultry students by hose or placing them in water barrels. The 'magic' of Cannington certainly had me captured for life. Work hard and play hard and you'll get the best out of Cannington and life. That went in 1954 and it still goes in 1992.

Kathleen Rogers (nee Prowse) 54/55 P..

Gilbert Little (1957/58)

I was privileged to be stationed in the New Block as it was called at the time and we were often raided by the younger element from the main building. After a number of sorties we decided to fill a bath with cold water ready for the next assault. It was with great satisfaction that two students were duly immersed in the bath. Mr Hawkins, the Warden at the time wondered why there was a trail of water across the courtyard. I cannot recall the names of the students duly dunked. This was one of many incidents which occurred and one for which I was grounded for the weekend in the strict regime of the time, having to sign in every hour. *(COSA Magazine 2005)*

Susan Kerr (nee Nixey) 1957/58

There was one other poultry student and her name was Bridget Garnett. We did all our studies and work at the Poultry Section at the top end of Cannington with Miss Quinlan. SFI kept RIR and Light Sussex. The hens were kept in the trap nest boxes when they laid their eggs, so we had to keep going round releasing them, take the number from their leg and write it on the egg. All the eggs were recorded in a big book and at the end of the year we could total up how many each hen had laid. When the eggs were incubated each had her little wire box with her number and eggs in it. When hatched we wingbanded the baby chicks with two numbers, one its mother's and the other its own to be put on the ring when it was put on its leg when it was big enough (p.48).

(below: from the 1957 [left] and 1956 COSA Magazines)

Judging Root Singling Competitions.
Messrs. B. Thomas, A. J. Marval and "Stan."

The New Science Laboratory.

1950/51 Easter Hat Parade

1950/51 - Caste of **IOLANTHE**

Chapter 10 - Cannington in the 1960s

The New Farm Institute - by the Principal

There has been a great deal of talk going around about the possibility of a new farm institute at Cannington. The talk has not been all "hot air" as we shall see in due course. (Editor's note: Perhaps it might have been better for Cannington if it <u>had</u> all been "hot air"!).

The report by the de la Warr committee made it clear that old buildings, particularly historic buildings, should not be adapted to try and fulfill the functions of a farm institute. The report indicated that it was "not considered that old buildings provide a suitable environment for modern technical education. Nor can they be very satisfactorily adapted for residential purposes" (Para.106). In addition to deciding that new buildings are necessary the report indicates that "there must be a substantial increase in the number of students and that about one hundred places is the minimum size to be aimed at" (Para.95).

It was therefore decided to provide eighty single study bedrooms for men and twenty bedrooms for women with the necessary warden and staff accommodation.

In the first installment it is proposed to erect a forty bedroom block with common room and warden's flat, an agricultural machinery workshop and demonstration room and certain other offices.

Because of the late start in the present financial year it is likely that the first instalment and the second instalment may be merged and the two instalments more or less built together. With this combination a main hall, lecture rooms and administrative offices will be built along with the sleeping and workshop buildings.

A field to the west side of front field, of about six acres has been purchased to make a compact block of about twenty acres on which to build the new institute and establish playing fields, roads and car parks. The Court Farm buildings, workshops and Principal's house will be demolished to make room for some of the new buildings. A new Principal's house is to be built, probably on the east side of front field. It is intended to build the Agricultural Engineering workshops along the top of the Downs to link up with the tractor shed and machinery storage space. The new cattle yards for forty milking cows with facilities for self feed silage and other types of feeding experiment will be to the south of the present tractor shed on the Downs. The fattening piggery will remain and a poultry unit of three thousand to five thousand birds in batteries and deep litter will be housed near the piggery.

How long these developments will take is difficult to forecast, but at the time of writing, mid October, the **Ministry of Education** want us to start at once and to be well through with the whole programme in about four or five years.

As these new developments progress, the outlying fields, such as the poultry department and the Court Orchard in Mill Lane will be sold and if the proposed development of the horticultural department is allowed to proceed as planned, then the present sports field will be developed for horticulture with the necessary packing and store sheds. The glasshouses and sheds in the walled gardens will cease to be used and extra glasshouses, potting sheds, stores, etc., will be built at Crockers.

It is to be hoped that a much more detailed report will be possible in twelve months time.

W.W.Ballardie (Principal: 1951-64).

Dairy cows strip grazing

Already changes were taking place: "A major change to note with regard to livestock is the Committee's decision to start a herd of British Friesian cattle . . . . ." (1956 COSA mag. p.26).

Further Changes - Combining Wheat

1964 STUDENT COURSES

COURSES

Full Time

The courses offered are GENERAL AGRICULTURE, DAIRY FARMING, DAIRYING, COMMERCIAL HORTICULTURE and GENERAL HORTICULTURE (Parks). This alternative course in Horticulture is especially designed for young Parks and Garden Employees who are primarily concerned with decorative horticulture.

These courses extend over three terms, each of approximately twelve weeks duration.

Block Release

The courses offered are DAIRYING for the Dairy Industry extending over three years and MILK PROCESSING AND CONTROL for City and Guilds No. 160 final.

Examinations

Students are prepared for one or more of the following examinations:

NATIONAL CERTIFICATE IN AGRICULTURE

NATIONAL CERTIFICATE IN HORTICULTURE or CITY AND GUILDS
    STAGE II HORTICULTURE (GROUPED COURSE CERTIFICATE)

ROYAL ASSOCIATION OF BRITISH DAIRY FARMERS' CERTIFICATE
    IN DAIRYING

CITY AND GUILDS No. 160 final

CITY AND GUILDS No. 160 intermediate

CITY AND GUILDS No. 270 FARM MACHINERY OPERATION AND
    CARE

ROYAL HORTICULTURAL SOCIETY GENERAL EXAMINATION

BRITISH BEEKEEPERS' ASSOCIATION PRELIMINARY CERTIFICATE IN
    BEEKEEPING

Day Release

Courses are staffed from the Somerset Farm Institute and held at fourteen centres throughout the county of Somerset in Agriculture, Horticulture, Agricultural Engineering and Milk Processing and Control.

Short Courses

Short courses are held where time and accommodation permit for school children, day release students and those interested in special subjects such as gardening and cheesemaking.

Annie Sherborne Remembers

The first funny incident I remember happened on a farm walk in the first term. The practical lesson had been cancelled and we were accompanied by Mr Gwynne and the Dairying Group. We followed Mr Hoskins and a group of Gen. Agris. around at a safe distance apart until right by the River Parrett. On Court Farm we had to go through a very muddy gateway - that was my undoing, because very gently and gracefully I fell in it, with all the Gen Agris watching. Embarrassment and cold made the walk back seem endless.

The next happened in the dairy. Mr Gwynne in charge again. Sidney Smith and I were using the pasteuriser. While I had my back to it the machine was switched on, the plates weren't tight enough and I was drowned in freezing cold water. Mr Gwynne's face was unbelievable shock, laughter and tears all in one. Mr Gwynne left at the end of that term to go abroad; things were never the same again.

At the Christmas show, produced by Mr Lawson, Sidney dressed as Mr Marval with cotton wool cheeks, Janet Adlam as Mother, John Robbs as son and many more working for the big night.

Ten minutes in, on the 'Night', there was a power cut, but the show went on. With Tony Davey's magical help the power was restored but it was well into the second half. I wonder if Nick Brake has ever forgotten the cow he calved that night or if the Friesian 'sheet cow' has ever got over it.

Many more things come to mind - a party in the bee garden where Norah forgot what lived in the little hives and sat on one. Margaret's lovely Ford Popular, and a talcum powder fight (not to be recommended) and of course a beach party with Rave Dave Robinson and his friend Roger.

And does anyone know the whereabouts of Victor Tucker?

(Annie Sherborne 1966/67 D)

WORK WITH SECONDARY SCHOOLS

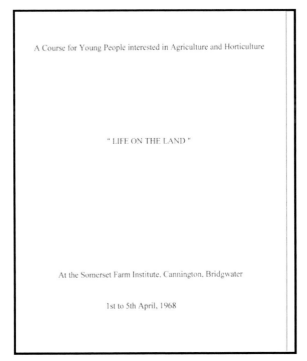

A Course for Young People interested in Agriculture and Horticulture

" LIFE ON THE LAND "

At the Somerset Farm Institute, Cannington, Bridgwater

1st to 5th April, 1968

Above is a copy of the front cover of a 1968 booklet describing short courses designed for children of school age. The courses involved are described on the following pages.

INFORMATION ABOUT THE COURSE

Everyone concerned with the organisation and planning of the course hopes that you will enjoy it and will find the time spent at the Somerset Farm Institute a worthwhile experience. They feel this will be so if you take an active part in the programme of work and in all other activities. Time is short — so make the most of it.

Times of Meals		
	8.0 a.m.	Breakfast
	10.45 a.m.	Refreshment Break
	1.0 p.m.	Dinner
	5.30 p.m.	High tea
	8.30 p.m.	Hot drinks

House Rules

1. You must report at once to your tutor if you are ill or suffer any accident.

2. You may not smoke at any time during the course.

3. You may not leave the Institute or surrounds without permission.

4. You must change farm and garden footwear in the downstairs cloakroom before going up to your bedroom.

5. You must make your own bed each morning after breakfast and leave your room tidy.

6. You must be in your own room each evening at 9.30 p.m. Lights are put out at 10.0 p.m.

Staff		
Course Organiser	—	Miss B. M. Gibson
		County Rural Science Organiser
Tutors	—	Mr. Ashley — Keynsham Mr. Falvey
		Mr. Bennett — Wellington
		Miss Duckham — Wells
		Mr. Morris — Taunton
		Mr. Talbot — Backwell
		Mr. Webley — Midsomer Norton
Matron	—	Miss Hobbs
Warden		Mr. Russell Smith
Principal of the Institute	—	Mr. P. Keen

Editor's Note: Courses of this type were arranged by Miss Gibson, the County Rural Science Organiser. Visiting tutors included teachers of Rural Science from several Somerset Secondary Schools. One of these visiting Tutors had earlier been Mr Roy Ashley, born at Queen Charlton. (His name is now crossed out). Mr Ashley had graduated in Horticulture at Reading and was at this time teaching Rural Science at one of the Keynsham Secondary Schools.

The Horticultural Department at this time, in conjunction with the County Rural Science Organiser, provided 'refresher" courses for teachers of Rural Science in Somerset Secondary Schools, and teachers (such as Mr Ashley) who had attended these courses and knew the Cannington set-up provided Visiting Tutors for the residential courses described here.

PROGRAMME

Monday 1st April

4.0 p.m.	Assemble at the Institute and report to the Enquiry Office
5.15 p.m.	High Tea
6.0 p.m.	Tour of the Farms and Gardens
7.30 p.m.	Assemble in Hall (New Building)

Welcome and Introductions — Miss Gibson

"The Farm Institute" — a talk by Mr. Keen

The courses were well structured.

And no fear of getting lost!

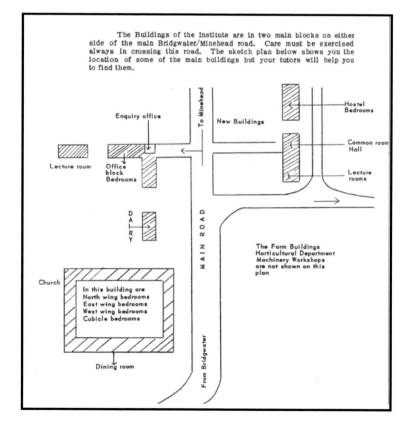

The Buildings of the Institute are in two main blocks on either side of the main Bridgwater/Minehead road. Care must be exercised always in crossing this road. The sketch plan below shows you the location of some of the main buildings but your tutors will help you to find them.

Agricultural Group

FARM GROUP

Farms — Court Farm and Rodway Farms

Staff — Pigs — Mr. Hoskins
Cattle — Mr. Capel
Sheep — Mr. Heal
Grassland — Mr. Mead
Crops — Mr. Berkley

Tuesday 2nd April

9.0 a.m. – 10.45 a.m.	Lecture Room – Talks (1) Pigs – Mr Hoskins (2) Sheep Mr Heal
11.0 a.m. – 12.45 p.m.	Practical Farm Tasks – Group 1 – Pigs Group 2 – Sheep Group 3 – Cattle Group 4 – Grassland Group 5 – Crops and Machinery
2.0 p.m. – 4.30 p.m.	Practical Farm Tasks – Group 1 – Crops and Machinery Group 2 – Pigs Group 3 – Sheep Group 4 – Cattle Group 5 – Grassland
6.30 p.m.	Hall (New Building) Guest speaker – Mr. Peter Campion, Somerset Federation Young Farmers' Clubs "The Young Farmers' Club Movement"

Friday 5th April

9.0 a.m. – 10.0 a.m.	Talk – Guest speaker – Mr. A. F. R. Fisher, Regional Training Adviser – Agricultural, Horticultural and Forestry Industry Training Board
10.0 a.m. – 10.45 a.m.	Talk – Farm Figures – Mr. Summers
11.0 a.m.	"Points of View"
12 noon	Final session with the staff and final words from Mr. Keen

Wednesday 3rd April

9.0 a.m. – 10.45 a.m.	Lecture Room – Talks (1) Beef Cattle – Mr. Capel (2) Dairy Cattle – Mr. Capel
11.0 a.m. – 12.45 p.m.	Practical Farm Tasks – Group 1 – Grassland Group 2 – Crops and Machinery Group 3 – Pigs Group 4 – Sheep Group 5 – Cattle
2.0 p.m. – 3.15 p.m.	Thatching Demonstration by Mr. Whitemore Groups 1, 2 and 3 Notebooks and Diaries – Groups r and 5.
3.15 p.m. – 4.30 p.m.	Thatching Demonstration by Mr. Whitemore Groups 4 and 5 Notebooks and Diaries – Groups 1, 2 and 3.
6.0 p.m.	Hall (New Building) Guest speaker – Mr. Brian Whitemore, Ash Priors, Taunton Talk – illustrated by film and slides onthe work of a thatcher
7.30 p.m.	The Bridgwater Young Farmers' Club present "The Auction" – a play in Somerset dialect.

Thursday 4th April

9.0 a.m. – 10.45 a.m.	Talks 1. Grassland – Mr. Mead 2. Crops – Mr. Berkeley
11.0 a.m. – 12.45 p.m.	Practical Farm Tasks – Group 1 – Cattle Group 2 – Grassland Group 3 – Crops and Machinery Group 4 – Pigs Group 5 – Sheep
2.0 p.m. – 4.30 p.m.	Practical Farm Tasks – Group 1 – Sheep Group 2 – Cattle Group 3 – Grassland Group 4 – Crops and Machinery Group 5 – Pigs
6.0 p.m. – 6.45 p.m.	Hall (New Building) Talk and Films on "Farm Safety" Mr. Broom, Ministry of Agriculture
7.0 p.m.	Social

Horticultural Group

Staff — Mr. Brookfield, Head of Department — Fruit
Mr. Little, Park's Department — Turf, Nursery work
Mr. Sutton — Potting Shed Operations
Mr. Heyward — Machinery

Tuesday 2nd April

9.0 a.m. – 10.45 a.m.	Demonstration and Practice – Potting Shed Operations – Mr. Sutton (Crocker's)
11.0 a.m. – 12.45 p.m.	Practice – Nursery Work – Mr. Little (walled in Gardens)
2.0 p.m. – 4.30 p.m.	Horticultural Machinery – Mr. Heyward and Garden staff (Crocker's)
6.30 p.m.	Hall (New building) Guest speaker – Mr. Peter Campion, S.F.Y.F.C. "The Young Farmers' Club Movement"

Wednesday 3rd April

7.0 a.m. – 8.0 a.m.	Practical Work – Crocker's and Gardens
9.0 a.m. – 10.45 a.m.	Demonstration – Turf culture – Mr. Little
11.0 a.m. – 12.45 p.m.	Demonstration and practice – Fruit Tree Pruning – Mr. Brookfield
2.30 p.m. – 4.30 p.m.	Garden machinery
6.0 p.m.	Hall (New building) Guest speaker – Mr. Brian Whitemore, Talk illustrated by film slides on the work of a thatcher
7.30 p.m.	Bridgwater Young Farmers' Club present "The Auction" – a play in Somerset dialect

Thursday 4th April

9.0 a.m. – 10.45 a.m.	Demonstration and practice – Potting shed operations II – Mr. Sutton (Crocker's)
11.0 a.m. – 12.45 p.m.	Demonstration and practice – Fruit tree grafting – Mr. Brookfield (Court Orchard)
2.0 p.m.	1. Visit to Rylands Nurseries, Wellington by kind permission of Mr. F. Rowe
	3. Visit to Vivary Park, Taunton – Park Superintendent, Mr. Taylor. By kind permission of Borough Surveyor
6.0 p.m.	Talk and films – "Farm Safety" – Mr. Broom, Ministry of Agriculture
7.0 p.m.	Social

Friday 5th April

7.0 a.m. – 8.0 a.m.	Practical work
9.0 a.m. – 10.0 a.m.	Guest speaker – Mr. A. F. R. Fisher, Regional Training Adviser, Agricultural, Horticultural and Forestry Industry Training Board
10.0 a.m. – 10.45 a.m.	Talk – Farm Figures – Mr. Summers
11.0 a.m.	"Points of View"
12 noon	Final session with the staff and final words from Mr. Keen

Milk Processing Group

MILK PROCESSING GROUP

Staff — Mr. Galloway and other members of the Dairy Department

Tuesday 2nd April

7.0 a.m. — 8.0 a.m.	Dairy Routine
9.0 a.m. — 10.45 a.m.	Dairy practice — Butter-making
11.0 a.m. — 12.45 p.m.	— Cheese-making
2.0 p.m. — 4.30 p.m.	Dairy practice
6.30 p.m.	Hall (New building)
	Guest speaker — Mr. Peter Campion, S.F.Y.F.C. "The Young Farmers' Club Movement"

* * * * * * * *

Wednesday 3rd April

7.0 a.m. — 8.0 a.m.	Dairy routine
9.0 a.m. — 10.45 a.m.	Dairy practice — Butter-making
11.0 a.m. — 12.45 p.m.	— Cheese-making
2.0 p.m. — 4.30 p.m.	Dairy practice
6.0 p.m.	Hall (New building)
	Guest speaker — Mr. Brian Whitemore, Ash Priors, Taunton. Talk illustrated by film and slides on the work of a thatcher
7.30 p.m.	The Bridgwater Young Farmers' Club present "The Auction" — a play in Somerset dialect

Thursday 4th April

7.0 a.m. — 8.0 a.m.	Dairy routine
9.0 a.m. — 10.45 a.m.	Visit to Commercial Dairy
11.0 a.m. — 12.45 p.m.	
2.0 p.m. — 4.30 p.m.	Milk Testing
6.0 p.m.	Hall (New building)
	Talk and Films "Farm Safety" — Mr. Broom, Ministry of Agriculture
7.0 p.m.	Social

* * * * * * * *

Friday 5th April

7.0 a.m. — 8.0 a.m.	Dairy routine
9.0 a.m. — 10.0 a.m.	Talk — Guest speaker — Mr. A. F. R. Fisher, Regional Training Adviser, Industrial Training Board
10.0 a.m. — 10.45 a.m.	Talk — Farm Figures — Mr. Summers
11.0 a.m.	"Points of View"
12 noon	Final session with the staff and final words from Mr. Keen

Agricultural Machinery & Farm Crops

AGRICULTURAL MACHINERY AND FARM CROPS

Staff — Mr. Hudson and other members of the Machinery Department

Place — Agricultural Machine Shops and Farms

Tuesday 2nd April

9.0 a.m. — 12.45 p.m.	Practical Agricultural Engineering — Mr. Hudson and staff
2.0 p.m. — 4.30 p.m.	Practical Agricultural Engineering — Mr. Hudson and staff
6.30 p.m.	Hall (New building)
	Guest speaker — Mr. Peter Campion, S.F.Y.F.C. "The Young Farmers' Club Movement"

* * * * * * * *

Wednesday 3rd April

9.0 a.m. — 12.45 p.m.	Practical Agricultural Engineering — Mr. Hudson and staff
2.0 p.m. — 4.30 p.m.	Practical Agricultural Engineering — Mr Hudson and staff
6.0 p.m.	Hall (New building)
	Guest speaker — Mr. Brian Whitemore Talk — illustrated by film and slides on the work of a thatcher
7.30 p.m.	The Bridgwater Young Farmers' Club present "The Auction" — a play in Somerset dialect

Thursday 4th April

9.0 a.m. — 10.45 a.m.	Talks — Lecture Room (1) Grassland — Mr. Mead (2) Crops — Mr. Berkeley
11.0 a.m. — 12.45 p.m.	Practical Farm Tasks (with Farming Group) Crops — Mr. Berkeley Grassland — Mr. Mead
2.0 p.m. — 4.0 p.m.	Practical Farm Tasks (with Farming Group) Grassland — Mr. Mead Crops — Mr. Berkeley
6.0 p.m.	Hall (New Building) Talk and film on "Farm Safety" — Mr. Broom, Ministry of Agriculture
7.0 p.m.	Social

* * * * * * * *

Friday 5th April

9.0 a.m. — 10.0 a.m.	Talk — Guest speaker — Mr. A. F. R. Fisher Regional Training Adviser — Agricultural, Horticultural and Forestry Industry Training Board.
10.0 a.m. — 10.45 a.m.	Farm figures — Mr. Summers
11.0 a.m.	"Points of View"
12 noon	Final Session with the staff and final words from Mr. Keen

Expansion continued at Cannington in the 1970s, and in this extract from the COSA Magazine of 1985, the Pricipal P.H.Keen, DFC, BSc, summarises the changes:

College Update 1975-1985

By the early 1970s the Dairying Course had been discontinued and the Dairy Farming Course was being run in conjunction with the Agricultural Department. We had all felt that we should be offering National Diplomas at Cannington but it was for the Dairy and Food Technology Department to blaze the trail with the launching of the 2-year Diploma in 1973. We had remodelled the Amory Laboratory and introduced quite a lot of equipment to the Dairy to do with foods other than milk products. This will all be moved into the building now under construction on the old Court Farm site in the autumn. The building will be alongside the demountable classrooms and laboratories on the Sports Field, erected a couple of years ago for the Youth Training Scheme (YTS) Courses and the new one-year Certificate Course.

The Horticultural Department was the second in the "Diploma Stakes". The Advanced Certificate in Amenity Horticulture had been running since 1971 and the Glasshouse complex in the Walled Gardens was completed in 1972. The first Diploma intake was in 1976 and, this being a sandwich course, they returned for their third year in 1978. The number of students returning for a second year of study was becoming significant, which brought quite a change in college life. The Student Committee became more important, we had students on the Governing Body for the first time, the sports teams became more consistent and more and more students were living out in 'digs'.

The Engineering Department has had the most dramatic change because it now runs its own courses. The YTS courses and the full time Agricultural Mechanics course, together with the servicing of an increasing number of full time courses has increased the work enormously. The erection of demountable teaching rooms and offices on the Downs accompanied a reorganisation of the main structure and the addition of the poultry house alongside. The completion of the J. Humphrey Engineering Centre to the South now almost doubles the facilities, and with Hockey Field now operated by the engineers and an area of Downs also being used for practical work and machinery setting, the Downs now resembles a small industrial centre. The wrought iron forges, operating from the double Dutch Barn, add to this impression when they are in business and Frank Day's blacksmith courses add to the interest of weekend walkers on the Downs when the sparks are flying and hammers clanging. John Hudson now has fourteen lecturers which is the same number as in each of the Departments of Agriculture and Horticulture.

1971/72
Horti. Study trip to the Scillys

L. to R.:
Back row: M.Boller; R.Bates; R.Pickford; O.Walker; H.Wood; R.Cripps;
Front Row: M. Snellgrove; N.Butler; Kingi; R.Madley; R.Cluff; P.Millwood; G.Rollison

Ironically, the Agricultural Department was the last one to get its Diploma Course. When it came to deciding the regional pattern of courses, because we already had two diploma courses running, we had to wait for other colleges to catch up. 1980 saw the first course start by which time Dr Lishman and his team were based in the old Court Farmhouse now renamed 'Montgomery House'. This is also the home of the Management Department and it was from here that Ian Hoyland ran the Farm Based Information Centre before moving to Cornwall as Director of Agricutural Education.

The 1974 Tug of War

1 - Unknown

2 - Tim McLaughlin

3 - Stigg Quinn

4 - John Warfield

5 - Gordon Stone

6 - Campbell Parker

L to R: 1..............2.................3.............4................5............6

1 - Chris Anderson

2 - Stigg Quinn

3 - Phil the Boot Moseley

4 - Nick Phippen

5 - Marcus Guppy

6 - Campbell Parker

L to R: 1.........................2 ..3........4...........5................6

Angie Benson & Christine Gemmill

They're not even watching!

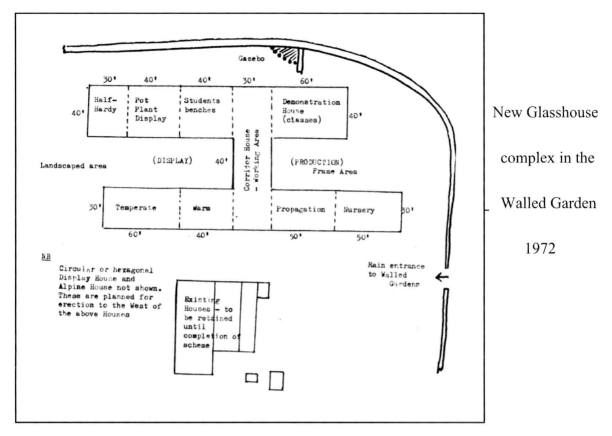

New Glasshouse

complex in the

Walled Garden

1972

"The old glasshouses in the walled gardens are to be replaced by a new block designed to cover teaching needs, and the first instalment is now completed.   The layout illustrated above is intended to afford good winter light for all houses with the display areas forming the western arms and the service areas and production houses to the east of the central corridor". (Stuart Brookfield - 1971 Magazine).

"The Glasshouse complex in the walled garden was completed in 1972" (*College Update. p.63*).

(And demolished thirty years later ? - Editor)

Nesta Hawkins (nee Lewis) introduces two visitors to Glastonbury's Rural Museum to the mechanical and technical aspects of butter making . . . Cannington style! This series of demonstrations is proving a tremendous success.

At

Glastonbury Rural Life

Museum in the 1970s

(A.R. Watkins, N.M. Williams, A.R. Hurd & S.P. Thomas)
1976/77Students outside the Student Pig Unit

The Student Pig Unit was established to give students experience in the day to day running of a stock unit, with all the day to day difficulties and problems that a modern pig farmer faces.

Students M.F.Perrington and R.S.Gatcombe 1976/77 make last minute preparations for their
re-entry into the world at large after their year at Cannington. An engine out of one car and into another.

Chapter 12. Cannington in the 1980s

<u>Farms</u>: Three farms 422 acres. Two herds of Friesians: 80 cows milked by a 4:8 herringbone and 70 by a 3;6 two level abreast parlour. Dairy replacements are bred and reared (and some dairy bred beef cattle) but there are no sheep and only a small poultry unit. 45 sows rear their pigs to weaning and there is a separate Student Pig Unit of 30 sows. The purpose of the farm is to provide the facilities for practical demonstrations to students, on machines, livestock and a wide variety of crops and grassland, "to provide the opportunity to participate in routine operations and provide situations and data for the teaching of farm management".

<u>Dairy</u>: Greatly expanded in recent years and now includes courses in Food Technology. The type of machinery is numerous and subjects range from butter making to yoghurt, food freezing and canning.

<u>Horticulture</u>   In this field the college has experienced the greatest change.   From the frozen cabbage patches and windswept orchards of the 1920s to the tropical glasshouses, pest-controlled by the 'Birds of Cannington' of the 1980s.   Of a total of 22 ha., 14 are devoted to commercial cropping, which includes 0.2ha. of glass, 4ha. of vegetables, 6ha. of fruit and 1 ha. of nursery stock.   The 8ha. amenity horticulture area is made up of walled gardens, grounds and playing fields.   Unlike the early days, the department is run on a commercial basis, and marketing is through a farm-gate shop, by 'pick your own' and through a local wholesaler.*(From the The 1980s Prospectus in the COSA Diamond Jubilee Magazine 1921-1981).*

A Day at Somerset College of Agriculture & Horticulture in 1981

Alarm clocks ring at 7.30 a.m. and we all turn over for another 30 minutes sleep before hurriedly stumbling out of bed at 8 o,clock to dress and rush up to the main buildings for breakfast before 8.30 a.m.

We all collect sleepy-eyed in our lecture room for subjects such as Food Chemistry, Management, Microbiology, and Food Processing. The lectures could well be described occasionally as organised chaos (especially the practical sessions).

Lectures finish at 12.25 p.m. in time for dinner at 12.30. after which it's all into the Common Room for a quick cigarette, social chat or a game on the 'Space Invader' machine until 1.30 p.m. when it's back to lectures until 5.00 p.m. when we have high tea.

After the meal it's back to our rooms to work for a few hours or for those not inclined that way it is watching the television or playing snooker.

Turned out of the Common Room at 11.30 and lights off when we think best,
Judith Saille, FT (Food Technology) 1980/81 - COSA Magazine - 1981

MISS M N HEYWOOD
THE LONGEST SERVING MEMBER OF STAFF

Miss Heywood, the College matron, is now the longest serving member of staff. She came from Tiverton to take up the position of assistant matron in April 1947.

In those days there were about 50 students, divided into 4 groups, agriculture, dairying, horticulture and poultry. Everyone was housed in the old priory building and it was a very close knit community. Rules were strict, no drinking in pubs, lights out at 10 p.m., no vehicles on the premises and a rigid regime of practical duties on the farm, the gardens, dairy or poultry units.

Today, sitting in her office, Miss Heywood made comparisons with the present. 250 full time and many more part time or short course students. She no longer has to supervise the kitchens and dining rooms but, nevertheless, has about 20 in her department.

She feels that the larger numbers and increased mobility and independence of present day students has changed the old "family" type atmosphere. In fact the staff at the College almost equal the numbers of staff and students 30 years ago.

The College also has an almost constant role of hosting all types of conventions and gatherings of the most unlikely types, many of which are residential.

Her memory for ex students is phenomenal and I was very grateful for the fact when checking up some details for the magazine She hoards a huge volume of files and other details of students and the O.S.A. in her office which, I am sure, will prove to be very valuable for members of the O.S.A.

(from the 1985 COSA Magazine)

Top left: New cubicles and the raised feeding passage.

Top Right: The Herringbone milking parlour under construction - 25-2-82

Left: Slurry pit, strainer wall and liquid effluent tank

Rodway Farm: Silaging in Shark's Field in 1981.   This part of the field was later owned by the District Council and became the site of the new village playing fields.

(Above photos: 1982 COSA Magazine)

SOMERSET COLLEGE OF
AGRICULTURE AND
HORTICULTURE

OPEN DAY
1985

CAR PARK: £1 PER VEHICLE, INCLUDING
FREE PROGRAMME.

OPEN DAY 1985

On the left is a reproduction of the cover of the Open Day programme of 1985 (reduced). The contents of the programme are recorded on the following pages, and give a comprehensive picture of Cannington activities at this time

Dear Visitor,

Welcome to the Cannington Annual Open Day.
I hope that your day with us will be enjoyable and that it will increase your knowledge and appreciation of the countryside and of some of the problems associated with food production.

P. H. KEEN, *Principal*

The college offers residential courses in

AGRICULTURE, DAIRY FARMING, HORTICULTURE

FOOD TECHNOLOGY AND ENGINEERING

Students taking these courses are prepared for the:

BTEC National Diploma in General Agriculture
National Certificate in Agriculture
National Certificate in Dairying
BTEC National Diploma in Amenity Horticulture
National Certificate in Horticulture (Amenity & Commercial)
Advanced National Certificate in Amenity Horticulture
BTEC Diploma in the Technology of Food
BTEC Certificate in the Technology of Food

Block release courses are also run for the Dairy and
Agricultural Engineering Industries.

Details of part time Day Release Courses including Management
subjects and also the Youth Training Scheme, are available
from the careers stand in the Main Hall.

For further details please contact a member of staff or phone
Combwich (0278) 652226.

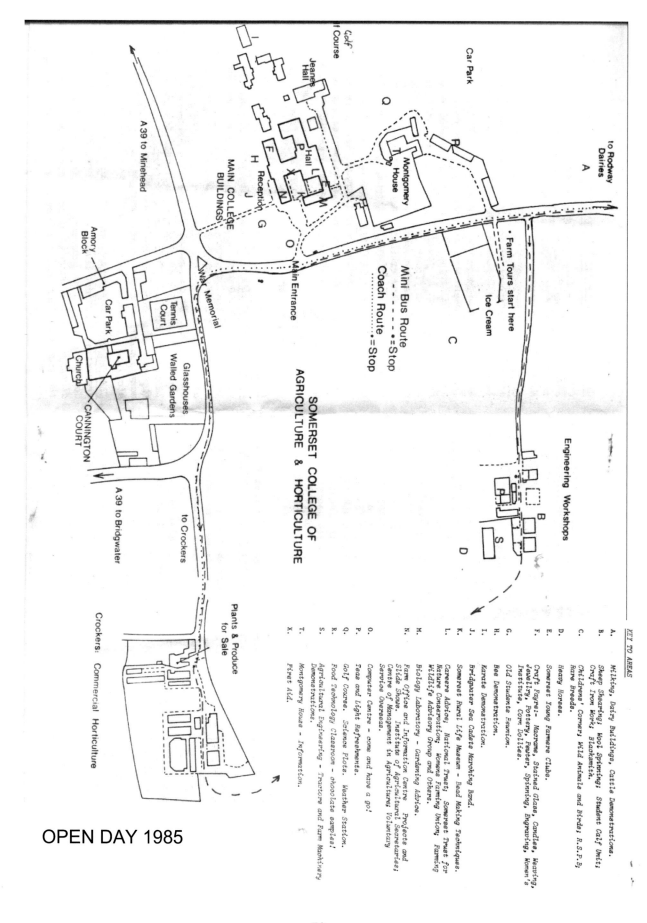

OPEN DAY 1985

SOMERSET COLLEGE OF AGRICULTURE & HORTICULTURE

KEY TO AREAS

A. Milking, Dairy Buildings, Cattle Demonstrations.
B. Sheep Shearing; Wool Spinning; Student Calf Unit; Craft Iron Work; Blacksmith.
C. Childrens' Corner; Wild Animals and Birds; R.S.P.B; Rare Breeds.
D. Heavy Horses.
E. Somerset Young Farmers Clubs.
F. Craft Fayre:- Macrame, Stained Glass, Candles, Weaving, Jewellry, Pottery, Pewter, Spinning, Engraving, Women's Institute, Corn Dollies.
G. Old Students Reunion.
H. Bee Demonstration.
I. Karate Demonstration.
J. Bridgwater Sea Cadets Marching Band.
K. Somerset Rural Life Museum - Bead Making Techniques.
L. Careers Advice; National Trust; Somerset Trust for Nature Conservation; Womens Farming Union; Farming Wildlife Advisory Group and Others.
M. Biology Laboratory - Gardening Advice.
N. Farm Office and Information Centre Projects and Slide Shows. Institute of Agricultural Secretaries; Centre of Management in Agriculture; Voluntary Service Overseas.
O. Computer Centre - come and have a go!
P. Teas and Light Refreshments.
Q. Golf Course.
R. Food Technology Classroom - chocolate samples!
S. Agricultural Engineering - Tractors and Farm Machinery Demonstrations.
T. Montgomery House - Information.
X. First Aid.

<u>SOMERSET COLLEGE OF AGRICULTURE AND HORTICULTURE</u>
<u>COLLEGE OPEN DAY</u>

SATURDAY 11th MAY 1985 2.00 - 5.00 p.m.

<u>Transport</u>

Coach transport is available between the College, the
Commercial Horticultural Section (Crockers) and Rodway Dairies.
Mini-bus tours go via the Workshop and Crockers Sales Stall
of produce and plants. Tractor and Trailer rides, with guides,
will take you from the Engineering Workshop area through
the farm to Rodway Dairies. You can then get a coach back up
to the Main Campus.

See the map further in the programme for the location of the
various features, exhibits, coach and mini-bus routes. For
further information please call at the Information Centre,
or ask a member of staff (they are wearing lapel badges).

<u>FARM FEATURES</u>

Rodway - milking and dairy buildings, cattle demonstrations,
possibly silage making (weather and season permitting).   **A**

Sheep shearing and wool spinning demonstrations.   **B**

Farm tours - by tractor and trailer (see above) weather permitting.

Student calf unit - demonstration of College's young cattle.   **B**

<u>OTHER ATTRACTIONS</u>

Children's corner - an interesting display of small animals
and pets to delight the young and the 'young at heart'.   **C**

Forge: Craft iron work.   **B**

B

Blacksmith: A farrier will be shoeing horses during the afternoon.

Heavy horses: Working the land below the Engineering Workshops **D**

Somerset Young Farmers Clubs have a participative display to do
with International Youth Year - well worth a look!   **E**

Wild animals and birds: We hope to have David Chafe with some
owls and his badgers and a fox. He will be talking about his
animals during the afternoon.   **C**

Rare Breeds: The Rare Breed Survival Trust will be showing
some rare breeds of sheep.   **C**

Craft Fayre including macrame, candlemaking, jewellery, weaving,
spinning, pottery, fabric printing and the Womens' Institute. **F**

Old Students Reunion - tent on front lawn.   **G**

Bees - have a look at the hive and demonstration on the front
lawn.   **H**

A Karate demonstration given by members of the Taunton Shotokan Karate Club will take place at 2.30 p.m. in the Sports Hall.   I

Bridgwater Sea Cadets marching band will entertain you throughout the afternoon.   J

Somerset Rural Life Museum will be demonstrating ancient bead making techniques.   K

There are also interesting stands provided by the Institute of Agricultural Secretaries, the Centre of Management in Agriculture, and Voluntary Service Overseas.   N

FEATURES INSIDE THE NEW BUILDINGS

Main Hall - Careers advice - Agriculture, Horticulture, Food Technology and Engineering.   L

Various other displays include the National Trust, the Somerset Trust for Nature Conservation, Womens Farming Union, Farming Wildlife Advisory Group and many others. L

Biology Laboratory - Garden advice and Plant Identification. M

Student work - Displays are to be found in Horticultural classrooms. Agricultural projects and slide shows of College events are in the room next to the Farm Office.   N

Farm Office and Information Centre - students will be working on the farm computers and in the Farm Office. They will be happy to explain the purpose of the Office and how it works.   N

Computer Centre - Students will be using the computers and you are invited to have a go yourself.   O

Teas and Light Refreshments - On sale in the dining room and machinery workshop area (2.00 - 5.00 p.m.).   P

The Open Day ended with an "Easy Prize Competition", consisting of five simple questions relating to aspects of the Cannington Open Day, and the the following sentence had to be completed: "*Cannington College Open Day is a great afternoon out because: . . . . "*

Horses are back at Cannington!

A group of students working under the supervision of the head groom.
(Ann Spencer - far left)

(from COSA Magazine, 1988)

Chapter 13. Cannington in the 1990s.

The Chronicle is grateful to Katriona King who provided nearly all the 1990s material: She writes:

In September 1990 I attended Cannington College BTec National Diploma in Land Based Industries (Agriculture). The following were the course members:
  Naomi Clegg; Sarah Hawker; Jonathan King; Katriona King; James Weeks.
Other options were Horticulture, Food Science and Countryside Management (I think).

In September 1991 I returned having enrolled for the BTech National Diploma in Agriculture, which was a 3-year course with the 2nd year on practical placement.. Course members were:

Rachel Chittenden	*Deborah Cossey*	*Hugh Foster*
Jonathan King	*Katriona King*	*Paul Kingston*
Nicholas Leach	*Keith Sparks*	*James Weeks*
Michael White		

Course Tutor: *Sue Bateman in year 1 and Richard West (JRW) in year 3.*

Lake District Study Tour: Angela, Steve, Jim and David Capel

During the first year of the NDA, along with the NCA, there was a rota arranged to carry out the farm duties as below:
  Dairy/Milking: Start at 5.00 am and 2.00 pm reporting to Ivan Wareham.
  Young Stock: Start 6.30 am and 1.30 pm : Graham Gibson
  Machinery: Start 1.30 pm: Tim Moore
  Pigs: Start 6.30 am and 1.30 pm: Keith Woollerson
  Calving Duty: Check cows at 10.00 pm
  Bulling Duty from November 1st.

Our study tour was an exchange with East Germany: they visited Cannington 23rd to 27th March 1992 and we visited Germany in June 1991

13. Cannington in the 1990s

The staff who taught us from 1990 to 1994 were: *Barry J. Gimbert (Principal), Roy Pumfrey, Richard M. Newman, Graham Corner, Steve Bryant, David H. Capel, PWT; JND; RHH; AH; WVGB; BJB; Robin Ballerdie.*

<u>Farm Staff</u>:

Farm Director	*Steve Bryant*
Herdsman	*Ivan Wareham*
Assistant Herdsman/Shepherd	*Malcolm Porch*
Pig Unit manager	*Keith Woollerson*
Stockman	*Graham Gibson*
Tractor Driver/ Relief Pigman	*Steve Dart*

National Certificate Students for 1991 were:

Tony Brice	*Paul Carp*	*Mark Catley-Day*
John Chapman	*Philip Cotterell*	*Don Creed*
Matthew Creed	*Jo Cruze*	*Eric Down*
Colin Grainger-Allen	*Darren Heal*	*Glen Humber*
Richard Lewis	*Nick Parker*	*Ian Shepherd*
Ben Stitch	*Katherine Wilson*	

End of Course Photograph (NDA3 - 1994)

Back Row: *Paul Kingston; Ian Shepherd; Rachel Hole; Deb Cossey; Katriona King; Michael White; James Weeks.*
Front Row: *Hugh Foster; Nick Leach; Richard West; Eric Down; John King.*

NDA First Year Study Tour exchange to Germany ; June 1991
Left to right: Keith Sparkes, Nick Leach, James Weeks, Robin Ballerdie, Hugh Foster,
Katriona King, Lecturer "Bill" (WVGB), Paul Kingston, Deb Cossey, Rachel Hole
(nee Chittenden), Michael White, John King.

SPORT

Ladies Indoor Hockey Team - 1990
(3rd in SCAT Tournament)
Back: L toR: Vicky Porent; Anne-Marie Mathew;. Natalie Kirk;
Nicola Whitworth; Maria Burton.
Front: Jo Cross; Penny Weymouth; Helen Bigge;Jo Hounsell

Hadlow 7s Hockey Tournament 'Plate' 1994
Eric and Nick (Katriona King : Capt.)

75

Yeovil Centre Report

This year has proved to be a very busy but interesting and satisfying one, in which there has been a steady increase in course options, student numbers and resources.

Following the successful introduction of full-time BTEC First Diplomas in agriculture and horticulture last year, it is pleasing to note that these courses boast an increased group size of 33% for the academic year 1993/94.

Increasing demand for full-time courses within the South Somerset area has prompted Cannington to offer further options at both BTEC First Diploma and National Diploma levels. The options available for September 1994 are as follows:

First Dipoma in Floristry, Countryside Management, Agricultural and Horticultutal

Mechanics, Animal Care and National Diploma in Animal Care.

Also due to the rapid progress made by students on NVQ level 2 programmes, we

expect to have a large cohort of day-release students advancing to NVQ level 3

programmes (Incorporating Management competencies) early in 1994.

The Amenity and Commercial students have benefited from the new glasshouse constructed during the summer. It also incorporates a Floristry workshop which has accommodated part-time floristry courses during the autumn term. In addition it also provides a useful growing area for our increasing collection of commercial House-plants.

During the autumn term, the Youth Training Foundation Group acquired the tenancy of a 0.5 hectare (1.25 acre) local authority plot of land. They have recently completed the arduous task of removing the majority of weeds and have begun planting vegetable crops. Much of the cleared debris and some unwanted wood was used to construct a large bonfire, much to the delight of several local playgroups and schools on Guy Fawkes night.

This year's study tour was spent at Ambleside in the lake District. Students completed an interesting and enjoyable week. It consisted of a mixed programme of practical work and visits. The Yeovil students benefited from integrating with fellow colleagues from Cannington.

During the year, groups completed various conservation projects for local Schools, Farmer/Growers, Golf Clubs, Nurseries, Local Councils and the National Trust. These were all appreciated and provided immense stimulus for all students involved.

Lastly, may I thank all the students, local farmers and growers who have repeatedly made resources available to us during 1993.   (COSA Magazine 1994).

21st December 1993 - A Mr Blobby impersonation, which was part of the Cannington Christmas Party, was followed by a rendering of *An Alternative Christmas Carol* sung by Andy Morris (NDCM2), Michael White (NDA3) and Katriona King (NDA3) - who else (!) They are said to be impersonating the SMT team - Barry, Lynn and Richard. (Editor's Note: Don't ask me!). *(from COSA Magazine 1994)*.

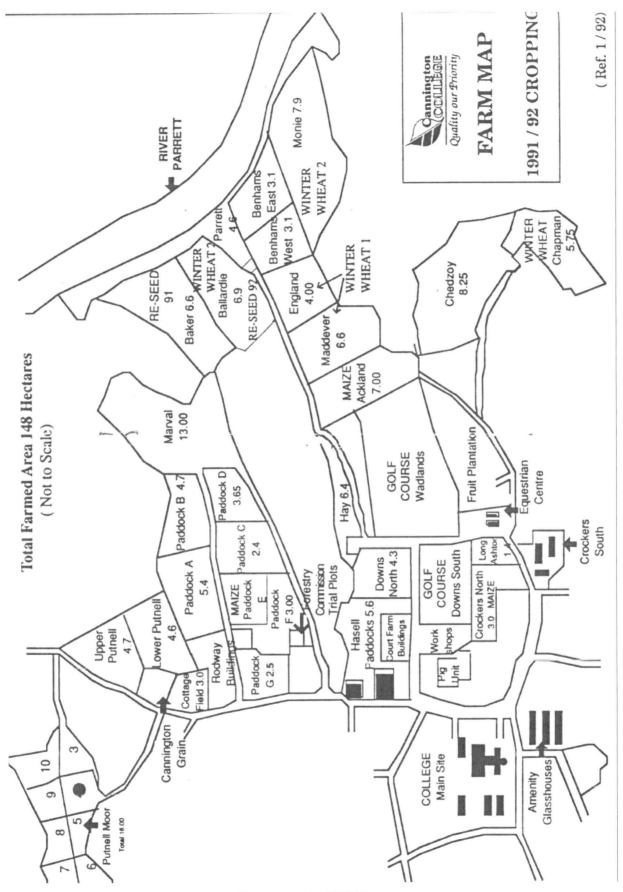

Cannington in 1991/92

13. Cannington in the 1990s

LIVESTOCK NUMBERS AS AT 1.4.92

DAIRY	136	Cows
	55	Heifers under 1 year old
	56	Heifers in-calf
BEEF	12	Pedigree Aberdeen Angus cattle
	28	Aberdeen Angus x Friesian suckler cows & calves
	28	12 m.o. suckled calves
	40	Cattle under 1 year old
SHEEP	150	breeding ewes: N. Country mules and halfbreds
	1	Charollais ram
	3	Texel rams
PIGS	78	breeding sows
	4	gilts
	4	boars
	126	suckling piglets
	304	weaners

CROPPING SUMMARY 1992 CROP YEAR

Permanent pasture		89 acres
Long Leys		148 acres
Winter Wheat		74 acres
Maize		42 acres
Roads and buildings		12 acres
	TOTAL	365 acres

ROTATIONS

Six of the fields on the flood plain are in a six year rotation of two wheats, beans, two wheats and oilseed rape, although at present the rotation is complicated as new fields are introduced and existing fields go back to grass.. Maize is grown in fields which are suitable, some being used continuously, others having maize as a cleaning crop prior to re-seeding to a short term ley.

DAIRY HERD

Until April 1988 the College ran two dairy herds. Since then the herds have been amalgamated and run as one. The herd consists of 160 pedigree Holstein Friesians and the breeding is aimed at producing a dairy type animal. The herd is milked through a 14/14 herringbone parlour.

The herd is predominantly autumn calving and the majority of cows (with one or two exceptions) are bred pure to provide herd replacements and surplus heifers for sale. The worst 20% of the herd are bred to beef breeds (predominantly Belgian Blue) to provide calves for the beef unit or for sale. Dairy heifers are also bred pure, with a beef bull used to sweep up.

THESE CHANGING TIMES - The Chairman of the Governors writes:

The incredible pace with which all Colleges have evolved since incorporation is inevitably posing an enormous challenge to all further education establishments. At Cannington the 25% increase over three years in student numbers, combined with a massive reduction in funding, has forced far reaching changes. New courses have been developed, modern methods introduced to streamline systems and workloads substantially changed and increased.

Faced with the culture shock of meeting these targets, set by our paymaster The Further Education Funding Council (FEFC), everyone is concerned to retain the traditional character and ethos of the College. The balance between tradition and change is delicate and will never suit all parties. That both should have their place in a College of Cannington's reputation is undisputed.

It is not surprising, therefore that tensions should develop. It is now a matter of record that the management style of the Principal, in keeping the College on line to meet its targets, has triggered some loss of confidence in some quarters. As a consequence an Enquiry has been set up to recommend a just and lasting solution to this issue. Meanwhile, during the period of the Principal's suspension, the expanded senior management team under the careful leadership of Lynn Dudley is, with cooperation of all staff, ensuring the smooth running of the College.

Cannington may be suffering some temporary but inevitable growing pains in establishing itself as one of the foremost Colleges for 'rural industries' under the new regime. Despite strong finances, excellent resources and dedicated staff, a touch on the tiller will be needed from time to time to steer the right course between tradition and change.

John Alvis - 1995 COSA Magazine

Chapter 14. Untrained Staff?- Nonsense!

The changes mentioned on page 78 were not all for the better. The well-meant conclusion that "Despite strong finances, excellent resources and dedicated staff, a touch on the tiller will be needed from time to time to steer the right course between tradition and change" was too optimistic. Unfortunately bureaucratic helmsmen from Whitehall had steered the barque of Cannington among the rocks of the Dept. of Education and much more than a "touch on the tiller" was now needed to avoid shipwreck.

"Most teaching staff are well qualified in their subject discipline, but only 67% hold a teaching qualification" says the unfavourable 2003 OFSTED Report on Cannington College. Who can blame the Bridgwater Mercury of 13/5/03, for reporting that "a third of the teachers were untrained". What else were jounalists and other local people to think? Not having a teaching qualification means "unqualified" or "untrained" to most people. But it meant only that a third of the professionally qualified lecturing staff did not have a Certificate or Diploma in Education, often called a "Teacher's Certificate", or the "parchment".

In fact the staff so described were no more "untrained" than W.D.Hay himself had been. Back in those glory days of W.D.Hay no member of staff had a Certificate or Diploma in Education. Under Ministry of Agriculture rules it was not necessary. Neither W.D. Hay himself had a Cert Ed, nor A.D.Turner, Miss Saker, Miss Masters, Miss Monie, Miss Taylor, J.W. Dallas, Miss Maddever or any of the other stalwarts of the time. If Ministry of Education rules had applied then, they would all have been classed as "untrained" because they did not have a Certificate or Diploma in Education. They were "not qualified to teach", and therefore could never have been employed at Cannington under those rules!

OFSTED shock for

A DAMNING report into the state of Cannington College has left the future running of the historic institution in doubt.

OFSTED inspectors found a third of teachers were untrained, management and leadership was unsatisfactory, value for money was poor, student numbers were declining and pass rates on many courses were poor, according to a report published on Friday.

And the decline in the college's fin-

ances since the last OFSTED inspection in 1998 has left the governors pondering its future.

The college has made an operating loss for the past three years, a budget surplus has been converted into a significant deficit, budget controls are weak and reserves are low and declining, according to the report.

The principal Richard Hinxman has been placed on extended leave since the beginning of last week after the

By News Editor SEAN SMITH

newsdesk@bridgwatermercury.co.uk

contents of the damning report became clear.

Matters have been made worse by the fact that the college has been unable to appoint a financial director for over a year now.

Two of the three areas of the college's curriculum – horticulture and agriculture and countryside studies – received the second lowest mark att-

The report from the Bridgwater Mercury of 13th May 2003,

Fortunately, in the great days of W.D.Hay Cannington was not ruled by the Ministry of Education, it came under the Ministry of Agriculture, which demanded only that Lecturers should have recognised professional qualifications, which were mainly Diplomas awarded by the RASE or RHS (like the allegedly "untrained" staff of 2003), and be keen to pass on their knowledge to their students.

How many members of COSA noticed when, in the 1970s, "Cert. Ed" appeared among the qualifications of the Cannington Staff, indicating that the Ministry of Education had taken control? It only happened post-1960. But by 1971 ten out of 38 staff members had Cert.Ed. By 1985 the number had risen to 20.

14. Untrained Staff?- Nonsense!-

What had happened was that responsibility for Agricultural Education had been transferred by Central Government from the Ministry of Agriculture to the Ministry of Education. As a result, Ministry of Education rules now applied throughout Agricultural Education - including, of course, Cannington. (See Dept. of Education instructions on page 57). One of the most entrenched long-term rules of the Ministry of Education was that all teachers or lecturers - except graduates, originally - must hold a Certificate or Diploma in Education (the hallowed "Parchment") with its Registered Number recorded in the archives of the Ministry of Education in Whitehall So all new Cannington staff appointed had to have a Cert. Ed. or Dip. Ed. and all existing staff were pressed to do a course to acquire a Cert Ed. by one or other in-service scheme. Soon even graduates were expected to have a 'parchment', and even Ph.Ds were not exempt. The Editor became aware of these facts when looking for a post after Anthrax and Swine Fever (following F&M) forced him out of farming in 1963, and he spent the following year acquiring a Cert. Ed. (He considered it a waste of time, and still does, and never normally admits to having one!).

Studying for a Diploma or Certificate in Education brings people under the baleful influence of educational psychologists, theorisers beloved of the Ministry of Education, whose interests are in psychology and sociology and not in education. In the Editor's view, such "experts" have very little interest in or knowledge of education (and, of course, no knowledge whatsoever of farming), but the resulting Certificate or Diploma qualifies the holder to teach a wide range of subjects to a wide range of ages, which anyone with any commonsense will realise is unrealistic.

But does it matter? Perhaps insistence on a Cert. Ed. is just a mild idiosyncracy of the Ministry of Education, a nuisance, but well meant and harmless. Not so! The rule was well meant and useful a century ago, when it raised standards among non-graduates generally, but particularly among "pupil teachers" (youngsters of fourteen or so, straight out of school and knowing little more than the three Rs). But it was never necessary in agricultural education, and is not necessary now.

In fact the demand for Cert.Ed. helped to sink Cannington as an independent entity by labelling many of its staff as inadequate.

The Official College Announcement

Cannington College
COLLEGE OF THE COUNTRYSIDE

As you are aware Cannington College underwent an OFSTED Inspection in January this year. We were understandably disappointed with some findings and fully recognised the need to improve some aspects of our provision.

Since then, much progress has been made to bring about necessary improvements. The Corporation is analysing the strategic direction of the College, to ensure clear vision and direction in the future. The Principal has been on extended leave since the end of April 2003.

The report rightly recognises Cannington College's key strengths, such as good pastoral support for students, good use of the estate for teaching, good progression opportunities and effective links with specialist centres.

OFSTED Inspectors focused only on our Further Education provision. The last inspection of our Higher Education provision was graded by QAA as excellent. We are also regularly and satisfactorily inspected by various examining boards.

As usual we have seen more successes this term, including approval from the Royal Horticultural Society to build two gardens at this year's Hampton Court Palace Flower Show. The winning designs were created by our Higher Education horticulture students, Russ Joyner and Bridget Hobhouse.

We also enjoyed glittering success at the Bath & West Show at the end of May. Cannington College's Yeovil Centre won a Silver Medal for their 'Spring Garden' designed and built by mature students with the help of horticulture lecturer, Hervé Le Reverend.

These achievements, coupled with our 80 year history, demonstrate the importance of Cannington College within the land-based sector and the community. We have a dedicated staff and have received resounding support from the LSC and other stakeholders. We are confident and determined to continually improve our services and shall endeavour to keep you informed of future developments.

David Tremlett
Chair of Corporation

Editor' Footnote: It is rather laughable, if shocking, to learn that the Department of Education in early May 2006 issued a 22 page guide for OFSTED Inspectors called *Guide to Ofsted's House Style*. This booklet included a guide to spelling such simple words as "underachieve", "timetable" and "teamwork" but also gave examples of how to use "its" and "it's". (Daniel Boffey, Daily Mail, early May 2006). OFSTED Inspectors apparently need help to achieve even Fourth Form Secondary English Language level but are nevertheless believed to be well enough qualified to outlaw Cannington!

Chapter 15 - Decline and Fall.

(Contributed by Caroline Woolley and Benny Goodman)

During the last decades of the Twentieth Century in Britain, fundamental changes surrounding the status of agriculture, its support funding and future policies were beginning to have adverse consequences on its infrastructure, of which one - that of agricultural education - was especially affected.

Such was the nature of these distractions that former long cherished priorities were cast aside and replaced by seemingly more democratic and cost effective avenues of development - more suited to the modern era of perceived 'need' in Society.

Tried and tested ways of doing things were abandoned for experimental and new managerial techniques, run by often inexperienced and less informed officials.

In short, the terms "Agriculture" and "Farming" were suddenly expunged from the language of the day and replaced by such phrases as "Land Based Industries", "Countryside Care Initiatives" and "Rural Resources", et alia!

Once the profitable future of small and medium sized livestock and mixed farms in the West Country had dwindled - hastened by BSE and Foot and Mouth outbreaks in the 1990s - a discernible shift away from the agricultural Sector to a new creature called "Land Based Training" came about, backed by dubious financial funding.

This outcome was influenced by unilateral County decisions not to send agri/horti students out of the County for further education at specialist colleges enjoying a high profile in the industry. Instead, 'in-county' systems of training were set up and supported, resulting eventually in much higher costs of per capita training, piecemeal courses and downgrading of results. The overall shift of prosperity away from rural areas in the 1980s and 1990s engendered much resentment and distrust of the regulating authorities. This trend was aided by Central Government's reorganization of County boundaries which, at a stroke, reduced the size of Somerset by 33% and its population by some 66%.

No longer were Somerset's proud rural industries accorded the employment priority status of bygone years. Attitudes changed to the extent that from the 1980s onwards there was a reluctance on the part of the Careers Service to send students into the 'land-based' sector because of perceived low pay, low status and diminished career prospects.

Central Government then decided to make FE colleges "Self Sufficient" and set up the Further Education Funding Council (FEFC) through which all FE colleges would bid for their funding. In fact this funding was pegged at a given rate on a sliding [downward] scale over ten years. This pegged unit rate used a complex formula for scaling support up or down depending on the type of course offered. For example, for IT and hair dressing, training rated as an A which equaled low funding while chainsaw, tractor driving etc rated an E and a higher rate of funding. It could be argued perhaps that this system tended to encourage higher numbers rather than an improvement in end product quality!

The independent status of FE colleges also meant that County Councils were no longer responsible for the financial support or personnel arrangements for the colleges. Moreover, College principals and senior staff now had to manage a business including the responsibility of buying in their own services. They were of course first and foremost educationalists by training but had to grapple with accountancy, marketing and business disciplines with which many were not familiar.

What was at first an exciting concept became a millstone in so far as much of the available funding was expended on these (business) services rather than on the development of college courses and their marketing. In respect of Cannington, the untimely death of the Principal appointed in 1991 who was guiding the college through 'Incorporation' and on to 'Independent' status, dealt a severe blow to the future of the college. Subsequent appointees were unable to keep the college on a steady course and external pressures to tackle change, and to perform, only exacerbated instability and internal dissension. At one stage the Chair of Governors who saw the College through its transition from an LEA establishment to a FEFC College resigned.

In the ensuing years the College's financial status further declined accompanied by recriminations all round. Despite a last desperate attempt to restore its fortunes, it was finally realised, too late, that the College could not continue due to indebtedness and under funding - in short, Cannington was too small to survive on its own. Had this fact been acknowledged earlier and arrangements made to link up with another college/university whilst retaining its own autonomy, the College would have had a future.

However, by the end of 2002 it was abundantly clear that Cannington was a failed college and it was necessary for the Further Education Funding Council and the Learning and Skills Council to step in and sort out the problem of Land Based education in Somerset. Aided by substantial funding, Bridgwater College took on the task and have endeavoured to save as much as possible at Cannington whilst analysing the financial viability of the establishment overall in addition to specific training courses in particular.

The ongoing and rigorous re-vamp of Cannington continues to be a painful process but at the same time offers hope for the future. Current investment at Cannington is aimed at a new Animal Care Building and also an upgrade of the accommodation block to a high conference standard. In the spring of 2006, appointed consultants are assessing the College farm with a view to introducing a modus operandi enabling its educational status to be retained while ensuring profitability.

Regrettably, in these tough times, there may yet be more casualties.

Comment from Benny Goodman: One is tempted sometimes to ask why it is the Anglo-Saxon British are so peculiarly adept at allowing priceless entities to be cast aside, only later to regret bitterly their passing - too late. In the West a few of so many examples include: Long Ashton Research Station, the Somerset & Dorset Railway, the Southern Railway and Great Western Railway branch lines, Cornish tin mines, Brendon Iron ore, North Somerset Coal, Mendip early strawberries, Devon violets and proper farmhouse clotted cream.

Editorial Comment: Cannington's paymasters and controllers, the *Further Education Funding Council* (FEFC) and its successor the *Learning and Skills Council* (LSC) appear to be non-elected quangos appointed and financed by Central Government. Such bodies appear to have little knowledge of or connection with local affairs, and are often based on "Regions" which cover several counties but have no economic or historical basis in this country. It is sad that local government in Great Britain, the birthplace of representative government, has come into the hands of such unrepresentative bodies.

An Encouraging Message from Stuart Brookfield

After years of turmoil, with two Principals in succession suspended and the troubles with far reaching changes in the financing of Agricultural Education, it is heartening to hear of hopeful developments now that Cannington College is part of Bridgwater College, with new management headed by Principal Fiona Macmillan, whose success at Bridgwater has been noticed in national reports. One example of the cheering news is that plans are now afoot for the building of a new glasshouse in the walled gardens. It must have seemed strange for horticultural students to study at a centre without anything to replace the large and carefully designed set of amenity glass put up less than forty years ago and demolished thirty years later.

Let us hope that the renaissance of Cannington as a regional and nationally important centre for Agriculture, Horticulture and broader based studies in environmental and countryside management will succeed, and that the "old" students association will flourish similarly.

Best wishes to all staff engaged in the present developments and to all ex-students and especially to members of the association. *(COSA Magazine 2005)*

From Stuart Brookfield, Head of the Horticultural Department at Cannington, 1952/85 and Patron of the Cannington Old Students Association.

A Pictorial Medley

In the Chemistry Lab.

Analysis of soils or feedingstuffs, no doubt

(*It's called titrating - and she's got a good reading*)

Young top fruit trees on various commercial rootstocks ?

Bath and West Show: Above: Horticultural Exhibit.   Below: Butter-making Demonstration

Straight faces all - this is a serious matter!

Above: Week-old chicks. (Being reared in a paraffin heated hover).
Below: Point-of-lay pullets reared in out-door arks - very healthy.

Cannington's last horse. But what's his name?

Well at least changing a wheel is less

trouble than shoeing an 'oss!

Editor's Note:
Right: A Standard Fordson. The fuel tank held 17 gallons of TVO which might last 8-10 hours, so for a long hard day you had to carry extra fuel! They all started on petrol, of course. (But they were not motor- cars: if you idled them on TVO for more than three minutes the plugs would oil up!).

This early model had a water-filled air cleaner, just above the (optional) pulley wheel, holding a gallon or so. The story goes that when a newly arrived and well trained Land Girl filled one with water before starting up, the farmer 'went up the wall', and rang the 'county' War Ag. to complain: he had had his Fordson for a year but had never put water in the air cleaner, and thought his prized tractor was ruined. (But that was in Warwickshire - I'm sure Somerset farmers had more sense!).

One of these tractors, a high geared Green Spot, although out of doors all the year round, would start at the fourth pull up of the starting handle (for the Editor, then aged 17) even in freezing weather. On the one occasion when it would not start (after enduring pouring rain outdoors for a week) it started immediately after the magneto had spent half an hour in a slow farm oven. Timing? The mag could only be refitted in two positions, and you marked which was the right one when you took it out! Simple, sensible engineering with mud on its boots. But the Ferguson with its sophisticated new hydraulic system superseded those old Fordsons, and with an obedient plough which could be adjusted, backed and raised with a forefinger, ploughing became less of a long acquired art, and the trailed plough disappeared. Eventually really sophisticated comfortable monsters appeared (Bottom photo, page 88).

But without those old standard Fordsons we might not have beaten the U-boats: Cannington's wartime plough-up campaign under W.D.Hay depended on them. All the same, it is rather sad that it was those lovely old basic Standard Fordsons which sounded the death knell of horse cultivation ion in Britain.

A dangerous game, this oxy-acetylene welding - and you have to concentrate to get it right.

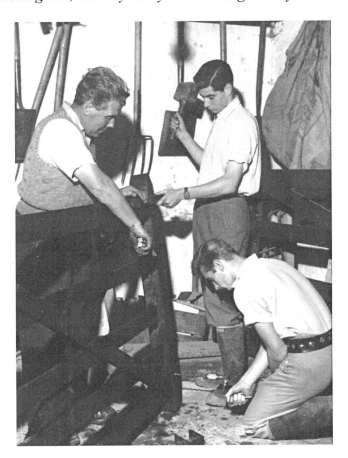

1961-62

Low-tech, this. but

watch his fingers!   That

mallet looks dangerous!

L - R: Tom Sprott, (Lecturer)
*   Michael Valdes-Scott*
*   Gerry Smart*

"That's the sump. Always keep the correct oil at the correct level."

"Careful now! Watch that post. It's not as easy as backing an 'orse."

Then there was real high tech!

Spring - spraying apple trees in blossom

*Not rockets ready for take-off!   Just Carbon Dioxide
for the tomato crop.*

From Hand milking to Parlour Milking

Hand milking in the mid 1930s

"Don't lean your head against her flank" - Miss Taylor

Bucket type machine milking in the 1930s
(Rare before 1935)

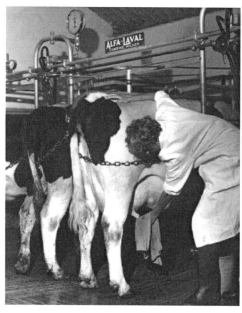

Machine milking in a one level abreast parlour - (1960s)
(Not uncommon by 1941/2)

(Then came two level, in-line and herringbone parlours, semi-automatic and automatic ones and so it goes on)

Collecting Cut Flowers can be back-breaking

Mixed perenial border -

Shrubs with Herbaceous

Plants can be labour-

saving and attractive

Then the Exam!

With Mr Cramp, once a lecturer, now External Examiner

Land Girls and their Parents outside the 'Kings Head' - 1941/42

Mr and Mrs Croaker - Retirement - 1947

Dairy students on a visit to Clare's of Wells - 1947/48

Court Farm Barn -   Mixing Cattle Rations with Pat Pile - 1949

1961/62 First Dairy Farming group with A. J. Marvel (Vice-Principal)
'A. J.' was also Lecturer 'Foods and Feeding' – "You can say ...."
Also in the photograph with one of Rodway's finest are from the left -Caroline Woolley
(nee Collins); 'A J'; Gerry Smart; Richard Collins (no relation to Caroline);
Alan Bracey; Michael Valdes-Scott; Bill Crook and Jane White (nee Loomes)

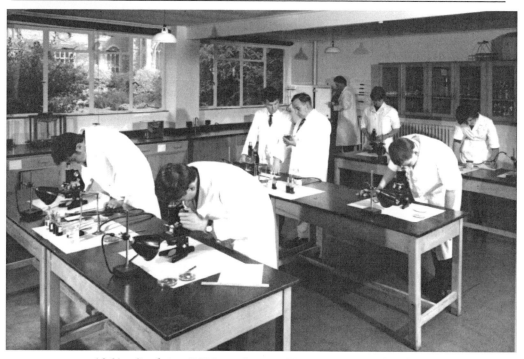

1961 - Studying DNA, perhaps. No names, I'm afraid

Miss Hobbs with her Netball Team

Richard Crane   Richard Sneyd   Stuart Jackson   Jim Pratt   Pat Sweet   Mike Dawes
Des Reeder   Pame Lowe   Sam Harcombe   John Hewson   Jill Packer
Mary Frost   Alena Kratochvil   Judy Rose

Hockey Team 1964/5?

95

This photograph, from Mr John Norton, is titled County Council Cheese school and dated "about 1880". Elizabeth Ovens, thought to be 10th from left, holding sack-trucks, married Richard Norman, who farmed at Lamyatt. Mr Norton is their g.g.son. They moved to Evercreech in 1911. (see page 1).

"Hullo John ! Getting late early these days isn't it?" *(Photo by G. Jarrett).*

AND LAST BUT NOT LEAST - STAN ACLAND

MISCELLANY

Looking Back - by W.D.Hay

On the 1st February 1922, Mr James Mackie became the Principal of the Farm Institute and County Agricultural Organiser. I also started work the same day as his assistant. Unfortunately, Mr Mackie died as the result of war wounds. He was one of the finest men that I have ever known, and his death was a great loss to the institute and country.

A Committee meeting was called and, greatly to my surprise, I found that I was the new Principal and County Agricultural Organiser. It is interesting to note that I was on my own for some months, doing all the lecturing on agriculture to students, running the farm, and doing what I could in advisory work in the county. I was busy! I found out that if you want to know a subject, teach it! Second thoughts - there was Mr JW Dallas out in the county. (JWD did not join SFI until Sept. 1924 - Ed).

I was lucky again, as within a few years we had one of the most capable and efficient staffs manning the main departments, agriculture, dairying, and horticulture. Poultry developed a little later. Somerset was a great farm-cheese-making county in those days, with thousands of acres of natural grass (very poor stuff by modern standards) and dairy shorthorns, dry from two to five months during the winter and back into cheese making in the spring. It was during the thirties that the pattern of the breed of cows began really to change. The Institute was a great reservoir of trained cheese makers, who were in great demand.The whole situation was ideal, the Institute also being the headquarters of the dairy advisory staff.

In looking back (and students can corroborate this), punctuality and hard work were number one in my view, and very few differed with me. If they did I did not hear about it.

In writing this article, I have refrained from mentioning names, but one I must mention "Stan". We all know him and remember the nice bit of temper which appeared when slipshod work was done!

All farm work was done by horses, the mower and the binder being the harvesting tools (I think it was in the early 1940s that the first combine appeared - a bagger). Every farmer grew an acreage of roots, mostly mangolds, the best yielding cows being fed on mangolds and hay and *mostly* home grown concentrates, winter beans being a standard crop on many farms. Hay-making was carried out mostly by hand in the 1920s, but machines began to appear; only two fires in the Dutch barn!

I have mentioned cows, but we also had beef, sheep and pigs. Beef cattle were very popular on some of the marshes, sheep were also very successful where the land was suitable; Down sheep on the better lowland farms and Devon Closewool etc., on the hill farms. Pigs were a most important asset, especially on the cheese-making farms where whey was plentiful.

It was quite obvious that something had to be done about the grassland, but it took a number of years to find out exactly how to improve it without spending too much money, furthermore we had to get the confidence of the farmer. As a great believer in "seeing is believing", we carried out a large number of "experiments" in conjunction with Bristol (University) before we finally decided what to do. We had laid down a large number of trials of fertilisers and seeds mixtures etc.

The three-year ley system of farming was very popular in the West Country - three years ley, then cereals, roots and cereals. After the second year with the ley, there was very little keep, and when ploughed up and oats sown, the result was a very poor crop. The reason for this was that the clover had died out during the second year - it was supposed to be Wild White, but unfortunately it was Dutch White - after writing to some 15 leading seedsmen in England and Scotland for 1lb of Wild White seed, these were sown at Cannington and we found that only two samples were true to type (one from England and one from Scotland). From then on, all the seeds mixtures for our trials came from that one source, with tremendous results. The succeeding oat crop was so lush on some farms that it went down. This was the turning point in our seeds mixtures for three-year leys. We even used up to 40 units of nitrogen on some of our plots! Weren't we devils!

Quoting from an Advisory Report for 1935: "Since 1924 official Manurial Trials have been made on 125 farms (178 fields), etc. When we started these trials (including grass seeds), we had to take a lot of knocks, claiming that they were 'a waste of money', etc. We had many critics, but ultimately these critics were our greatest supporters.

One big demonstration was attended by the Minister of Agriculture, Lord Cranworth, and his Land Fertility Committee, plus Somerset MPs, the County Agricultural Committee and most of the notable people in Somerset Agriculture. To ram the lesson home, Mr Hayes of Nurcott Farm came to the microphone and said: "As one of the bitterest critics of this work he wanted to admit his error and to say how much he had benefited by adopting this new type of farming on his land". (This was a lot for an Exmoor farmer to say).

Somerset was one of the most prominent counties in England and Wales in regard to the Young Farmers' Club movement. An Organiser was appointed at an early date, with Headquarters at Cannington. This was very useful, as the agricultural and dairying staff could help the Young Farmers' Organiser. A County Federation of Young Farmers' Clubs was formed in 1934, one of the first, if not *the* first, in England, with a total of nearly 20 members.

Many special functions were carried out during the 1939/45 war, but I will only mention the Women's Land Army. The Institute took a big part in training the WLA, and a very large number passed through our hands.

The horticultural department developed during this period, working in collaboration with the Long Ashton Research Station. Funds were not available to go all out as the horticultural superintendent would have wished.

During my 20 odd years in Somerset, there were many changes in the farming pattern. For example, one man milking a dozen cows per day. Instead of ploughing 1/2 to 2/3 of an acre per day, 10 acres was not uncommon, machines taking the place of men, and still it goes on. No, I think I lived in the right age, or was the right age at the right time for me? (*From "Fifty Glorious Years - 1971*)

PRINCIPALS OF THE PAST 50 YEARS

Left to right: W. J. England, W. D. Hay, P. H. Keen, A. J. Marval, W. W. Ballardie.

From "Fifty Glorious Years" - the 1971 COSA Magazine Fiftieth Anniversary Edition

----

99

The Milk Marketing Board

This organisation was formed in 1933 to counter the ruinous conditions faced by dairy farmers in the great depression of 1929-1932.

In essence, because of the perishability of milk and the small size of dairy herds, the individual dairy farmer had little bargaining power to secure the price needed to remain in business; the exceptions were those producers whose milk supplies were close to towns and cities.

The serious state of the farming industry was recognised by Government and the Agricultural Marketing Acts of 1931 and 1933 were passed to encourage organised marketing of basic foods. In the case of milk, a comprehensive scheme was drawn up, endorsed by a ballot of milk producers and it became the Milk Marketing Board.

The Board's fundamental principles are extremely important and are as follows:

1. Co-operative organisation of milk producers, and three members appointed by the Minister of Agriculture

2. Monopoly statutory power as first hand buyer of all milk supplies. It should be remembered that by the same token, the MMB has a statutory duty to buy all milk supplies offered; this may involve uneconomic measures at times of peak supply.

3. All revenues from milk selling are pooled. In the main these monies are received from buyers by the tenth day following the month of production and are paid out promptly as "pool price" subject to compositional quality (viz: butter-far and solids-not-fat) and seasonal and regional variations.

Furthermore, under paragraph 59, of the Milk Marketing Scheme 1933, far-reaching "Miscellaneous Powers" were allowed and these have been of great value in developing the commercial strength of the producers' organisation.

Following the Agricultural Act of 1947, British agriculture depended on the fairly simple policies of guaranteed prices and deficiency payments for the next thirty years. Since 1st January 1978 the Common Agricultural Policy of the European Economic Community has been in operation with its many complexities; as this period has coincided with severe cost inflation and reduced profit, many dairy farmers find themselves confused.

Fortunately the MMB has proved to be a resourceful organisation and is busily adapting itself to these challenges.

Since the formation of the MMB in 1933, creamery capacity has been built up steadily and with the purchase of the 16 Unigate Creameries in 1979, the Board now operates 32 creameries throughout the western half of England and Wales, this business now operating under "Dairy Crest" is manufacturing no less than 40% of the butter and skimmed milk powder made annually.

One of the most impressive results of MMB operations is the daily collection of ex-farm milk and its delivery to dairies and creameries. This is an area where rationalisation to ensure least cost is very effective; so much so that the MMB now owns and operates 55% of the tanker fleet involved.

Milk recording became almost defunct during the Second World War, but was rescued by the MMB in 1943 to become national Milk Records; the Bureau of records followed soon afterwards and this laid the foundation for Breed Societies, AI organisations and dairy farmers generally, to begin using milk records for both breeding and management purposes; today no less than 40% of out dairy cattle are officially milk recorded.

Undoubtedly there will be problems arising from the severe recession, CAP measures to restrict milk production, the importation of liquid milk from other EEC member states and the serious decline in the UK butter market.

But without the MMB there will be little hope of securing a proper return for the dairy farmer's investment and constant effort.

Part of Article by Denley Brown, (Guest Contributor), COSA Magazine, No.5. 1982.

Young Farmers' Clubs in Wartime - by Miss Maddever

When I came as a member of staff to Cannington in March 1932 (three years after I had been a Dairying Student at the Institute) I was given the job of Dairying Instructress in the Elementary Schools Dairying Scheme. Three of us lived at week-ends in the splendid cottage behind the Principal's house (alas! the cottage has been pulled down). There was at that time a young man on the staff called Tony Trew who was said to be the County Secretary of Y.F.C.s - at that stage I had no idea what he really did! - he had an occasional visitor from Y.F.C./H.Q. in London called Marcus Drew, the latter was an assistant of the late Major Hiles. (I believe there were three staff at H.Q. to deal with the *whole* country!)

After two years "on schools" Miss Taylor sent me into the Dairy Department to be Miss Monie's Assistant and so one was often asked to talk to Y.F.C.s. You see, Mr W.D.Hay as Principal of the Farm Institute was also County Organiser for Agriculture and in the latter capacity he ran the Y.F. Clubs and Tony Trew was a member of his staff. All staff were expected - of whatever department - to help with Y.F.C. programmes and lectures.

Tony Trew was soon succeeded as County Secretary by Jim Congdon (1928) - a gay energetic Cornishman - indeed he was the only member of the staff who was allowed "to tease" Miss Monie!

When the Second World War broke out in 1939 Jim Congdon being a member of Somerset Light Infantry left immediately to join his Regiment. For some two years Mr Hay had much pressing business dealing with the despatch of all the current batch of students, so that the first 70 Land Army Girls (W.L.A.) could come for training. Then there was the "Policy of the Plough" to get over throughout the county, where most forms of arable farming were unfamiliar, for most farms were grassland dairying farms so this was a marathon task. Annual General Meetings of the Y.F.C.s were suspended for two years but in 1941 a meeting was called, there was no Secretary and I well remember Mr. Hay looking across the room and saying to me "You could be County Secretary - you *will* be County Secretary!". There was no question of arguing with authority in those days. I was by this time Miss Taylor's Senior Assistant on County Dairying (cheesemaking and milk production) and she said "By all means take on the Y.F.C.s so long as it doesn't interfere with your normal work!!" One has to remember there was strict petrol rationing and driving with blacked-out head lamps was really dangerous and many of our clubs covered large scattered rural areas.

What were my first impressions? Well it was that one must get to the clubs somehow, so farm visiting was arranged in the areas where the Clubs monthly meeting was due. As there were 23 Clubs it was possible to attend practically every monthly meeting. D.M.Phillips who was also on the County Dairying Staff helped me very much. (She arrived on the staff the day all the signposts were removed - a good job she was a first class map reader!

Most of the Clubs reared 'Calves' and this exercise seemed to be much more important than a well balanced programme! When the calves came to be sold after the show, some enthusiastic Dads bid a big price for a rather overfat calf - yet many boys and girls learnt a lot and were so proud to lead their animals at the Annual Show. Some Clubs had dances *very* frequently and very little else of consequence!. The again what did these 'membership' numbers mean? For some enthusiastic Dads had entered their children almost as soon as they were born, so the numbers "on the books" bore no relation to the numbers who came to the meetings! All was somewhat confused because with petrol rationing those who lived several miles from the Club meeting place couldn't come anyway - so after a few months a few Clubs met at various farm houses.

A "Y.F.C. History" of 1942-43 which I found in my office not long ago recorded wartime competitions of Silage Making (a fairly new thing!), Collections of Grasses, Vegetable Growing (brussels sprouts, tomatoes and onions) also mole-catching.

The Clubs were magnificent during the war, they worked so hard (especially for the Red Cross) and we started Carol Singing. Something else which had a premiere was a Public Speaking Competition because in those days many members were not prepared to make any comments at meetings (times have changed, haven't they?!). I always remember the late Hon. Lady Langman (who was President of the Wincanton Y.F.C.) saying "It's all very fine getting these young people to talk - your problem may be stopping them!".

Part of the article by Miss K.D. Maddever in COSA Magazine No.7 (1984).

Miscellany

Miss Honor Henslow (1935/36) returns to Cannington in 1985.

How worth while to have made the occasion. Not just to relive old memories but also to discover with astonishment the new and forward looking college well established on fields where cows once grazed; surprisingly I felt as much a part of it all as in the older areas. The building attractively surrounded by trees and gardens seemed just as much a part of the village of Cannington as the old one always will be. I had returned there during the wartime to work in the gardens, but that made a different chapter from my student days. The two periods remain quite distinct in my memory: both were happy and full of good friendship.

It was bound to be with a feeling of nostalgia that I wandered slowly round the deserted gardens after my arrival, on a warm evening. Remembrances crowded in of the old times, old ways of cropping and working, and the faces of one's past companions rose to mind and faded into the air. There were two girls with me that year, and about twelve boys. Sadly I believe some of those lads did not return from the war but that was our future yet to be. We were a hardworking group, very obedient under our energetic and good tempered instructor Mr Engledow, who kept an eagle eye on the manual labours of sixteen year olds, and no malingering! It was a very healthy discipline for the working years ahead.

Such a pleasure to see once again the solid old rose stone House and the fine garden walls, sadly no longer covered with trained fruit trees. A sign of these days - no longer economic to grow and tend. Well, they are certainly a test of stamina, pruning and tying in on bitterly cold days. One or two old shrubs still lived in their same corner. Amazing! There stood the old potting shed! Well I never! Still the old prop house just about to go I suspect, and the "new" fruit store, grown old. That dated me! I missed the fine old Well Head once covered in ceanothus, it always felt like a piece of history. Once a vast compost heap filled a corner of the same garden, warm and squelchy to our chilled booted feet on cold early dawns when detailed to turn it over; the smell none too pleasant in its steamiest stages of kitchen and garden waste decomposition!

Finding the new bee garden was a delightful surprise. Our Bee instruction took place on hot summer evenings between the fruit store and the prop house. The instructor, Mr. Withycombe, a tiny man like a bee himself, and very deaf, travelled the country on a bicycle with a little box behind his seat in which he carried the latest swarm! (what faith in its security!) Inviting us to hive the swarm with bare hands as he did - there were no takers! No one wore protective clothing, so we were happy to leave it to him! He could tell when the supper bell rang by the instant look of profound relief on the young faces round him. I wonder if the same acceptance and self control would be the same today!

Great changes in numbers 1 and 2 gardens, I remember it with espalier apples by the path so smothered in blossom the air was heavily scented for weeks. The garden now reconstructed behind the house where Mr Turner and then Mr England lived has been developed most attractively.

The extensive changes in the central gardens are very impressive, with the vast amount of modern plant work for amenity horticulture, which has totally changed the type of training students take, compared with the one year course in basic commercial food and flower growing, mostly as open crops. No present day student can lack the qualifications for many interesting openings after being trained in such a mini-Kew, set over the land we dug and double-dug, sowed and hoed and spread compost over manually. At least we developed muscle!

I appreciated Miss Heywoods kind thought in giving me a room overlooking the front of the old building; at the side, the dairy which to my ears still echoed to the clatter and bustle of Miss Monie's day. Though silent now, the nimble girls in fresh applegreen dresses covered in sparkling white aprons and caps will I think always gently haunt the area.

A peep into the old building to see the round hall, our one-time lecture room, and where we danced on Saturday evenings and sang on Sunday evenings, organised by a dedicated Matron whose name sadly escapes me; and then down the steps to the changing rooms. I could not believe my eyes that our old locker room was still there unaltered, as though it was yesterday we'd left it; except for the spiders' webs spun where we tossed our boots off, hungry for our lovely home-cooked meals, real farmhouse fare then! . . . . for me it was wonderful to see Miss Maddever at the gathering, for she links me back to the days I recall, bright at the top table in her Reading blazer, not so long arrived there herself, I recall.

So the dignified old house and fine tower remain at the college core, dreaming a little of its yesterdays and of all those who have gone with time, but also stating a sense of sturdy continuity into the new days and new ways of modern life and its demands for a high standard of learning and practice. Nothing can alter the serene old building presiding at the heart of Somerset.. A College and its life, one hopes, for as long as ever! So that the students there now, will will have as happy a recall in the next century as I did in 1985.*From Miss Honor Henslow (COSA Magazine No.9 1986). (See photograph on page 33) - Sadly Miss Henslow died in 1992 - COSA Magazine 1998*

The Gale and the Bulldozer

The Gale of March 1987

One wonders if the bulldozer damage was worse than the gale damage!

All Cannington must have been in a cheerful mood on Thursday 26 March, having just beaten Hampshire (Sparsholt) in the third round of the Norsk Hydro Farming and General Knowledge Quiz.

Mr Keen tells the story: "The Hampshire minibuses disappeared into the darkness for their long journey home. The night was dark, the wind was getting up and driving rain beat against the windows. At about 9.30 the electricity failed and with no lights we groped our way to be to contemplate the success of the evening and the storm outside.

Most of the facade was blown down

By morning the gale was at full blast. Gusts of wind made the trees bend over and the suspended ceilings in the new buildings heave and creak. Tony Davey, in his caretaking duties sensed danger and warned the students in Collingridge Room to move out to the safety of the Jarrett Room. Suddenly there was an exceptional gust. Day release students in Amory Block could not believe their eyes as they saw virtually the whole of the facade to the right of the portcullis of the main frontage of Cannington Court collapse with a 'crump' onto the roof behind. The noise of the wind reduced the sound almost to imperceptibility and it was not until later that it was realised that a tall chimney on Court House had crashed onto the adjoining roof.

Gradually the impact of the event began to dawn. All the upstairs rooms had to be evacuated. In the downstairs rooms the dust had accumulated and cracks appeared. "The whole area must be cleared" was the verdict of the architect when he arrived on the scene. The YFC office and downstairs bedrooms were included and then out came the ropes to cordon off the area and the bollards to indicate 'no-go to traffic'. And what about the services? Water pipes, electricity, the fire alarm system? Within hours a photographer had appeared for the architect, the press were on the phone and before the weekend was over scaffolding and tarpaulins were in place.

Incredibly no-one was hurt and viewing the scene later it seemed incredible that in the temperate climate of tranquil rural Somerset such havoc could have been caused in so short a time by a gust of wind". *(P.H.Keen - The Principal, April 1987 - COSA Magazine No.10, 1987)*

Miscellany

The Bulldozer

For those students who can remember the erection of the original building of the original dairy complex at Rodway, which became known as Rodway 1, we have to announce the passing of an era. Over the last few years the college has had a problem of too much dirty water being produced on the Rodway site, about 30% of that dirty water originated from the Rodway 1 buildings, buildings which for some time had been earmarked for demolition and redevelopement. And so it was last autumn (1997) that we bit the bullet and drove a bulldozer through the lot! In its place we have erected one barn 126 feet wide, 265 feet long, and 18 feet to the eaves. It covers an area of 33,390 square feet (0.75 acres), and at present houses bulling heifers, dry cows, the ewe flock (due to lamb in April) and the pedigree Aberdeen Angus cows and calves. Eventually when funds allow it will also have a calf unit and workshop (thus allowing the farm to vacate the buildings on the Downs). *(Steve Bryant, COSA Magazine 1998)*

The Old Court Farm Buildings

 Demolition

The Replacement going up

For many of you as former Dairy and Agricultural students, the demolition of the barn and surrounding buildings at Court Farm will mean the final disappearance of "The Farm" as you knew it, particularly if you were students of the Farm Institute era. However, change takes place and the area is now primarily being utilised for the erection of a Food Hall for the Food Technology Department. The farm has not been provided with a replacement covered storage area but, as the activities and acreage of the farm had retracted recently, it may not be necesary, particularly if a smaller farm is envisaged.

Alan Brownsey , COSA Magazine 1985

Above: Cannington - 1947: © - Crown Copyright.   Below: the Campus 19??

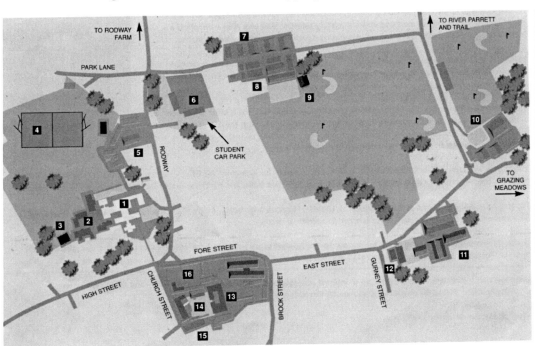

KEY

Car Parks

Administration Centre

Residential

Glasshouses

Teaching Buildings

1 Main Administration Centre:
  Reception, Offices, Refectory,
  Laboratories, Library,
  Classrooms
2 Residential Accommodation
3 Sports Hall
4 Sports Field
5 Food Processing Hall
6 Animal Care Centre
7 Forge

8 Mechanisation Centre:
  Workshops, Classrooms,
  Offices
9 Golf Club House
10 Equestrian Centre: Indoor
  and Outdoor Arenas,
  Paddocks, Stables
11 Crockers: Agriculture,
  Equestrian and Countryside
  Management. Offices,
  Classrooms, Glasshouses,
  Workshops

12 Arboriculture Workshops,
  Teaching Facilities
13 Cannington Court: Offices,
  Classrooms, Residential
  Accommodation, Clifford Hall
14 Court Dairy: Floristry Centre,
  Offices
15 Priory Barn: Classrooms
16 Heritage Gardens

Miscellany

Editor's Explanation, Excuse and Apology.

"How did an outsider get involved with our Chronicle?" I can hear all COSA members saying it!

My excuse is that I was born into a Somerset farming family so I am not an outsider, and in any case it's not from choice that I missed Cannington! My boyhood ambition was to "go to Cannington" and only brucellosis and Hitler stopped me. In 1937, when I was fourteen, fate stepped in. By September only one of our autumn calving cows remained in-calf. All the rest had aborted and then refused to hold to the bull, and remained barren! Either we had bought in brucellosis or it was on the new farm we had moved into on Lady Day. With no prospect of winter milk Father had to give up farming. Later my parents opened a private school at Gillingham, Dorset, but meantime Cannington was out - and in any case was training Land Girls when I left school just as the war started in 1939.

I already had a lot of "practical". When I was five I sometimes helped to drive our 60 cows in for milking and I helped to polish the brass of our governess car and its pony's harness. I caught, harnessed and handled bigger horses from the age of ten, hand-milked from eleven and milked regularly from thirteen. But I needed theory. I read *Watson & More* studiously, I scanned the *Farmer & Stockbreeder* avidly every week, and read all I could of W.D.Hay, H.I.Moore and Prof Stapleton. But I knew it was not enough. Then in 1942 I joined the RAF. When the jocular corporal who marched recruits up and down Scarborough sea front wanted to raise a laugh, he would loudly proclaim that he had never heard of a flying farmer before, and he was sure one was enough! (I was the first to solo in a Tiger Moth, but that's another story!). After the war Cannington provided only short courses and there was a waiting list for Reading - and other English colleges. Scottish Colleges gave immediate priority to ex-Servicemen, so my brother Don and I were admitted at once to Edinburgh for NDA - with NDD at Auchincruive.

After briefly enduring being bored lecturing at Shuttleworth and managing a 200 acre Cambs. farm, I managed an 850 acre Somerset mixed farm for ten years, and still have a letter of thanks from J.W. Dallas for hosting the 1956 & 1957 NIAB Wheat Trials and a NAAS Farm Walk at Hardington (opposite). But anthrax and swine fever in 1963, following F&M in 1958, forced me out of farming. To survive I went into secondary and special education (in London!) and as a hobby acquired a history degree. Thirty years on, even with new hips and a new knee, I had to give up sailing my cherished 25 foot 1900 vintage yawl, *Hesiod,* which I had rebuilt, and as a less strenuous hobby wrote books on farming and farming history. One of these mentioned Harold Hebditch of Stoke-under-Ham, from whom, early in the war, I had learned a lot about arable and sheep farming as "assistant living in as family", as it was then called. At that time your indefatigable Magazine Editor Nan Eaves, then aged about thirteen, was one of the six engaging Hebditch girls. I sent her a copy to find out if the family minded being mentioned, and the outcome was that I was asked to help with the Chronicle, so at last I am at Cannington, if only on paper.

I hope there are no mistakes, but some are possible because of my lack of grass-roots knowledge. But no mistakes will be quite as glaring as those in a 1971 "Farms and Farming" book which labelled a Standard Fordson as a "Fordson Major"! And described the ancient miserichord illustrated below as depicting cowmen having trouble milking a cow. Wrong again! As I am sure you know, it is a warning to neighbours not to quarrel: two farmers are contesting ownership of a cow while a lawyer milks the profits (see his wig?). It was such examples of silly publisher's mistakes plus the principle "Beware the middleman" which persuaded me to be my own (hobby) publisher. And in any case "Hands on" is the sure way to get a job done as you want it done. So if there *are* any mistakes they are mine and I apologise for them now, as well as for the unavoidable poor quality of some of the old photographs. GAJL

MINISTRY OF AGRICULTURE
FISHERIES AND FOOD

SOMERSET AGRICULTURAL
EXECUTIVE COMMITTEE

Any reply should be addressed to the

COUNTY AGRICULTURAL OFFICER

quoting 825

Your Reference ....

Telephone : TAUNTON 3694, 4491

WHEATLEIGH HOUSE
TRULL ROAD
TAUNTON
SOMERSET

12th July, 1957.

Dear Mr. Loxton,

Farm Walks and Demonstrations

I write to thank the Radstock Co-operative Society and you on behalf of the Executive Committee for so kindly allowing the Farm Walk to take place last evening.

My Committee greatly appreciates this form of co-operation and it is particularly pleasing to the Committee to work in conjunction with you in this way, and to be able to show such good and unusual farming for the district.

The attendance, despite the weather, was an indication of the interest in your successful activities, and I hope that the Society and you feel rewarded for all the thought and work which has been devoted to this rather large enterprise in recent years.

With the Committee's thanks.

Yours sincerely,

(J. W. Dallas)
County Agricultural Officer

G. A. J. Loxton, Esq.,
Hardington Farm,
FROME.

"Unusual" Farming for the district: I grew more arable crops than most farms in that heavy land area: 850 acres with 200 wheat, 20 potatoes, 50 barley, 70 late-sown strip-fed kale, 50 strip-fed IRG, 20 (steep) permanent grass, remainder 3 year strip-fed ley. 100 acres self-fed silage, 100 hay, 450 cattle (180 cows), 50 sows for baconers, 50 plus poultry. Mr. Dallas told me that 70 odd farmers attended - I was too busy to count.

COSA MAGAZINE 1985: Mr. Dallas came to the Farm Institute on 1st September 1924 when he was met at the station by Mr. Hay (who had recently returned from his honeymoon!) Mr. Dallas was ASSISTANtT AGRICULTURAL ORGANISER and lived in the Institute until he himself was married on 24th December 1924. In the Spring of 1930 he left Somerset to become County Agricultural and Horticultural Organiser for Bedfordshire: he was also W.A.E.C. EXECUTIVE OFFICER there dutring the War. At the inception of the N.A.A.S. In 1946, Mr. Dallas became County Agricultral officer for Bedfordshire, returning to Somerset in the same capacityin 1950 where he worked until retiring in 1960. We extend our congratulations and Best Wishes to Mr. and Mrs. Dallas who now live at Mill Cross Cottage, Kingston St.Mary, Taunton. NB. Mr. Dallas died in 1991 at the age of 95.

A Small Village in a Small World.
(An Editorial Meander)

"It never occurred to me when I left school at 15 to start work at Church Farm, Queen Charlton, that I would end up working for the future King of England. Now there's name dropping for you!"
(Terry Summers in the 1994 COSA Magazine).

This introduction to an item from Terry Summers in the 1994 COSA Magazing attracted my eye. Back in the 1920s it was from Church Farm that the Hembers used to bring their hire steam traction engine to thresh our wheat, oats and beans at Charlton Farm in that same village. One of the Hember boys was Bob, who later was on the sales staff of Hext Bros, and the other, the youngest, was Jim, who was an RN Petty Officer during the war and sadly did not survive. Another farmer's son from that tiny village did not survive - William Ford, shot down over Germany in 1943.

Queen Charlton, where I was born, is small: so small that in my boyhood days it rarely appeared on maps of the area, much to my annoyance. It is somewhat larger now, with several new houses as well as numerous conversions of barns, stables and cow-houses, and it is now marked on most road maps. It has been thoroughly gentrified - our shepherd's cottage is now occupied by a famous writer and our farmhouse is now called Charlton House. There is only one farm left - instead of five - Kenneth Baber's Manor Farm. The remainder of the land is farmed from outside the parish.

But why my particular interest? Because Cannington has another link with Queen Charlton, indeed with Church Farm. Graham Dawes (Ag.1948/49) lives there! His house is built in the old Church Farm orchard and when he first arrived at Queen Charlton to learn farming, Graham used to live in the house in which I was born - and left in the 1930s! Sadly it is not a farmhouse any more, there is no land attached to it, and as I said, it is now called Charlton House.

The first time I met Graham, while researching the history of the village, and before I knew he had been to Cannington, he regaled me with hilarious stories - in the vernacular - of events involving village people I had known. One of them, about Tom Pike, who was of an old village working family, who had become a roadman, tells Tom's detailed account, in his own words, of the occasion when Tom was stung by a wasp which flew up his trouser leg as he cycled home one summer evening, and how he coped with the situation. Graham's rendition ought to be recorded, but I have heard since that he was well known for such stories even when he was at Cannington.

Michael Comer (49/50 GA) in a letter in the 1984 COSA Magazine writes: "I recently discovered whilst reading the Western Daily Press that Graham Dawes (49/50A) only lives a few miles from here. His daughter Penny hit the headlines in the Young Farmers Movement. Graham and one of his two sons assist Graham Spencer (50/51A) on his farm. His other son is an agricultural engineer. Graham Dawes told me that he was a Special Constable for 30 years and often went on duty with Mary Smith (49/50D) who served 25 years as a professional Police Officer in the Somerset and Avon Force".

Graham:Verger Sacristan   Not only was Graham Dawes a Special Constable for many years, and thus a well known figure beyond the parish boundary in that sphere, but he was also for many years Churchwarden of St Mary's at Queen Charlton and latterly Verger Sacristan, and leading bell-ringer (and Tower Correspondent), so he is also very well known throughout the Bath and Wells Diocese.

Second reason for my interest: Terry Summers describes his work with the Duchy of Cornwall, Gatcombe, etc., and it must seem unusual that a career so close to the Royal Family should start from such a tiny village. Except that Terry was not alone! Brian, the editor's brother, born at Queen Charlton, was for many years Consultant to H.M. the Queen for the Royal Farms at Windsor, as Ralph Whitlock records in his 1980 book "Royal Farmers" (Page 125). A small world indeed.

How did <u>YOU</u> get to Cannington?

<u>Margaret Francis (Gilson - "Gillie") 1922. Dairy</u>

'Old Students' - well I certainly was one of those - in January 1922 I and my trunk travelled to Bridgwater Station and then on to Cannington. I've wondered how many of the originals were still around. Sixty years is a long time. Then I received the 1982 Magazine. Yes, there was Molly (Miss Mackie) and Bunchy (Mrs Pittard) and a letter from Tom Parsons.

In the year prior to my arrival at Cannington, in April 1921, I attended the cheese school at East Pennard. Miss Willis in charge, and there I heard all about the forthcoming opening of the Farm Institute. Miss Saker came one day and I was very interested and expressed a wish that I too could go.

But being the eldest of five children there were problems. As long as I could remember my mother had always made cheese during the summer months, in fact with very few exceptions so did all the neighbouring farmers' wives as well, and helped milk the cows. This job of milking fell to my lot at eight years old. Anyhow, to cut a long story short, as we say in 'Zummerzet', obstacles were overcome and I was pleased to join the students at Cannington.

As far as I can remember the course was in the form of a four week rota: 1). Dairy cheesemaking; 2). Buttermaking 3). Platform duty, including making various soft cheese, receiving the incoming milk daily, and testing the same; and 4). Poultry feeding and killing - I killed my first and last cockerel and when I got home I showed my father the right way, which he then always followed.

I wonder if the bell that Mr Crocker rang at 7 a.m. and meal times is still in the 'Quad'. After a hurried 'cup' in the dining room we hastened to our appointed places. Cheesemaking was always my favourite week. I shudder to think what Miss Saker would say, when I see on TV the electric curd cutters, and always say - to myself - what about the fat content going out with the whey. Most of the work duties, I remember, were done before lunch - afternoon lectures - Wednesday's recreation - for many years my leg suffered from "Bully-off" hockey, and there was badminton, or was it Battledore and Shuttlecock, in the Quad? Friday evening was a social evening. Once a concert and entertainment was put on and the village people invited. Matron was Irish, so in her honour the theme was St. Patrick's Day and prizes given.

Of Miss Saker, my lasting memory was of her kindness, especially one day when I received a letter from home, an outbreak of Johne's Disease - they call it another name today. Any way I was very upset and she persuaded me to go off duty for a couple of hours.

A tuck box from home usually ended in a midnight feast: 'lights out' at 10 p.m. was strictly adhered to. I returned to take N.C.D. Summer Term 1922 and my most vivid memory of this was churning butter at 5 a.m., or was it 4.30 a.m.? Weather so hot - no ice or freezers then. It is all so different now.

<u>Mollie Mackie</u> (also 1922).

Miss Saker was in charge when we started. Some of us were there all the time but some only came for a week or a few days and we all had to do a bit of gardening and farm work. We were a very mixed bag but we had great fun; some were quite good but a lot of them hadn't a clue, it was really rather primitive. I was only sent there because my father was Chairman of the Committee, but I would very much have liked to have done the whole course and gone on to Reading. Unfortunately I had to remain at home as I had a very weak heart. *(1981 COSA magazine).*

1922 - *Cheese Dairy with*

Molly, Gillie & Kitty.

(from the 1983 COSA Magazine)

Miscellany

Mrs F.G.Chamberlain (formerly Crane) 1927/8D.

My introduction to Cannington College came soon after leaving school and was a result of a visit arranged by the N.F.U. at which my father was a participant. My mother, thinking the visit would benefit me more than her suggested that I should take her place. How was I to bless her for so doing! Suffice it to say that I was hooked and, when we returned home, implored my parents to allow me to apply for entry. My father was not so enthusiastic. "Was there not plenty of opportunity for practical farming at home?" So there was, and no brother to benefit from it. But an unexpected ally apppeared. Captain Douglas Wills, who I believe was a member of the governing body at Cannington, came with a party to shoot over our land. When he heard of my interest he persuaded my father to let me apply.

Mrs Chamberlain (right) and Walter (Head Boy)

with Miss Monie 1927

I came in 1927, returning the following year to take the B.D.F.A. examination. Among my contemporaries were Kate Maddever and Lady Rosemary Baring.. Miss Monie was head of dairy. Our good friend Mr Croaker was at hand to extricate us from all manner of scrapes. (COSA Magazine 1994).

Ivor Crane 1944/45

When I left grammar school in Taunton in 1944 I was given information about scholarships to be awarded to the sons and daughters of small holders and agricultural workers for a year's course at the Somerset Farm Institute at Cannington. As my father was a tenant of one of the County Council holdings I decided to apply.

In due course I was asked to attend an interview at the College. I set off on my bicycle to ride the eleven miles there, not being quite sure of the way. En route I met another lad on a bicycle who was also a bit lost and it turned out that he was also making his way to the interview. He was Peter Hayman who at that time lived at Kingston St Mary. We were both accepted at the end of September. I arrived to begin a year's course in Agriculture.

The Institute had been closed during the war for the training of Land Army girls, but although the war had not quite ended it was opening up again. There were about fifty students, about half of whom were boys who were doing Agriculture with the exception of two who did Horticulture. Nearly all the girls were doing Dairying. Today's students would consider it a bit tough with everyone having to be in by 8.30pm and all the pubs out of bounds. However we soon became one happy family with the normal student romances. (COSA Magazines 1988, 1995)

(The photograph shows Ivor at his last milking before retiring).

(COSA Magazine - 1988)

How Dr Winifred Hector became a student.

Winifred Hector's ambition, on leaving Bishop Fox's in Taunton for London University in the twenties, was to become a professor of Anglo-Saxon. But after a year of study at Bedford College for her B.A., a Harley Street specialist said she must stop reading, because of her short sight, which meant abandoning her course.

"I retreated to Somerset, baffled and depressed, I knew of nothing else to do except gain another scholarship: this time it was to the Somerset Farm Institute at Cannington, where I was to study poultry husbandry"

In her eighties Dr Hector has written and published her lively autobiography: *Winifred Hector:Memoirs of a Somerset Woman.* In it she writes that the year's course had its rewards. "There were boys in abundance, and this was the first time I had met them at close quarters.".

However, soon after she left Cannington she discovered the disadvantages of agricultural life. She decided to become a nurse instead and left Somerset for good, to train at St. Bartholomew's Hospital, London. Her book, besides decribing life at Cannington, is a robust acccount of her life as a nurse, university lecturer and naturalist.

It is illustrated with photographs, including one of her and the poet John Betjeman. As well as writing nursing textbooks which became best-sellers, she appeared in television programmes, including one with Betjeman on the history of Barts. Hospital. (*Laurence Dopson: COSA Magazine, 1998*)

John Symes 44/45

My first contact with Cannington was in July 1944 when I first appeared before a selection committee. The meeting was held in the 'new' building, on the right as you enter the car park, approaching the old buildings, which in those days comprised the whole of Cannington' I was 16½ years old, and there was some doubt as to what I'd do, as the results of the School Certificate Exams had not come through. I believe that going straight from school to Institute/College isn't possible now.

You may wonder at the reliability of recall, after half a century, but I have good reason to remember it well. Amongst the members of the selection committee, only W.D.Hay was known to me, from his talks to Young Farmers' Clubs. I'm not sure how much extra-mural work is now done by the present College teaching staff. During the war years, and for some time after, Mr Hay, Miss Maddever, Bob Bell, Ted Lovell and so on, were kept busy 'educating' young and not so young farmers, at evening meetings, usually in the winter. It is probably not appreciated by anyone under 40, just how these stalwarts spread the word.

In a matter of 4 or 5 years after 1945, tremendous changes took place in farming. Weed killing sprays, of which MCPA was the first to be widely used, put paid to charlock and a host of other weeds. The sulpha drugs virtually ousted the quack elixirs common in every cowshed. And penicillin intra-mammary injections did away with the cussing and cajoling needed to get a drench down a cow.

Anyway, back to the interview. I said that I remembered it well. Indeed the name of one of the inquisitors is permanently burnt into my brain, as with a red-hot iron. Mrs Miller-Barstow felt, "dontcha know, that this applicant was too young and inexperienced to gain much benefit from the course". Depth of despair.

Now 'Bonny' Hay did have a reputation for whispering sweet nothings in young ladies ears. Just what he said to Mrs M-B I don't know, but the outcome was that not only was I accepted, I got a scholarship, to boot. This was to be the first course when the Institute got back to normal after years of W.L.A. training.

So to W.D. 'Tripod' Hay goes the credit for my student days. I always felt he had such very good judgment. I realised later that also on the jury was Jack England, who was Principal by the time we started in September. I never did learn if he was equally enthusiastic.

Looking back I am horrified at my naivety at the first experience of a co-ed existence but for someone with my shyness it was a real culture shock. Fortunately G.G., bless her, helped me to overcome some of the worst of the traumas. And a few weeks in the company of Cherry, Jill and Liz on the farm worked wonders.

Benny Goodman 49/50

I often reflect how fortunate I was to have been introduced to the delights of Cannington purely by a chance meeting with W.D.Hay in, of all places, Aberdeen. I was outside the North of Scotland College of Agriculture on demob leave in 1949, walking down Union Street. I had passed by a large granite block with carved numerals painted gold on it. "40½ Union St." they declared, and as a Somerset man it was the first time I had seen a "½" in an address.

Thereafter I was royally entertained. Fishing on the confluence of the Dee and the Don rivers and receiving a letter of introduction to W.J.England, then the Cannington Principal. I also took home a 6.lb sea trout (with instructions on how to cook it!), via the Flying Scotsman express and the 9.15pm West of England train back to Taunton.

That was a real experience and of course I eventually arrived at the pearly gates of the then Institute - into a thoroughly friendly and caring world of great interest and with a community spirit, which I feel sure continues unabated to this day. I have lectured to all, bar four, County Agri/Horti Colleges or Institutes in the UK during my career (Including Eire and Ulster), and nowhere did I encounter other than respect and praise for Cannington and all it stands for - *COSA Magazine 1995*. [Benny went on to take a BSc. (Hort.) at Reading and became U.K.Technical Manager for May & Baker - Ed.].

Messrs Thorne, Rowe, Lovell and Goodman in serious mode.
(1953 magazine)

David Gwilliam 49/50

To gain entry to SFI one required to have gained a 'General Certificate' at school - far too high a target for me! Fortunately my well known farming employer, Ted Owens, was on the SFI board and overcame that obstacle in spite of most places being awarded to farmer's sons/daughters or ex-service personnel who were being encouraged to rent County Council small holdings to feed the nation after WWII. So aged 17 (one of the youngest that year) I left home for the final time in September 1949.

Having little money I decided to earn some by cutting fellow students' hair. At one shilling a go (5p since 1972!) it was far cheaper than the 1/9d to 2/3d charged in Bridgwater. My cubicle bedroom was my 'saloon' which certainly did not please the cleaning ladies. One shilling - 100% profit - life had never been this prosperous before!

Stan Acland was the farm foreman, a real life character, but in retrospect not a tutor of 'modern ' farming - even in 1949. He was a man from the previous century. As far as I can recall he never went near anything mechanical. His main skill was the teaching of the best way to hoe mangels - not very useful in those days! He called every student "Johnie" - boy or girl - yet his image brings back fond memories of my days on the Cannington farm.

I make it clear that I was NOT involved in a prank that went slightly 'over the top'. The old Priory then housed the whole institute including the dormitories, kitchen, canteen, and the Clifford Hall. The new campus over the road by the farm was several decades away. Contractors re-tarmaced the quadrangle which is surrounded by the Priory buildings. They laid boards through the archway and across the tarmac to prevent tar being trodden into either the boy's or girl's accommodation. The mistake was leaving their motorised roller parked by the tennis court wall over the week-end. Several students found a way of starting the machine and decided to help finish rolling in the tarmac - boards included! It took the contractors more than a day to retrieve their boards and to reinstate the tarmac surface. There was 'all hell' to pay but no individual was punished as it was basically the contractor's fault.

The year at the Somerset Farm Institute changed the lives of numerous students by instilling basic values and the will to earn a living. Every student of our year who has attended a re-union has succeeded in their field of expertise. Thanks to the Principal - Jack England - and his dedicated staff.

Gill Southerington (nee Wyatt).

After a very unhappy year, due to a broken engagement, I had come to the conclusion that I just had to move away from all the sad surroundings of my, up till then, contented village life, and seek my fortune and make new friends. For the last four years I had been happy working in the mental home in the village. First of all in the gardens and then in the fields. The other girls I worked with were all in the W.L.A. but I was just another 'farm worker' helping to win the war on the land.

This was the very first time I had been away from home, and I was not very happy about that. My parents had been wonderfully kind to me and the last year must have been as miserable for them as it had been for me, because I had felt myself beginning to grow bitter and I know that they were very worried about me. So, here I was, away from the family for the first time and determined to make the most of life whatever it might hold for me. One thing was certain - I would make up my mind to work hard and to put all thoughts of men and marriage out of my mind for ever. Work was what I needed, and friends, of course. What I would really do when my student days were over was not at the moment important. I was a modern Mr Macauber 'waiting for something to turn up' but never dreaming of what that 'something' might be.

Once inside the Somerset Farm Institute I felt as if my fate was now sealed and that for better or for worse I had to endure the following year. I was shown to my bedroom, which was right over the main gateway and quite the nicest room on the landing, where my room mate was already unpacking her belongings. We had the last room as our names were at the end of the alphabet - Warry and Wyatt. There was a Withers somewhere in the building but she was younger than either of us so was in 'the nursery'. Sue Warry also came from Bristol and she too was a Horti. student. Somehow I always think Sue resented having to share a room with me because I was so much older than she was and I knew she looked on me as a real old maid. Still, we got on surprisingly well together considering how different we were.

1947/48 Horti students were named 'The Select Sixteen' by Mr Lewis our head lecturer. We were 8 boys and 8 girls, a very varied cross-section of the community. Most of them had been 'educated' at good schools and had come to Cannington with some idea at least of Botany and Chemistry. At the very bottom of the scale were the Council School Lot, in other words Bill, Dave, Warry and me. Our only lessons in Botany had been learned through Nature Study walks with our teachers, while tramping the country lanes in our school days. For me especially those days were many years ago. To get back to studying again after so long at work. We five hardly knew a stolon from a rhizome if we met one, but we did know a buttercup! The mysteries of N.P.K. and CO_2 were completely unknown, and it was just as well at that time, because if any of us had any idea of what was in store for us we would have left immediately.

The SFI in those days was not just somewhere to study our chosen subject in, it was a real home. We only went to our parents at Christmas and Easter for the usual holidays. After one term I was absolutely shaken and a little bewildered to find that in my heart I had no real inclination to go home at all, and would have been more than content to stay at the Institute and continue studying alone. Could it be that at last I had found what I had been looking for for so long, good friends and the chance to really stand on my own feet and really 'do' something?

Within a few days I was completely happy in the new surroundings. Philippa and Betty were my special girl friends and I (who had intended never even to look at another man) was getting on famously with the boys on the course.

Most students had jobs to go to when they left the Institute, but I was one who did not. Then we heard that four of us were to be given the chance to stay on and work there if we wished. I was one of the lucky ones, also Betty.

The next year's students duly arrived and among them was a boy from Lincolnshire - Frank Southerington. Now, Frank was in the same position as I had been - a council school boy with a minimum of education, but very willing to learn. He was specially good at practical work because he had worked as garden boy in a large estate garden for the last six years. In February 1950 Frank and I were married.

It does not seem thirty years and more ago that I walked through the 'quad' to a completely new life. The new building of S.C.A.H. is not like the old Institute. That lovely old place holds so many memories for us 'old uns' and will be for ever and ever . . . . . OUR SECOND HOME.

(from the 1995 COSA Magazine).

113

Letter from Bill White

I started at the Institute in 1925 when it consisted only of Court Farm, with a herd of Shorthorns. The cowman was Alf Tambling, assistant cowman Mr. Larry White. The Farm Manager was Mr. Aitken, Ten Shire horses were kept; Jim Priddam, Walt Quartly and Tom Burge were the carters.

That same year Mr. Aitken left and Mr. Stan Acland (dec'd) was made foreman.

In 1927 Mr. Furze came with the NIAB Trials.

In 1928 came Miss Welsh, Miss Masters (dec'd) and Miss Maddever. They lived at the Retreat (the former Principal's house) and were away week-ends, coming back on motor bikes and sidecars.

A change came in 1930 from Shires to Percherons, a French horse, which were bred from two brood mares, Sapital and Pappatie by name. The came the change to Ayrshires.

Miss Taylor was County Dairy Instructress and Miss Monie was Head Cheesemaker, with students to train in Court dairy.

I saw many changes during my 42 years at the S.F.I. *(1981 COSA Magazine).*

Walt Quartly and Bill White

Tom Burge who worked for the S.F.I for many years, always with horses. He was the first man to receive the long service medal at the Bath and West Show.

Letter from Thomas Cooke

I am in the Grosvenor Court Care Home, Margate, Kent. I had a couple of accidents which left me a cripple and unable to walk properly. Now in a self-propelled wheel chair, an electric one. The memory of coming to Cannington was one of the greatest things to happen to me, 69/70. Tutor Roy Cheek.

While working at Eleys at East Bergholt on the Suffolk-Essex border I remember one of those pony pulled grass mowers where it was dumped, with a big laurel growing through the blades. The estate had four large ponds 60ft long and 35ft wide which were filled up for growing rhododendrons - with a stream down the middle. The whole garden is now a Garden Centre.

Do you know of anyone with an Old Student Magazine 1969/70 for sale?

I am sending a £10 Postal Order for the book "Chronicle of Cannington" with the hope that it can be passed on.

I wonder if you have Roy Cheeks address.

With best wishes,
Sincerely,
Tom Cooke
(As soon as the Chronicle is available Tom will get one - Ed).

A Lancashire Lad from Crook's Peak.

I was born in Lancashire a long time ago. Not from farming stock, father was a Bank Manager. Left school and completed an NDA after an NCA at the Lancashire College of Agriculture now known as Myerscough. I was there for three years altogether; specialised in sheep and then rented a small farm in Lancashire.

Disagreed on a rent increase, wondered what to do, and then over a pint one night someone said why didn't I go teaching and I said 'not in a month of Sundays' but then thought about it and started looking for teaching posts. Saw one advertised in Somerset and came to the county in 1965. Started working with 'Day-Release' students in Weston-super-Mare. That was under the City and Guilds Stage 1 and Stage 2 system - the forerunner of Phase One and Two which still operates for some subjects, like accounts.

These lads - and occasionally there were girls - all farmers' sons and daughters, did a two year release course. Most of them were employed on the family farm. I was based in Weston-s-Mare and it was a full-time post - Bridgwater on a Monday; Weston - Tuesday; Chew Valley - Wednesday; Bridgwater; Long Ashton - Thursday and back to Weston on a Friday. A lot of miles. Nowadays I understand that all day release students go to Cannington and there is but a handful. In those days there were at least four of us covering the county and probably over 400 part-time students.

One course, run by Dick Heal in those days, had 32 students on it at Langford House near Churchill. There were 28 motor-bikes and one car, parking was at a premium. Looking back, we had some cracking students, had a lot of fun, had problems of course but they were always ironed out there and then. We were given the freedom to do the job and our practical skills were recognised by the college management. I worked a great deal with Dick Heal, who was my assistant when I first went to Cannington and he worked part-time, and then when I bought the farm here in 1970 we swopped over and Dick became my 'line manager' as it is called these days.

The day always consisted of part theory and part practical. Local farmers were always willing to provide a venue for various stock tasks and some of the tractor tasks as well. We provided basic stock, arable and machinery for all students. The machinery practicals were concentrated at Cannington where Goff Berridge reigned. He was a bit of a character. He was one of those people that if you wanted to learn then Goff would teach you. If you messed around he would tell you to begger off and that was that. Nobody ever beggered off! Knew his stuff! I think my claim to fame with Goff was that he knew how to set a plough and I knew how to drive a tractor and the students never worked out that I didn't know how to set the plough and Goff couldn't drive a tractor! We worked that for years and years!

In those days everyone worked as a team - working to each others strengths and weaknesses. No jealousy, everyone supported everyone else. And we worked with the students and got dirty just as they did.

Somewhere this has got lost. The 'jobsworth' people came in who did not work after five o'clock and felt that it was not their job to get dirty because that's what students were for. They were there to learn and staff were there to teach them but they earned a salary and students got in the way of meetings!

In those days if you wanted to go to college, you had to have something about you because they did not take everyone. Nowadays if you can stand up and breathe, you can get in. Also these days if you don't feel like turning up then you don't but then it did not enter people's heads not to turn up for classes. When I lived in at the college I looked after the 'office block' as Warden and everyone had to be in by 10.30. I would do my rounds at 10.25 and not notice the wire ladder parked adjacent to a drain pipe which was the escape route after 10.30. Of course I did not know anything about this and as long as folk turned up for their morning duties I was not overly bothered. They genuinely thought I didn't know and all obeyed the golden rule 'thou shalt not get caught'!

There was a camaraderie amongst staff and students, and all would help each other if there was a bother.

I worked for five years full time with part-time students, a little bit with full-time students, but not a lot, up to 1970 when, as I said earlier, I bought the farm. Lived in during the first term and then bought a house in Sandford not far from here.

After I bought the farm here I concentrated more on sheep skills and shearing and taught hundreds of people to shear. Got my British Wool Marketing Board Shearing Instructor's badge after a lot of blood, sweat and damned hard work. In fact I've lost my badge, come to think of it! Helen must have tidied it away! Also became an NPTC examiner in shearing and the last people I assessed was about six years ago. I still shear my own flock but it takes me a considerable time longer than before!

Hard work with shearing but a hell of a lot of fun. Best time I had was with the YTS (Youth Training Scheme). One year I was told that all YTS students had to do a shearing course and that half of them would not turn up, so I went and briefed the groups that if they said they were coming then they had to turn up. There were 84 students and only one failed to turn up and that was because the cowman at home had broken his leg and he was needed. All did their four day shearing course and together with the full-time students we got through 4500 sheep that year - sheep provided from Exmoor to Highbridge.

Farmers looked after us well, supplying tea and coffee except for the one who pointed to the tap in the yard! The further you got away from the centres of population the better the hospitality. Farmers were getting their sheep shorn free of charge and we did earn our snacks! Three of my students became European shearing champions. A shearing course at Gupworthy on Exmoor resulted in the farmer equipping himself with a tea urn and kept us supplied with tea all day as it was blistering weather. At the end of the day he said that he had arranged for everyone to nip down to Ralegh's Cross for a beer on him. He was a committed teetotaller but was so impressed with the lads' performance and the condition of his sheep that he was prepared to lay his principles to one side for this occasion.

Those students seemed to love genuine work and shearing is a classic example of being able to see the result straight away. Ploughing is another. A field of hay well turned is another. Because you always get farmers peering over the hedge full of criticism if the lad was not getting it right. I suppose we used to take a pride in our work then to satisfy our self-esteem. Where has this gone?

Finished in August 1992. Fun had gone out of it. 60's, 70's, 80's - we had some good times. The staff were committed to the students. Worked hard in the summer but took it a bit easier in the autumn and spring terms but then the whizz kids came in and the place started to go downhill fast. I was told by one of the senior staff that according to staff room gossip I couldn't teach. This said, despite my students getting very high marks and the Inspectorate being entirely happy with my performance. So I took the 'package' and came home.

I have remained here ever since, farming up to 300 ewes at one time with the Devons, but now it is getting near time to give up stock altogether. For next year I probably will have 20 sheep. Cannot move away from here, though - just look at the view!

David Capel, Day Release Staff; 1965 - 1992.
(From Caroline Woolley's conversation with David Capel).

SYLLABUS FROM THE 1935/36 PROSPECTUS
(there is little change since the 1920s)

A LIGHTHEARTED PREFACE TO THE SYLLABUS
(Why "Wild White" Hay?)

'Man o' Mendip', who for many years was a Somerset correspondent for the Western Daily Press, in 1932 attended a Grass Seeds Mixture Demonstration above Porlock Hill, conducted by W.D.Hay, and he reported the event in the WDP on 5th November 1932. (Man o' Mendip is said to have been Gray Usher, a Cannington student between 1922 and 1924).

Here I was 900 feet up on Porlock Hill admiring the Grass Seeds Mixture Demonstrations arranged by W.D.Hay, our progressive County Agricultural Organiser. They are showing excellent results, particularly on Mr W.J. Westcott's Birchanger Farm. There was a large company from all over the county present. Mr Hay [showing an admirable knowledge of St Paul's Epistle to the Corinthians, Chapter 13 - Ed.] commented that when we are without charity we are nothing, but he added that without Wild White Clover farmers were a minus quantity. One of the most popular gentlemen farmers from North Somerset asked me if we could not also offer a sentiment. Here it is:

NEBUCHADNEZZAR ON PORLOCK HILL - by Bridget

The Devil's Chimney soaring high
Stands out in gorge as we jolt by
Through tow'ring rocks and passes.
No time have we to sense the thrill
But on we go to Porlock Hill
To learn of land and grasses.

From Dunkery Beacon, Bridgwater Bay,
Lynton and Lynmouth, Minehead way,
To a land of beef and barley,
They come through bog and water-reed
The Exmoor men on sturdy steed,
For farming talk and parley.

To change from moor to verdant strand,
Good grass to grow on barren land
Needs certain seeds and grasses.
Indigenous ones do often tease,
The farmer must get rid of these
And good ones grow in masses.

Ryegrass (Italian), Cocksfoot sure,
Ryegrass (Perenniel) Trefoil pure,
Are right the country over.
Rough stalked meadow grass, Alsike too,
Only the best of these will do,
Mixed well with Wild White Clover.

Use Clover - red kind, flowering late
And Clover - red kind, broad - its mate.
The Speaker says - he's a Scot moreover,
"Wi' Creasted Dogstail dinna fash,
'Tis neither good for beast nor cash
But mind ye Wild White Clover".

When talk is done and daylight ends
We say 'goodbye' and homeward wends
Each tired and hungry rover.
All need some vittles right away,
For all we've had in a long, long day
Is Grass and Wild White Clover.

11

SYLLABUS OF INSTRUCTION.

Text Books as advised.

COURSES.

AGRICULTURE.

This course consists of three terms each of 12 weeks' duration, and therefore covers a full year's operations on the farm. Each student is required to take part in all kinds of farm work including dairying and poultry-husbandry, under the direction of the Staff, and must attend all the lectures and demonstrations forming part of this course.

FIRST TERM.

AGRICULTURE. Soils—Their origin, variations, adaptability, effects of cultivation, water supply, temperature, air supply, altitude, aspect, indications of fertility, methods of soil improvement.

Livestock.—Breeds of cattle, sheep, pigs and horses.

Farm Building Construction. — Building materials, arrangement of farm homestead, erection of cowsheds, dairy, implement shed, stable and piggeries.

Implements and Machinery.—Construction, mechanism, care and cleaning of farm implements and machinery.

Dairy and Poultry Husbandry.—As in the short Dairy course.

GENERAL SCIENCE. Matter—solids, liquids, gases, atomic weights, elements, compounds, acids, bases, salts, chemical change, elementary physics, the atmosphere and water.

Structure and growth of plants—roots, stems, leaves, flowers, fruits, seed. Life history of plants.

VETERINARY SCIENCE. Anatomy of farm animals, generative organs, circulation of the blood, respiration, temperature, digestion and assimilation, secretion, dentition. Parturition. Internal and external parasites, infectious and common diseases of farm animals and their treatment.

Water supply, ventilation, disinfection, control of disease etc.

FARM ORCHARDING AND CIDER MAKING. Fruit growing on farms. Farm orcharding—selection of site, planning and planting, varieties, renovation and care of orchards, principles and methods of pruning, grading and marketing.

Cider-making equipment. Varieties of apples, collection and storage, milling, pressing, fermentation.

13

SECOND TERM.

AGRICULTURE. Manures—Their origin, peculiarities, classification and use. Selection, valuation and mixing of manures. Farmyard manure. Green manuring. Manuring of farm crops. Residual values of manures, lime, chalk and marl. Effects upon soil and crops. Manurial values.

Rotations for different soils and conditions. Farm crops, their cultivation, manuring and harvesting.

GENERAL SCIENCE. Composition of plants and source of elements present—plant nutrition, composition of soil, available and unavailable constituents, mechanical analysis of soil. Effects of cropping, cultivation and place when mixed and applied to soil.

Seed testing. Identification of plants and seeds. Weeds, their habits of growth and methods of destroying them. Descriptions of cereals, grasses, clovers and forage plants. Reproduction, propagation, selection of seed mixtures, seeding.

BOOK-KEEPING. This includes a simple system of book-keeping suitable for farmers. Use of the diary, cash book and ledger, interest, discount, cheques. Books to keep on the farm. Annual balance sheet, profit and loss account.

FARM ORCHARDING AND CIDER MAKING. Propagation of fruit, trees and grafting. Stocks for grafting, pruning. Winter and spring spraying, appliances, spray fluids. Cider-making, control of fermentation, filtering, bottling.

THIRD TERM.

AGRICULTURE. The feeding and management of cattle, sheep, pigs and horses.

GENERAL SCIENCE. Composition of the animal body, animal nutrition, composition of farm foods, nutritive values, composition of milk, butter and cheese. Changes taking place in dairy processes.

Bacteria and fungi. Life history and description of common fungoid diseases. Preventative treatment. Insect pests and how to deal with them.

LAND SURVEYING. The use of the chain and optical square—measurement of areas, sub-dividing fields, etc., plotting and calculating areas. Cubic contents, measuring manure heaps, stacks and timber.

15

HORTICULTURE.

This course consists of three terms each of 12 weeks' duration. Students will be required to take part in all types of work in the gardens and plantations under the supervision of the horticultural staff.

The aim of the Horticultural Course is to provide practical instruction and training in growing fruit and vegetable crops by methods which should equip students with practical experience and information and enable them to take up commercial Horticulture as a career, either in private or commercial work.

Special tuition is given to those students who decide to take up one branch of Horticulture as a speciality and assistance can be given, if desired, to students to pass examinations held by the **Royal Horticultural Society** and other bodies.

FIRST TERM.

GENERAL HORTICULTURE. Introductory—Branches of commercial horticulture, fruit farming, market gardening, nursery work, glass houses. Soils suitable for horticultural crops, classification of soils and their adaptation to horticultural purposes, selection of land for fruit growing and market gardening, district, aspect, soil, equipments. Implements and tools used in horticulture.

FRUIT CULTURE. General introduction Selection of sites for special systems, influence of weather and other conditions. Top and soft fruits, cultural and market values. Recognition and choice of varieties, their cultural and marketing values. Types of trees, systems of planting, methods of cultivation. General management of fruit plantations.

Estimates of expenditure, capital outlay, marketing, book-keeping, labour.

Propagation by cuttings and layers.

GRASS ORCHARDS. Laying out, planting and maintaining. Renovation of grass orchards. Grading, packing and marketing autumn and winter fruit. Storage of fruit.

VEGETABLE CULTURE. General introduction. Suitability of special soils and situations. Intensive and extensive systems of cropping and cultivation. Preparation of land, soil working and cultivation. Systems of rotation, inter-cropping and catch cropping.

16

Cultivation of the chief market garden crops. Selection of varieties.

Storage of crops, grading, packing and marketing vegetables.

FLOWER CULTURE. General introduction. Cultivation outdoors and under glass, for market.

SECOND TERM.

GENERAL HORTICULTURE. Manures and their application. The living plant. Chemistry of soils. Manures. Horticultural materials.

FRUIT CULTURE. Pruning fruit trees, general principles and methods according to type of tree and other factors. Manuring fruit trees in relation to kind of fruit, age of tree, stocks, method of pruning.

Propagation of fruit trees by grafting and budding. Fruit tree root stocks, their value and effect, propagation of root stocks. Manuring and pruning as applied to grass orchards. Winter spraying materials and spraying appliances. Power sprayers.

VEGETABLE CULTURE. Manures for vegetable crops, mixing and application of manures. Seed beds. Vegetable seeds, seed sowing. The use of frames and hot beds.

Tomato and cucumber culture under glass.

FLOWER CULTURE. Seed sowing under glass and in open. General treatment of young plants, pricking out, potting. Propagation of plants by cuttings and division. Cultivation of pot plants. Forcing bulbs in pots. Marketing of flowers and plants. Heating. Ventilation and watering frames and glass houses.

THIRD TERM.

GENERAL HORTICULTURE. Economics of commercial horticulture, general statistics. Laws relating to horticulture. Costs of establishing fruit farms, market gardens and nurseries. Estimates of costs and returns under various systems. Valuations, tenure, buildings and equipment of a holding. Book-keeping.

17

Systems of marketing produce, methods of packing.

FRUIT CULTURE. Insect pests and fungus diseases. Methods of control, prevention and treatment. Summer spraying. Summer pruning and training fruit trees. Nursery work in raising fruit trees, bushes and root stocks. Picking, packing and marketing soft fruits.

VEGETABLE CULTURE. Insect pests and fungus diseases and their examination. Methods of control.

Summer and autumn cropping. Harvesting and marketing summer and autumn crops. Packages. Methods of sale. Summer cultivations.

FLOWER CULTURE. Hardy and half-hardy plants and flowers grown for sale. Marketing. Insect pests and fungus diseases, under glass and outside.

CROPS GROWN UNDER GLASS. Introductory to subject. Construction of houses, heating, ventilation, water supply. Systems of cropping, culture of chief glass-house crops.

BEE-KEEPING. Instruction in practical bee-keeping is provided for students of the horticultural course. Lectures are given during the winter months, followed by practical work in the apiary in May, June and July.

FARM ORCHARDING AND CIDER MAKING. Horticultural students are expected to take instruction in these subjects with the students of the agricultural course.

19

DAIRYING.

The full course consists of three terms each of 12 weeks' duration. Students will be required to take part in the handling of milk, and in the making of butter and cheese, etc. All students must take the full syllabus of instruction. It is an advantage to be able to milk before taking up this course.

A 12 weeks' course is also arranged. The work will be a simplified form of that taken during the long course.

Short courses on dairying will be given during each term. Students attending will do practical work along with those taking the longer course; but the lectures which they must attend will be of a more elementary nature.

Short refresher courses for those who have already attended the Institute are also arranged.

Students are prepared for the **British Dairy Farmers' Association** Examination for Certificates in butter and cheese making, and these examinations are held annually at the Institute. The results of the examinations held have been most satisfactory, over 90 per cent. of passes having been obtained.

Up to the present there has been no difficulty in finding posts for students who have taken full advantage of the training given.

LECTURES AND DEMONSTRATIONS. Milk—Its nature, composition and uses. Secretion of milk, treatment and sale of milk.
Cream — Methods of obtaining cream. The sale and ripening of cream.
Butter—Composition and methods of manufacture.
Cheese—Its nature, composition, food value and uses. Control of acidity. Ripening, storing and marketing of cheese. Faults and troubles in cheese-making. Varieties. Rennet, whey, whey butter.
Equipment of dairy.
Dairy Farming—Breeds of dairy cows. Foods and feeding. Effects of foods on dairy products. General management of cows. Common ailments of dairy stock.

PRACTICAL DAIRY WORK. Buying, handling and general management of milk, milk testing, pasteurization and cooling of milk. Care and management of separators. Treatment of cream for sale and butter making. Butter making and potting of butter. Cheese-making, soft, blue and hard pressed varieties. The making of whey butter. The keeping of dairy records. The care of dairy plant.

POULTRY HUSBANDRY. Dairy students attending the long course receive instruction in poultry husbandry, which includes practical work, lectures and demonstrations.

In so far as accommodation will permit, students are received for shorter periods for specified instruction in any branch of dairy work.

21

POULTRY HUSBANDRY.

The full course consists of three terms of 12 weeks each.

The Institute is now approved by the National Poultry Council as a centre for the training of students in preparation for the **National Certificate in Poultry Practice.** Only students taking the full course are eligible to sit for this.

Shorter courses can be arranged to suit the requirements of individuals.

Syllabus of Lectures and Practical Work.

FIRST TERM.

BREEDS. Suitability for different branches of poultry husbandry.

BREEDING. Selection of stock. General principles of breeding. Suitability of crosses for various purposes. Breeding for egg production. Importance of pedigree. Progeny testing. Recording and culling.

FOODS AND FEEDING. Description of feeding stuffs and suitability. Mixtures for different classes of stock. Mixing of foods. Wet and dry mashes. Cooking and preparation of foods. Supplementary foods. Methods of feeding.

MANAGEMENT OF ADULT STOCK.
General treatment and detailed management of the breeding and laying stock throughout the year. Artificial lighting, trapnesting and recording.

TABLE POULTRY. Breeds and crosses for fattening. Age at which to fatten. Preparation of foods for fattening. Methods of killing, plucking, shaping, trussing, packing and marketing.

ANATOMY. The detailed anatomy of the fowl. Skeleton. Muscular system. Elementary Histology of the animal cell and tissues.

PHYSIOLOGY. Respiration. Circulation. Digestion. Excretion.

ELEMENTARY BIOLOGY. The structure and mode of life of Amoeba and Hydra treated in an elementary manner.

GENERAL SCIENCE. (As Agriculture 1st Term). Elementary knowledge of Plant Histology.

BOOK-KEEPING. Value of Accounts. General principles of Book-keeping. Use of waste book, journal, cash book and ledger.

SECOND TERM.

HATCHING. Selection and care of eggs for hatching. Testing. Natural hatching. Management of broody hens. Artificial hatching. Types of incubators. General management.

REARING. Natural rearing. Types of coops. General management. Artificial rearing. Types of brooders, indoors and outdoors. Feeding of chickens and growing stock.

HOUSING. General principles. Description and arrangement of various types. Intensive and semi-intensive houses for large flocks. Houses for chickens and growing stock.

RUNS. Area required. Management of grass, soil and covered runs.

PHYSIOLOGY. Reproduction. Metabolism.

EMBRYOLOGY.
The elements of embryology as exemplified by the development of the chick.

CHEMISTRY OF FOOD AND DIGESTION.
Elementary chemistry of the proteins, amides, fats and carbohydrates, so far as it is related to the composition of animal tissues and feeding stuffs.

The appearance, composition and use of the common feeding stuffs.

The importance of mineral salts and accessory food substances. The chemical changes taking place in the various stages of the process of digestion, and the relation of these changes to enzyme and bacterial activity.

BOOK-KEEPING.
Open and closing the accounts in the cash-book and ledger.
Sales and Purchase books.
Trial balance. Valuations and depreciation.
Trading, Profit and Loss and Capital Accounts. Balance Sheet. Assets and Liabilities.
Banks Accounts and Cheques. Bills of Exchange and Promisory Notes.
Consignment Accounts.

23
THIRD TERM.

DUCKS, GEESE AND TURKEYS. Description of breeds. Selection, hatching, rearing, housing, and general management. Egg and meat production. Marketing.

MARKETING. General principles of buying and selling. Co-operation. Grading, testing and packing eggs for market. Packing cases. Methods of preserving eggs. Packing stations. Collecting depots. Direct sale.

DISEASES. Common Diseases, treatment and prevention.

PATHOLOGY.

Bacterial diseases.—Bacillary White Diarrhoea, Cholera, Avian Typhoid, Tuberculosis.
Diseases due to Filterable Virus.—"Roup," Fowl Pox.
Protozal diseases.—Coccidiosis, "Blackhead."
Diseases due to fungi.—Aspergillosis, Favus.
Prophylaxis.—Infection, Contagion, Isolation, Disinfection, Immunisation.
General diseases.—Impaction of the crop, Simple Diarrhoea, Gout Rickets, "Leg weaknesses." Paralysis.
Vicious habits.—Cannibalism, Feather eating.
Diseases of the reproductive organs and abnormalities of the reproductive function.
External and Internal parasites.
Tumours.

HYGIENE AND SANITATION. Water supply. Disinfection of buildings, appliances and runs. Treatment of poultry manure.

Construction of Poultry Houses and Appliances.

DESIGN. Elementary design and method of construction of houses and appliances in general use. Light—ventilation—capacity—interior fittings.

MATERIALS. Timber—fibre boards—asbestos—glass and glass substitutes—metals—brick—stone—lime—mortar—cement—concrete—roofing materials wire—fencing—wire gauges.

CONSTRUCTION. Use of tools—size of timber commonly used—construction of mash hoppers—nest boxes, etc.—type of floors.

MANAGEMENT. Treatment of houses—preservatives—paints and painting—prevention of rot.

BOOK-KEEPING.

Analytical book-keeping, Income Tax.
Special account books for poultry farmers.
Stocktaking. Simple costings.

Note: As far as time will permit, demonstrations will be given in preservation of fruit and vegetables and in domestic hygiene, to all female students taking the long courses.

Some Year Photos - 1921-1960

*Thanks to Nan Eaves (nee' Hebditch) for correcting,
as far as possible, the dates of the early copies.*

Some years and many names are missing. Why?

At some stage during the transfer of Cannington to Bridgwater College a large quantity of old Cannington documents and photographs were cleared out from their shelves and cupboards and Caroline Woolley and Nan Eaves are to be thanked for saving them.

However, some material disappeared in the process - before it could be saved - and this is no doubt why many annual photographs of staff and students are missing. Probably some of the lists of names attached to some of the photographs were lost at the same time - Ed.

THE FIRST STUDENTS

Photograph by courtesy of Mr. W. T. J. Cook

(1921/22 photograph - from COSA Magazine 1921-1981 Jubilee Edition)

SFI - 1922/23 - Loaned by A. Chamings, brother-in-law of Ernest and Arnold Hebditch

(This photograph is believed to have been wrongly dated as 1921/22 when it first appeared in the COSA magazine)

STAFF and STUDENTS 1923/24

Roe, Cutter, Miss Minette, –, Flashman, –, Miss Walker, –, –, –, Billington, Chancellor, McKensie Chapman, –, –, Miss Fuller, Mrs. W. Gould (nee Hill), –, Miss J. Day, –, –, –, –, Miss Snook, Taylor, Quick –, Mrs. Hay, Mr. Aitkin (Foreman), Miss Saker, Mr. Hay (V.P.), Mr. Mackie (P.), A. D. Turner, Matron, –, Miss Masters (Dairy) Champion, Chapman, Hebditch, Bowditch, D. Rowe, –, Kinsey, Palmer, Tavener, Milburn. The dashes signify some of the ones we cannot identify.

NOTE: Believed to be 1923/24, not of the date quoted in the COSA Magazine.

(1928/29 - from COSA Magazine - 2002)

1932/33

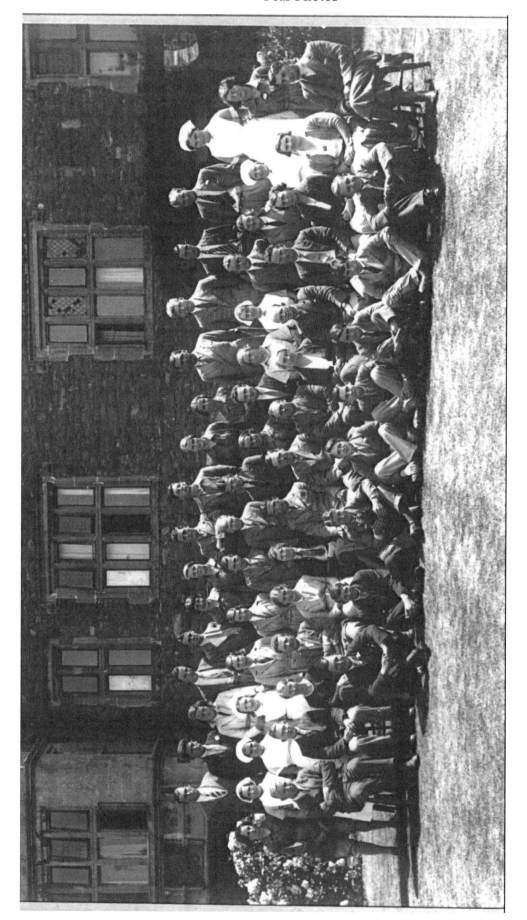

*1934-35 - from a dated but otherwise unmarked loose cutting from an
unknown local newspaper found in W.D.Hay's press cuttings book.*

1937/38

1938/39

1945/46

Back Row: Geoff Brooks; Clifford Leggett; Stanley (Schofield?); Roger Veale; George Lee; William Painter; Maurice North; D.H.K. Gilson.

4th Row: Jean Darknell ; Tom Elsdale; Robin Easterbrook; Tony Marsh; Cyril Lockyer; Ronald Dyke; Maurice Adams; Bryan Young; John Hill; John Mew; John Pearce; 'Tom' Tuckett; Joan Moore.

3rd Row: Mary Wentworth; Muriel Chinn; Andrew House; Pat Haymen; Noreen Rumley; Audrey Field; Myra Newbury; Lois Maggs, Sheila Naylor; Moira Uttley; Sheila Brown; Alison Spencer; Monica Brown.

2nd Row: Nan Hebditch; Una Farrar; Margaret Steer; Jan Denning; Meg Gall; Betty Clarke (?); John Holland; Bernard Tottle; Geoff Hunt; 'Jo' (E.W.) Trow; Norman Parker; David Barnes.

Front Row: Barbara Wright, Dorothy Muirhead; Marjorie Withers; ....; ....; Jenny Matthews; Thelma Chislett; 'Midge' ....; ....

(The names of the students of this year missing from the photograph appear to be: P.H.Smye; K. Wilkes; G.V.Parsons, D.M.Godfrey)

1946/47
(Many apologies. But it's this or nothing!)

1947/48)

1948/49

1949/50

	1	2	3	4	5	6	7	8	9						
Top Row	1														
2nd Row	11	12	13	14	15	16	17	18	19	20	71				
3rd Row	21	22	23	24	25	26	27	28	29	30	31	32	33	34	
4th Row	35	36	37	38	39	40		42	43	44	45	46	47	48	49
5th Row	50	51	52	53	54	55	56	57	58	59	60	61	62	63	64
Front Row	65	66	67	68	69	70									

Top Row
1. Malcolm Roberts
2. Mike Comer
3. Alan Whittle
4. Brian Cox
5. Pat Pile
6. John Harmer
7. Dick Hudson
8. Terry Summers
9. Keith Williamson-Jones
10. (Missing) John Smith

2nd Row
11. Graham Dawes
12. Bill Hayward
13. Arnold Coleman
14. Brian Harvey
15. Michael Bell
16. Michael Davey
17. John Bryan
18. Ron Beck
19. Dudley Trench
20. Benny Goodman
71. John Duvall

3rd Row
21. Maurice Davey
22. John Vile
23. John Rowatt
24. Jim Gore
25. Ken Booth
26. Margaret Knowles (Ball)
27. Mary Smith
28. Pam Mortimer (Tyler)
29. Mia Wall (Marler)
30. Bob Webb
31. Ian Hedderwick
32. Hugh Hammond
33. Jim Swaker
34. Bob Buffrey

4th Row
35. Arthur Lawrence
36. Brian Hack
37. John Fisher
38. David Gwilliam
39. Colin Welch
40. Richenda Keyworth
41. Pam Henderson (Newton)

42. Jane Everton
43. Shirley Daniels (Moore)
44. Janet Slade
45. Jack Palmer
46. Ken Harris
47. Ken Underdown
48. George Winslade
49. Derek Tottle

5th Row
50.
51.
52. N Scott-Miller
53. Miss E M Hobbs
54. Richard Swan
55. Miss E M Monie
56. A J Marval
57. W J England
58. W T Lewis
59. Miss Quinlan
60. T R Maitland
61. R C Rolt
62. Miss N M Heywood
63.

64.

Front Row
65. Barbara Glenn
66. Margaret Fortt
67. Molly Smith
68. Janet Peet
69. Valerie Gardner
70. Elizabeth Mosedale

ADDRESS'S WANTED

67 & 31

ANY CONTACT WANTED

10-17-21-23-24-34-35-40-44
66-71

1949/50; *Erratum - No.10 - actually Donald Smith (thanks to M. Bell)*
Omission - No.64 - (Ian?) Brown (thanks to Benny Goodman)

1951/52

1952/53

1953/54

1953/54

Key from the 1986 COSA Magazine

Back Row: Left to Right
John Danby, Martin White, Ben Whitting, Willie Weston, John Dunster, James Peters, John Quick, Ben (Clinker) Cole, Adrian Slack, Ron Burrell, David Lawson, Mike Clarke, Brian Croxton.

Third Row: Left to Right:
Westcott, Peter Manly, Reg Lewis, A.P.Jones, Roy Richards, Gerald Greenman, Hugh Land, Jock Alan Johnstone, Sparks Brian Jeffries, John Fisher, Leslie Jenkin.

Second Row: Left to Right:
Barbara Wharton, Josie Knowles, Jenny Swearse, Susan Crowe, Angela Dawson-Curry, Ruth Bartlett, Jenny Atkinson, Hazel Stephens, Sonia Hayes, Daphne Legg, Ingrid Clopperburg.

Front Row: Left to Right:
Mr Wiseman, Miss B. Pascoe, Mr B. Thomas, Mr I. Wright, Miss Monie, Mr Marval, Mr Ballardie (Principal), Miss Hobbs (Matron), Mr Maitland, Miss N. Heywood (Ass.Matron), Mr Rolt, Miss Deyermond, Mr J.B.Bulford.

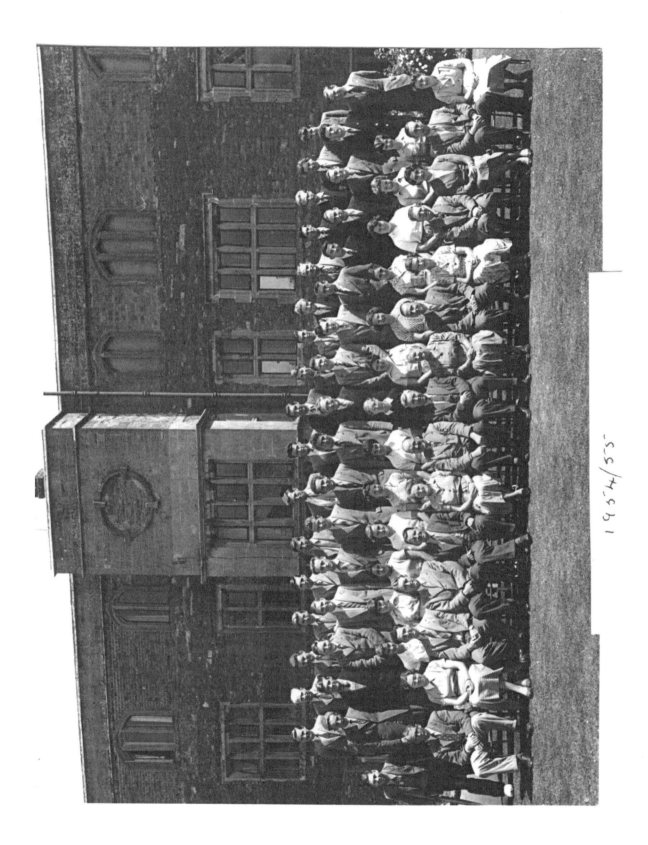

1954/55

Back Row

Alan Collins, Desmond Reeder, Jim Pratt, John Copestake, Richard Crane, John Bent, Brian Carlisle, Phil Bown, Colin Ellis, Richard Cooke, John Moor

Terry Hering, Sam Harcombe, John Perry, Stuart Jackson, Laurie Golding, Richard Sneyd, Eric Hewison, David Spyker

Row 2

Bob Speed, Mike Dawes, Milnes Priscott, David (chalky) White, Bob Baldwin, David Duplessis, Ken Dingle, John Hewson

Jim Boyt, Bob Main, Harry Lyfely, Pat Sweet, Nigel Goldsmith, Terry Harvey

Row 3

Alan (flash) Venner, Judy Rose, Alena Kratochul, Sheila Masters, Mary Frost, Madge Vearncombe, Bill Packer, Yvonne Father

Betty Dawson, Jo Sharplin, Kathy Plowse, Pam Lowe, Jean Butler

Front Row

Mr Wiseman, Miss Beryl Pascoe, Mr Brian Thomas, Mr Wright, Mr Maitland, Miss Hobbs, Mr Maitland

Mr Ballantine, Miss Monie, Mr Brookfield, Miss Bell, Mr Rolt, Miss Derman, Mr Balford

Miss Heywood

Above: 1954/55 names.   Below: Key to photograph on front cover (taken from the original).

Beryl Pascoe Mehdi Monsef Betty Dawson Yvonne
Mary Frost Madge Vearncombe Jo Sharplin Fathers
Dairy students of 1954/55.   Jean Butler   Miss Monie

147

L-R STAFF 1st Row (Bottom) Bryan Thomas, Miss N.Heywood (Ass.Matron), Bob Wright (Warden), Miss J.Bell (deceased), Major Matthews (d'sed) Miss Monie (deceased), Mr.A.J.Marvel (Vice-Principal), Mr.Ballardie (Principal) Mr.S.Brookfield, Miss E.Hobbs (Matron)(deceased), Mr.Maitland, Miss Deremond, Mr.J.Bulford, Beryl Davies, Tom Sprott. **2nd Row** Jim Peters,Claire Betts (Kellond), Gay (Appleby), Pat Gunningham (Besant), Gill Palmer (Powne), Ann Marsh, Yvonne Sayle (Croft), Ann Cuff (Snell), Gillian (Crombie), Pat Carr (Taylor), Elizabeth MacCrearie (Mortimer), Pam (Warner), Anna Vile (Burroughs), Ann Williamson (Merrit), David Willis **3rd Row** John MacMullen, Roy Caterer, Hugh Scott, Chris Humble. Ernie Tucker, R. Stevens, Colin Ryden, Martin Webber, Tony White, Alan Driver, Colin Jones, Peter Wood, Gordon Bragg, Bob Lovell, Paul Ludwick (deceased), Arthur Wilcox **Top Row** Pete Pritchard, ?, Robin Venn, Alan Ely, Ian Graves, - Heywood, Jim Atkins, Pete Coombs, John Beauchamp, John Clark, Basil Cuff (deceased), - Liston-Feulis, Maurice Marshall, Ted Joce, Bob Collard, Martin Shearn, - Johnson, David Gunningham, Chris Howard, Peter Sparkes, Martin Kellaway, Richard Frost.

1955/56

1957/58

57/8

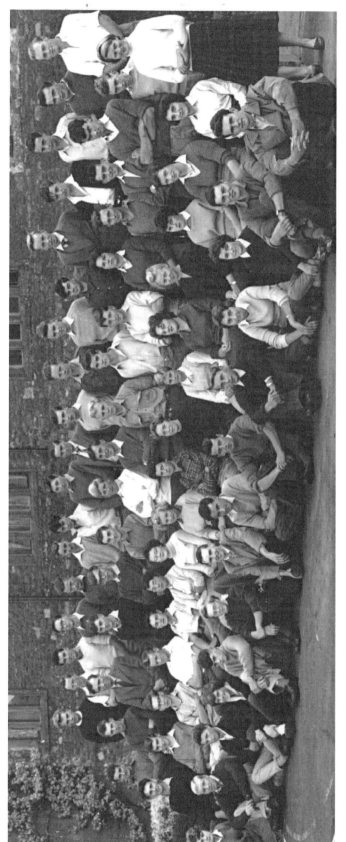

1959/60

AVAILABLE YEAR PHOTOGRAPHS 1961-1992

(Some years and most names are unfortunately not available)

(See note on page 127)

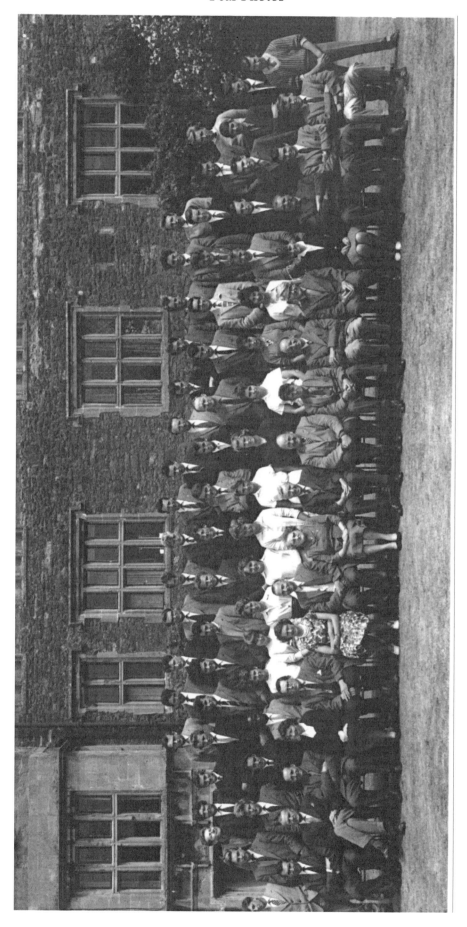

1961/62

1962/63

1963/64

Year 1963/64 Taken at Cannington Court before the days of the Car Park with 'Woodbine Cottage' in the background.
Top Row: (left to right) Michael Dunlop, Roger Cooze, Ted Watts, John Pinkerton, Alan Duck, Colin Edwards, Rodney Garbutt, John Spencer, Mike Wortley, Brian Kemp, Stewaret Loftus, Mike Carlisle, Peter Matthews, Hugh Brown, John Handel, John Flower, Roger Shearn, Maurice Ryan, Ted Bird, Chris Lintern, Dave Pursey, Alan Woodruff, Tom Cox.
3rd Row: John Goldsmith, Michael Rickers, Owen Thomas, Malcom Fewings, Pete Cook, Dave Harding, George Bayliss, Tom Hill, Clive Brooks, Geoff Bell, David Payne, Dick Line, Colin Rayson, Colin Hatherell, Tim Ayres, David Jewell, Alan Witcher, Richard Newman, Colin Wilkey, Steven Hussey, John Stone.
2nd Row: Terry Smith, Paul Briscoe, Chris Stevens, Tim Burden, Albert Affran, Brian Golding, Neville Mundy, Peter Butler, Ian Cockshot, Ben Osei, Ruth Heal, Dianne Coombes, Gale Johnson, Sheila Wheeldon, Cindy Cummines, Paula Marke, Roger Lane, Bill Pearce, Alex (Sandy) Ros, Mike Holloman, Peter Jewell, Michael Demnerley, David Snook.
Front Row: Steve Hewlett, Richard Bartram, Mrs Reynolds, Mrs Heywood, Mr Galloway, Mr Hoskins, Miss Syms, Mr Chambers, Mr Marval, Mr Ballardie, Mr Brookfield, Mr Reynolds, Mr Maitland, Miss Wootton, Miss Hayman, Dave Sheppard, P.J Sutton, Mr Mead. Ben Russell.

1964/65

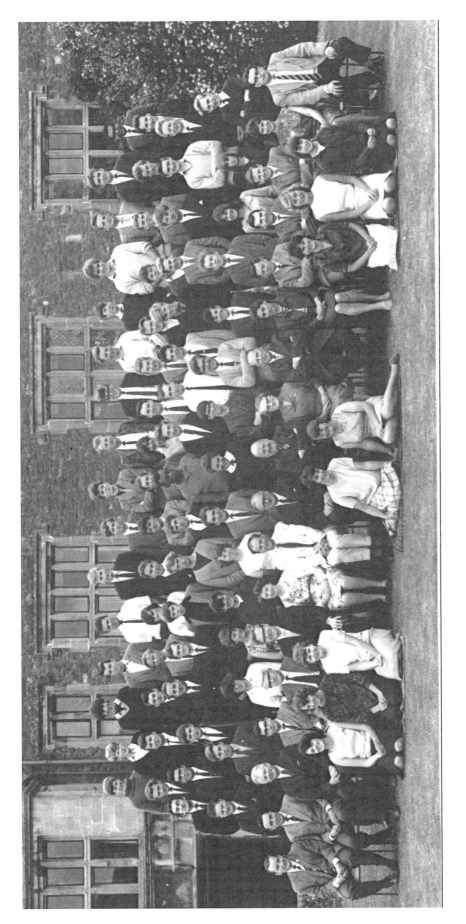

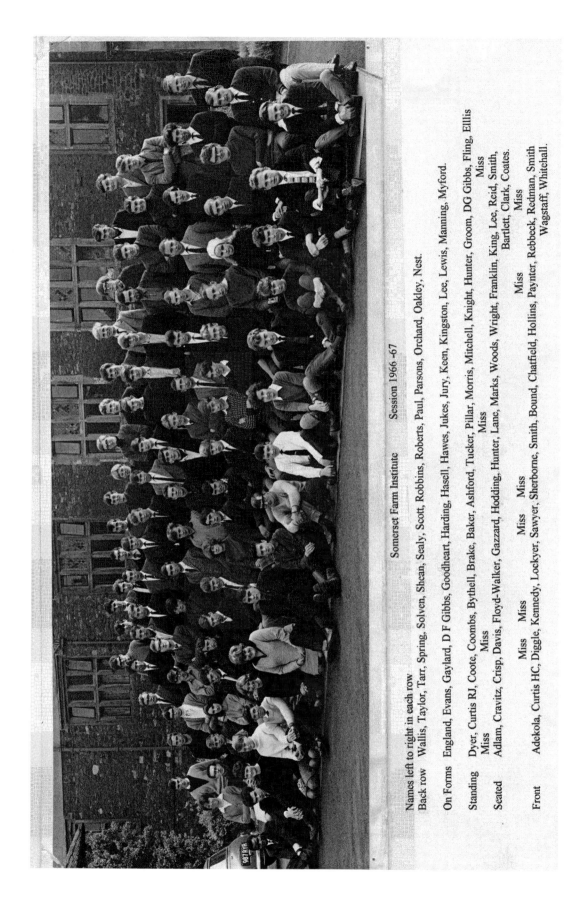

Somerset Farm Institute   Session 1966 -67

Names left to right in each row

Back row   Wallis, Taylor, Tarr, Spring, Solven, Shean, Sealy, Scott, Robbins, Roberts, Paul, Parsons, Orchard, Oakley, Nest.

On Forms   England, Evans, Gayland, D F Gibbs, Goodheart, Harding, Hasell, Hawes, Jukes, Jury, Keen, Kingston, Lee, Lewis, Manning, Myford.

Standing   Dyer, Curtis RJ, Coote, Coombs, Bythell, Brake, Baker, Ashford, Tucker, Pillar, Morris, Mitchell, Knight, Hunter, Groom, DG Gibbs, Fling, Elllis
            Miss   Miss

Seated   Adlam, Cravitz, Crisp, Davis, Floyd-Walker, Gazzard, Hodding, Hunter, Lane, Marks, Woods, Wright, Franklin, King, Lee, Reid, Smith,
          Miss   Bartlett, Clark, Coates.
                                                                                                                                             Miss

             Miss   Miss   Miss

Front   Adekola, Curtis HC, Diggle, Kennedy, Lockyer, Sawyer, Sherborne, Smith, Bound, Chatfield, Hollins, Paynter, Rebbeck, Redman, Smith
                                                                                                                        Wagstaff, Whitehall.

WHOLE GROUP:-

FRONT ROW (AGRIC.) LEFT TO RIGHT -

ALLEN, BALL, BULLEID, BURNHAM, BUTLER, BYTHELL, CANDY, CLARK, Miss CLYDE-SMITH, CROOK, CURRIE, FARRANT, GODDARD, HARTLEY, ISSAC, MARSTON

SECOND ROW (DAIRY FARMING):

Miss RHODES, PIPER, PEARCE, MOULD, Miss MERRIFIELD, Miss MANGHAM, JONES, Miss HART, Miss DONCASTER, BOYCE, Miss BOLWELL
(AGRIC.Contd.) - WEST, WEDMORE, STACEY, SHEARS, RAMSEY, PHELPS, MORRIS, McCAULEY

THIRD ROW (GEN. HORTICULTURE) - KNIGHT, JELLIS, HUTCHINS, HAMMER, ELLIS, DAVIES, AUCOTT, ADDISON
(CITY & GUILDS) - SMITH, POORE, POOLEY, Miss PENGELLY, NUNN, JOHNSTONE, JACKSON, HIBBERD, HILL, EARLEY, Miss CUMBES,
CLARKE, BYNOTH, BAKER, ADAMS

BACK ROW (GEN. HORTICULTURE Contd.) -
LITTLER, McLEAN, MORGAN, REES, SMITH, TREVAN, WALTERS, WOODMARK, (COMMERCIAL HORTICULTURE) - CROSSE, DOWN, ELLARD, GILLMAN,
GOSDEN, GRIGG, HOCKING, MARTIN, MEREDITH, RACKLEY, THORBURN, WHITE, A.R., WHITE, M.J. Miss WILTON

1968

1969/70 Session

k Row (General Agriculture) Left to Right:

ATTFiLL, CHANT, CLYDE-SMITH, CRANG, GRAHAM, GIBSON, HARDICK, HAYMAN, JONES, LLOYD, MILDON, MUSGRAVE, OWEN, RAWLE, REED, ROBBINS, RYALL, SIMMONS, SMALLDON, STEPHENS, SWIFT, TAYLOR, WATTS, WESTWORTH, WINGATE-SAUL, WHOOLEY.

Row (Dairy Farming)

ADLAM, MISS CLARKE, COX, MISS DENT, DOROTHY, MISS FLAHEY, MISS GREEN, MISS HAYWARD, HILLIARD, MISS HOBBS, MISS HUGHES, LEIGH, NEWPORT, MISS NICKS, MISS PAGE, STEADMAN, THOMPSON.

Row (Commercial Horticulture)

MISS ALLERY, BUNTING, BURCHETT, FISHER, HARDING, P., HERRING, JACKSON, MISS MATTHEWS, NELDER, POLLARD, PORTMAN, PRANGELL, SILL, STONE, STRIKE, SUMPTION, VOWLES.

Row (Amenity Horticulture)

AVERY, BOURKE, COOKE, CROSS, DOCKER, DOWDING, HARDING, N.S., HAVILL, HEY, HOAR, JONAS, JOY, LE TROQUER, McCANN, MANN, MRS. ROGERS, SAMS, TEMBWE, YOUNG.

t Row (City & Guilds Finals)

1970/71

1971/72

1972/1973

1973/74

1974/75

1975/76

1976-77

1978/79

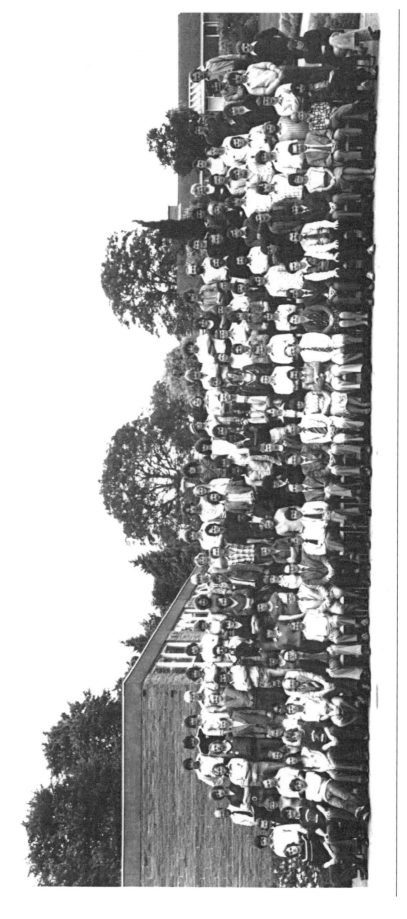

1981/82

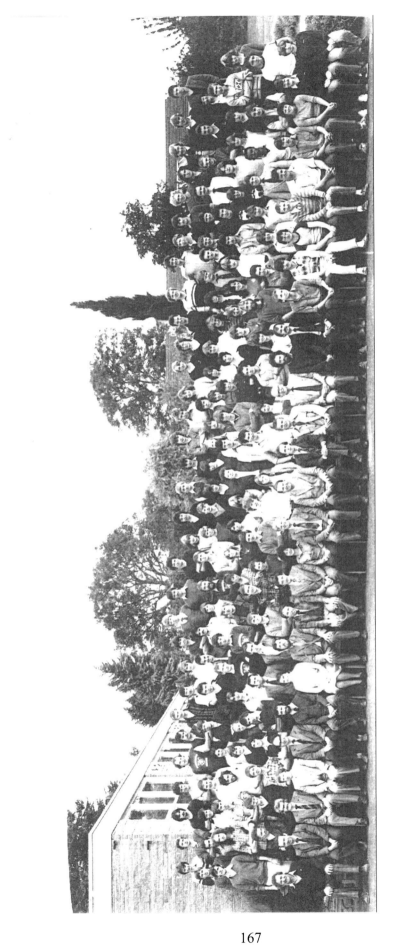

1983/84

1987

GENERAL AGRICULTURE

A.C. Adams, S.A. Baker, R. Bigwood, I.W. Booth, S.P. Breckenridge, P. Carnell,
N. Christensen, I.D. Cook,
S.H. Cooper, J.S. Cox, A. Crang, E.J. Eaves, A. Fewings, A.W. Foot, A.J. Howe,
M.T. Jackson, P.D. James, E.J. Landon, M.C. Lewin-Harris, A.T. Martin, D.J.P. Matthews,
D.J. Merritt, G.F.H. Munro,
C.R. Nicholls, R.M. Orledge, Miss J.E. Parfitt, Miss L.K. Rogers, G.P. Rumary, M.E. Sparks,
A.L. Taylor, A.G. Yardley, R.H. Heal.

1982/83

NATIONAL DIPLOMA IN AGRICULTURE YEAR III 1985/88

Bartlett R G; Cheffey M A; Davey R W; Fox J C; Hawthorne J R R (missing);
Lole M A ; Mitchell S D; Raine C F (absent); Tyler S J; Mr D Capel (missing)

1985/88

CITY & GUILDS 015 ENGINEERING 1987/88

Collins L; Cox A J C; Goodall A P;
Heydon C W; Woods C A; Mr I D Whitehead.

1887/88

Cannington COLLEGE
Quality our Priority

NATIONAL DIPLOMA in HORTICULTURE YEAR III 1988/91

Paul Allen   Toby Beasley   Nick Burgoine   Paula Churcher   Jon Darby   Martyn Davey   Richard Gwatkin
Richard Hobbs   Geoff Holden   Mark Hoskins   Brian Lane   Mick Little   Francis Nobes   Jon Pils
N RIGDEN   Jason Purcher   Andy Powell   Philip Rose   Andrew Rosenfield   Mark Thompson   Andrew Williams J P ADDISON

1988/91

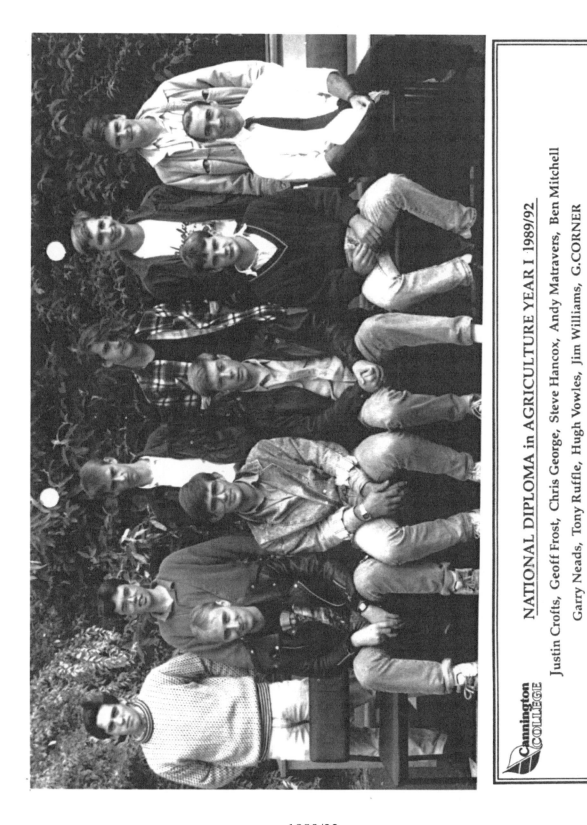

NATIONAL DIPLOMA in AGRICULTURE YEAR I 1989/92

Justin Crofts, Geoff Frost, Chris George, Steve Hancox, Andy Matravers, Ben Mitchell

Garry Neads, Tony Ruffle, Hugh Vowles, Jim Williams, G.CORNER

Cannington COLLEGE

1989/92

Memories of 1952 - 1985 - by Stuart Brookfield

I can remember clearly my arrival for interview for the post of Senior Horticultural Lecturer, as it was then called, in July 1952. I found far more likely candidates for the post assembled for the tour round the department and was not the only one surprised when I was chosen.

I was welcomed to my job by my colleagues, John Bulford, Tom Maitland (in charge of County Horticultural advice and lectures to outside bodies) and especially vivid in my memory is the cheerful, sun-reddened face of Bill Heyward, who was to be a life long friend and mentor.

I remember staying overnight in the old buildings with an antiquated bathroom and the kindness of Miss Hobbs, the Matron, and the acid wit of Miss Quinlan (in charge of Poultry and soon to be succeeded by June Bell, who died so tragically at a young age). Plus, of course, the inimitable and lovely Miss Monie in the Dairy.

At that time there was only one full-time horticultural course, day-release classes were only just starting and for Machinery, all students had weekly talks from the Machinery Officer of the newly formed NAAS, soon to become ADAS, a Mr Henderson, I believe.

The horticultural course was almost entirely commercial, with good orchards, market garden and the 1930s glasshouse unit in the walled gardens reinforced by two 100' long wooden glasshouses at Crockers, heated by primitive coke-fired boilers, sunk in deep stoke holes full of sulphurous fumes for the poor students doing glasshouse duties - it would be banned as a health hazard today.

Tom Maitland was very helpful and his staff provided support in the science classes he had established and a very successful Federation of garden Clubs which strangely petered out after some 15-20 years, only to have a strong rebirth during the end of my time at Cannington. A special event started by Tom and my predecessor, Bill Lewis, a year or two before I came to Cannington, was the Annual Bulb Show, held on the first Saturday in March. This grew and flourished greatly for 45 years and gave great pleasure to a large public in Somerset and provided exceptionally good experience for the students in organising and building a successful show - I was very sad when this closed during the tragic decline of Horticulture during the 1990s. It was a regular, unofficial reunion time each year for ex-students and staff.

In the early years of my stay at Cannington I was able to make the horticultural unit into a profitable and successful business and to modernise the famous orchards and develop the glasshouse unit at Crockers with a diversity of glasshouse types and enterprises. Gradually, however, the advent of specialist nurseries and modern techniques led to difficulties for such a small mixed holding and eventually in the 1980s the costs and falling numbers of students led to the abandonment of specialist commercial courses, while the more recently introduced course for Amenity Horticulture flourished and led to Horticulture, having - of all departments - the largest number of full-time students at the College during the second half of the 1970s and in the 1980-90 period.

The gradual switch to concentrating on Amenity horticulture started in a small way in 1962, with a course called 'Horticulture Parks'. Five students were enrolled but only four completed the course - one could not keep up with the pace! Then it became the 'National Certificate course in Amenity Horticulture' (NCH), with an 'Advanced course in Amenity Horticulture' (ANCH) following in 1970. Ordinary Diploma (OND) soon followed - a three year 'sandwich' course with the middle year spent in employment with selected employers making a total of 4 years in all, including the essential one year practical work before admission to the three year course. By the end of 4 years they were able and responsible people capable of holding down responsible posts in the diverse branches of amenity horticulture - parks, National Trust and famous gardens, War Graves Commission, nursery practice, arboriculture and many other branches. Quite a number went on to take the full National Diploma in Horticulture of the Royal Horticulture Society - the hallmark for many years of well qualified horticulturalists. I would encounter ex-students in major posts very often in future years when judging at county shows, Britain in Bloom etc. And I also enjoyed acting as examiner for the RHS and as Governor for Long Ashton Research Station.

Denzil Little, Michael Snelgrove and Mary Helliar (ex-student) were the staff responsible for the development of the walled gardens and new sites into teaching units for Amenity Horticulture with Denzil as the Senior Lecturer, to be succeeded by the redoubtable Roy Cheek, a great Plantsman with a strong parks background, unbounded enthusiasm, receiving high honours from the RHS.

Appendix

Other members of the horticultural staff over the years were John Bulford, who later became No.1 nationally for horticultural training with the Agricultural Training Board (ATB), Bob Caldwell, who later became Head Gardener for the Bishop of Bath and Wells, John Sutton who developed a strong student interest in his hobby of caving and helped develop the 'new' glasshouse unit at Crockers - this was to be reinforced in the 1970s with the 'New' Amenity Glasshouse range in the walled gardens, now replaced in its turn!

After John came Dick Harding who later became Rector (or Vicar?) of Pershore. Later on we had another religious switch in Elfrida Savigear, who was in charge of Science for some years before becoming Vicar for a group of parishes in West Somerset including Sampford Brett and Stogumber, where she still officiates. Stuart Chambers comes into this group in a way since he preached at Chilton Polden, as well as David Husband, a regular preacher at Spaxton.

These in turn were succeeded by Keith Sims - a loyal and faithful friend whom I often see regularly, Brian Thames, John Docker, John Bates, John Addison, Pam Holt and others who could all tell you interesting bits about the development and decline, unfortunately, of the Horticultural Department in the 80s and 90s.

All through these years the strong, well loved, Nina Heywood operated as Deputy Matron and then, after the retirement of Miss Hobbs, as full Matron and anchor figure for the OSA. She and Nan Eaves ought to be joint Patrons, known to all, unlike me - I was unknown to most agricultural and dairying students!

I should mention a few of the additional short courses we ran, such as 'Life on the land' for school children keen on Rural Science (p.59 - Ed.), regular one day courses for the visually handicapped gardeners, sizable (3 x 1 month) courses for Rural Science Teachers etc. As for Day-Release courses in Horticulture I must pay tribute to David Husband who worked tremendously hard for the courses at Cannington, Yeovil and Radstock. He was a fierce Scotsman who fought hard to see his students receive fair treatment and preached regularly at Spaxton Church. Sometimes his enthusiasm would lead him to use harsh words to those who seemed to oppose his ideas, followed by contrite periods. It was very sad that he should die from the effects of asbestos insulation at quite a young age.

I must turn to those Governors and their kin who helped horticulture become so important at Cannington. The Chairman of the Agricultural Education Committee when I was appointed was a quiet and formidable man, Mr Woodhouse, who, at a subsequent meeting reproached me for not addressing him as 'Sir', which rather took the wind out of my sails!

The Chairman of the Horticultural sub-committee was a dear man, a fruit grower from Milverton, Mr Wimbush, who gave me full encouragement and when he was nearing retirement, offered me the post of Manager at Ryvers Farm, which I declined with regret.

He was succeeded by a leading member of the sub-committee, Mr David Hebditch of New Cross Fruit Farm, who was a splendid Chairman and great friend for many years until, most unfortunately, he succumbed to the horrors of Parkinson's Disease.

A leading light on this sub-committee was Cliff Perry who was manager of the Hoskyns Fruit Farm at North Perrott and had been assistant Fruit Adviser under Mr Forshaw and took a deep and lasting interest in all that we did at Cannington, sending both his son John and daughter Sally to Cannngton as students, with whom I kept in touch for quite a long time - perhaps this will stir them to join me in what I call 'Pay Back Time'.

After the sad death of David Hebditch, our new Chairman was Philip Rowe, elder son of the famous Frank Rowe, chrysanthemum grower at Rockwell Green, Wellington, who retained the post until I retired in 1985 but who sadly died soon afterwards. We owe a great debt to these members of the sub-committee and in later years especially to two stalwarts - both ex-students from the early years of the SFI - John Dunster and Victor Verrier, the latter becoming Chairman of the Advisory Panel, as it became known.

For any important members of the committees and of the staff whom I have omitted to mention, please forgive the failing memories of an 86 year old! But I must briefly mention John Hudson, Head of Machinery for many years and his irrepressible helpmate, Goff Berridge, Tom Sprot - farm crafts instructor, and for most of my days at Cannington, the unique pair of Stan Acland and Bill White from the Farm. What a shame both of these were not made to reminisce on tape with their wonderful Somerset voices and humour. Perhaps others will enlarge on some of these and bring in AJ, Cy Bartlett and of course, dear Phil Keen at the helm.

Each year of most of my time at Cannington there were a number of highlights at which old students were to return in various guises.

There was the annual Spring Flower Show which grew and grew until it was attracting about 3000 visitors and a large number of professional and trade exhibitors. - probably the largest Spring Show in the south west. As a regular exhibitor, I was very proud one year to win the cup for most points given in memory of a student who was tragically killed in a road crash. The show gave rise to similar shows at Wisbech College and at least three schools in Somerset, by their Rural Science teachers who had attended our courses.

Then there were the Open Days developed largely under the friendliest of Principals, Philip Keen, which became major local events attracting thousands of visitors and many ex-students (p.69 - Ed.). Each Department drew up plans for involving all the students in demonstrating skills, often with an entertainment value involving young visitors - bait perhaps to entice future students. Guided tours and demonstrations of gardening techniques and plant sales were popular - and a great day out for the whole family. What a loss when these wonderful days petered out with the general decline of the college during and after the 'no good' nineties.

In common with our rival college at Askham Bryan in Yorkshire, each January saw a large number of management staff from the world of Amenity Horticulture make their way from all points of Britain, including Scotland and Ireland, to attend a 'refresher' course for 3 days with speakers of national importance - a miniature version of the Oxford Conferences held also in the post Christmas breathing space, effectively pruning the Christmas festivities for the horticultural staff. While Askham Bryan concentrated on attracting only the most senior Parks officers and the like, we seemed to be more appreciated by those with the middle and more diverse management responsibilities, putting the name of Cannington high on the list of centres for leadership in practical management development - the other occasions were also most agreeable and enjoyable reunions for our many friends in the horticultural world.

There are so many ex-students who have had most interesting careers and who have a great affection for Cannington, my plea to them is to repay sometime something of the magic which they had from us in the form of articles for the magazine, however short and pithy, and in the form of short talks at the AGMs of COSA - 'PAY BACK TIMES'. All of you ought to do so!

Stuart Brookfield
July 2006

Work Based Learning - Day Release Classes
by Caroline Woolley

The system of Education in the Land Based sector that underpinned the College from early days involved students working in their respective sphere of employment - be it agricultural or horticultural - and attending classes in the theory of their speciality mostly on one day each week for a prescribed number of terms, although sometimes this training was delivered in 'blocks' of weeks and the students became residents at the College.

These classes served the land based sector well and young people were able to assimilate practical skill and theory in a non-academic atmosphere.

Many young people then chose to go on to a full-time course already having completed a year of practical work. This pre-College year was part of the entrance requirements in the early days.

In 1960, on our day at college we studied Foods and Feeding, Grassland and Crops - one subject in each of three terms. At the end of the academic year we took a Union of Educational Institutes (UEI) Examination in those three subjects.

This was superseded by City & Guilds Phase I and Phase II Certification representing four 'years' of study. Crops and Livestock represented the major part and Machinery accounted for about a quarter.

There was also available Phase III and Phase IV - Accounts and Management - which together with Phases I and II led to a Full Technological Certificate (FTC).

The Youth Training Scheme appeared during the 1970s and this scheme enabled a variety of farmers and growers to support a young person on their holding while earning a Government Fee for so doing. The YTS person also received a small allowance with the knowledge that a job might be forthcoming at the end of it all. This was not always the case! Young people still regarded this as a possible pre-college year although this was not the intention. The YTS Scheme was devised to train the young person to employability within the sector.

Further refinement of this system moved away from allowances for farmers and growers, increased the allowance to the young person and required the employer to pay this allowance, pushed 'employed status' and introduced 'Modern Apprenticeships' where all young people had to be employed but allowed their time at college as part of the job. It was remarkable the stories that we were told about wily employers!

Gradually also the City & Guilds system of examination fell by the wayside as National Vocational Qualifications (NVQ) were introduced. No 'exams' but 'continuous assessment' in the workplace and proof of 'underpinning knowledge' from the participant were the only requirements. Students could gain a Level I - 'can assist with the task'; Level II - can complete the task; and Level III - 'can show someone else how to do the task'. This system is still in place. A course of study to Level III will take a person at least three years. The NVQ system is linked to the way in which colleges are funded since the Local Education Authority is no longer responsible for the fortunes of any Further Education College.

As mentioned elsewhere, there was a hive of 'day-release' activity from the 1960s until the middle 1990s - or 'extra mural' as it was better known for many years. There were 'out-centres' at Yeovil, as mentioned, Radstock, Taunton, Weston-super-Mare and eventually, Langford: University of Bristol Vet. Med. HQ, Liscombe, the experimental Grass Centre on Exmoor, Cannington main site, Blaise Castle in Bristol and Wisley Golf Club in London.

In one case David Capel started a Hill Farming City & Guilds Phase I and II at Liscombe with fourteen students (three employed by the centre) which eventually moved to Minehead when YTS took over.

Prior to 1965 there were Welding classes held in the evenings at Wincanton, working out of Yeovil College with a dedicated team of lecturers under the guidance of Neville Charles. His team included Claude Simpson: Machinery; Mike Smith and John Horsey: Horticulture; Frank Facey: Machinery; Ian Churchill, Tim Hunt and Graham Corner: Agriculture.

After Neville retired Yeovil changed tack, started full-time courses, moved to a separate building and later staff included Chris Baker, Gareth Hughes and John Snook.

Back at 'Main Site' in the 70s the late Peter Mead managed Extra Mural classes and all staff at the 'out-centres'. The team included Derek Bowden, Richard Newman, David Capel, Dick Heal, Steve Trice (Minehead), Trevor Powell, Peter Taylor, Alan Cannell, Phil Jowett, Roy Keyworth (sometime Head of

Machinery following John Hudson) Phil Kearn, Bob Smallwood, Richard Warburton, Malcolm Coat and Geoff Hester. By the time that the late Tony Udall joined the team from Brymore and had hundreds of young people on his books, the system had changed again and the out-centres were reduced to Yeovil only, Tony visiting all students in the workplace; and they were taught by designated College staff at either Cannington or Yeovil. Tony was then joined by Barbara Gray, Nigel Swaine and Caroline Woolley.

Years earlier Stuart Brookfield headed the Horticultural team at Cannington, and his staff included John Addison, Keith Sims, and Nick Rigden. Steve Hasell looked after horti. machinery.

In the 1980s Caroline Woolley was teaching something called 'Personal Effectiveness Skills' to reluctant young farmers as part of the early YTS Scheme, this 'subject' later became an integral part of the YTS philosophy. Jon Dubery was part of the team and of course, Stuart Christie. Later still Matthew Riddle, Geoff Millar, Marshall Clements and Chris Rusling became part of the underpinning knowledge delivery team.

The fortunes of the 'Extra Mural' Department have changed considerably over the years. Until the late 90s all staff were full-time and were responsible for their particular group as Tutors and for visiting the workplace. But as time moved on the funding system changed and so did the delivery method. Many staff are part-time only, there is now a central team who deal with all Government administration, some of whom set up the work placement and complete all the Health and Safety checks, while others are Assessors in their particular speciality.

Day Release has covered a wide range of subjects, not only agriculture and horticulture but also Agri. and Horti. Machinery, Green-keeping, Arboriculture, Floristry, Horse care and Butchery.

Many young people elect to work and learn this way, although the emphasis from Schools is on full-time college attendance - not always the system for guaranteed jobs, though.

The fortunes of the land-based sector are reflected in the numbers on the Scheme. For example, during the 70s and 80s over 600 young people were on the various extra-mural courses in Somerset; this went down to around 3-400 by the early 90s, and with the downturn in agriculture further reductions meant that this sector now has only about 100 students on Work Based Learning, as it is now called.

Wartime Rural Domestic Economy
by Nan Eaves

Gladys Cunneber (nee Adams) is in her late 80s but her memory is still very sharp (2006). She came to work at Cannington in 1946 in the rural Domestic Economy Department under Mrs. Chisholm.

Gladys tells me this section was opened in 1940/41 on Government advice to help the nation's (wartime) housewives make the most of all home produce and make do and save any article which could be turned to good use.

Mrs. Chisholm, another hardy Scotswoman, who taught bacon curing and treatment of other meat products or substitutes, headed a team of three. Her helpers were Miss Barr, Cookery Specialist, and Miss Coles who grew and preserved Garden or wild produce.

I can remember someone coming to our school and showing us how to make slippers out of dressing gowns and old skirts, and gloves and mittens from scraps. A Mrs Lester from Long Sutton demonstrated the making of hand sewn gloves, and the out-workers from the local glove factories were fascinated as they only ever did one process with their machines!

Fruit bottling and canning was demonstrated, Long Ashton being the specialist advisors, and, of course, wine and jam making.

Another of RDE's lines was household jobbery. - descaling kettles, rewiring, replacing tap washers and even how to replace window panes - any job the man of the house may have done had he been there.

All these R.D.E. activities brought many country folk to the SFI.

This department remained at Cannington until 1948, when it was moved to Taunton and became the Homecraft Service. They even added an urban specialist for the Townswoman's Guild. The service closed in the late sixties, when Technical Colleges ran classes in specialist subjects.

One amusing memory is that when there were W.I. open days the cheese made then had to be put away safely, out of the way of any visiting cheese factor. Invariably it had a strong taint of moth balls as the best coats of the WI members were preserved throughout wartime and post-war shortages by the use of these strong smelling moth repellents! It would not do for a cheese factor to notice the smell in case he condemned all the cheese as being tainted!

The Middle Years: 1952 - 1980
Compiled by Benny Goodman from COSA Magazines

In her introduction to these two sections, 'The Middle Years', by Benny Goodman and 'The Recent Years', by herself, Caroline Woolley writes: Each year includes a mix of highlights gleaned from the Principal's Report together with Editorial comment and here and there a word from the Chairman. Also mentioned will be notable occurrences from Magazine articles and dates to remember.

Attempting to pre'cis almost 30 years of magazine contributions will inevitably result in some vital piece of information being omitted. Sometimes, too, the year recorded may be wrong. Apologies, dear reader, if this has been the case.

1952. a notable year for the SFI when Life Membership of the OSA stood at 250 out of a total membership of 450 and cost two guineas per head compared with an annual fee of five shillings (25p,)!

W.D.Hay OBE B.Sc. commented that in contrast to pre WW2 days there was now huge competition for youngsters to get on the first rung of the farming ladder despite there being some 350,000 farm units in England and Wales. He extolled the virtues of dedication and hard work as the basis for a successful career.

Chairman R.J. Shattock urged old students to respond to the county's call for "greater effort in the production from the land".

While the county was adjusting to the death of King George VI earlier in the year, the agricultural industry was dealing with Foot & Mouth Disease outbreaks. and W.J. England left Cannington to go to East Africa (Kenya) and a new Principal W.W. Ballardie BSc, NDD was appointed.

Other notable changes at SFI were the departure of W.H.Lewis from the Horticultural Department to Studley College and Mr Scott-Millar, Agri. Dept., to Dunmow, Essex, to farm on his own account.

Notable arrivals included Mr Lewis's replacement - Mr S.H. Brookfield BSc and his assistant R.G. Bulford, who successfully engineered a whole new era for Horticultural Education at the Institute. In addition B.C. Thomas B.Sc., fresh out of Reading University joined the Agricultural Department to enhance extra mural studies activities.

Other 'snippets' emphasise the differences between 1952 & 2006: the attendance of ex Dairy student M.Esden at the Bath & West Show - held at Nottingham, and a reference to the Royal Show being held at Newton Abbott!

In these days of high fuel costs - a local agricultural machinery firm H.Kelland & Co of Combwich were promoting a Turner diesel tractor and Yeoman plough for efficient deep ploughing at only 9d (2p) fuel cost per acre!

1953. G. Jarrett, Editor of the COSA magazine made a stout defence of the SFI against outside criticism triggered by the poor financial performance at the Institute, especially in the Horticultural sector.

Chairman R.J. Shattock noted the rapid change from "greater production" in 1952/53 to an emphasis on "quality and marketing" in the field of Agriculture and Horticulture during 1954 and beyond. As so many times was his lot, A.J.Marval as Vice Principal ably stood in for the Principal Mr. Ballardie who experienced ill health during the year.

The Horticultural Department, under the guidance of S.H. Brookfield, streamlined its cropping policy to create fewer but better performing crops. The Dept. also provided 3 out of the 11 'credits' in the NCH Examinations nationally. Not to be outdone the Agri. Dept. received their first ever Combine Harvester - a Ransome 4ft trailer model.

On the social side the students had an active year - interacting with Dorset, Wilts, Glos and Devon Farm Institutes, and fielding a broad range of sports teams including Rugger, Soccer, Hockey, Table tennis, Netball, Cricket & Tennis - reflecting the huge contribution made by the SFI staff in energising the student body as a whole.

Page 38 - mention of Miss Loxton (ex SFI student) on staff at Seale Hayne. (Sister: Head of Dairying - Ed.)

A.J. Marval - after careful research was able to confirm that 1 in every 5 students who have passed through Cannington have actually achieved their life's ambition of farming or growing on their own account. Moreover, the vast majority of students have remained in Agriculture or Horticulture in various capacities - thus confounding critics who claim that Institute training is a waste of public money!

The 1953 Magazine included letters from ex students in overseas locations including Kenya, New Zealand, Canada, Holland, Denmark, Egypt and Cyprus - indicative of the spread of SFI influence worldwide!

G. Jarrett, SFI Magazine Editor sent a copy of the 1952 publication to H.M. the Queen on 28.4.53 and received an acknowledgment of receipt with thanks from her Private Secretary. One wonders what she thought of the 'goings on' in Crockers - if she ever read it!

1954. No surviving magazine copy.

1955. A year in which the summer was very warm in contrast to the previous two years. In 1955 the very first Annual Speech Day was inaugurated during which Earl Waldegrave presented the prizes and stated in his speech that Cannington was "now well known throughout most of the world and was held in high regard" etc. The year was one of consolidation on the Institute Farm with some preoccupation re testing of new silage preservatives.

Stuart Brookfield reported that the plantation yielded the highest apple crop ever, although the plum crop was almost non-existent.

Partially successful experiments were carried out on fruit trees using 245T - now banned.

Cannington was one of 3 countrywide Centres selected to conduct "Preliminary Field Trials" on behalf of NIAB - testing 14 new Winter Wheat varieties in addition to several new Spring varieties. The other centres selected were Cambridge and Edinburgh.

1956. Stan Acland, the doyen of Cannington farm staff was awarded the BEM in the Queen's Birthday Honours List. This event outshone even a visit from the Minister of Agriculture Mr Heathcote Amory to Cannington for prize giving. The Minister in his speech to the students & staff extolled the virtues of the Institute's courses and hoped that other young people would be encouraged to join the Institute to make up the temporary shortage of numbers, largely due to the demands of National Service call-up and vague rumours of the coming of the Nuclear Power Plant locally. There was also a drop in price of fat cattle which depressed farm profits generally over the County. Average 1955 prices £76 per head sold off the farm but in 1956 this had dropped to an average of £58 per head. Such setbacks in 1956 were exacerbated by drought conditions resulting in reduced yields with poor hay and silage yields also.

To boost farm profits Cannington elected to have two cattle herds - the existing Shorthorns at Rodway and a new Friesian herd at Court Farm.

1957. A year during which TV became available to farmers and Cannington/Combwich locality changed for ever due to the preparation work associated with the forthcoming construction of the Hinkley Point Nuclear Power Station. Road widening from the start of the Combwich Lane northwards resulted in the Village War Memorial being moved 'lock stock and barrel' westwards; the old familiar banks and hedges (so valuable for stock shelter) being eliminated with the Toll Cottage - all in aid of improving access to the construction site. The ancient sleepy port of Combwich was given a 'make-over" to prepare it for its major role in receiving heavy nuclear equipment imported by ship. Despite these enormous upheavals, the natives appeared to be philosophical about it all. The Principal, W.W.Ballardie reported that the previous year's drop in the farm's profit had been offset this year, with the help of the increase in milk production due to the new higher yielding Friesian herd created in 1955.

In September the SFI hosted its first international Conference of Young Farmers with delegates from such far flung places as Australia, Ghana, Southern Rhodesia, Germany, Channel Islands and Ulster.

1958. This proved to be an exceptionally wet season which hampered crop management and performance alike.

The SFI lost its longstanding N.I.A.B. trials this year while the farm discovered to its surprise that the new Friesian herd's average butterfat outperformed that of the Shorthorns by a comfortable margin! Murphy's Law dictated that the Horticultural Department, in conjunction with NAAS, held a successful irrigation demonstration in May. In this wet season few if any occasions occurred thereafter this year for irrigating crops in Somerset!

The extramural activities of the Institute have increased significantly with all manner of training subjects being catered for throughout the County, at centres including Yeovil, Taunton, Paulton, Wincanton, Frome, North Cadbury, Exmoor, Bath and many more.

1959. In contrast to 1958 this was a season of prolonged drought and fine weather - that caused many crop and livestock problems. The irrigation systems installed at Court Farm and elsewhere, hardly used in the wet 1958 season, proved invaluable this year. Stuart Brookfield reported that despite living under threat of closure of the Horticultural Department from the de la Warr committee report, prospective student numbers continued to increase. Only two years previously the then Minister of Agriculture, Mr Heathcote Amory, had selected SFI to become the centre for Horticultural courses in the south-west of England.. During 1959 de la Warr selected only 7 Institutes to teach Horticulture in England, with SFI excluded. (Damaging interference by politicians in the smooth progress of well established organisations is no new phenomenon!).

Appendix

This year brought the retirement of Mr W.D.Hay - one of the most influential agriculturalists of his day throughout the SW of England. He had been the Director of the Ministry's Experimental Farm at Martyr Worthy in Hants since 1949. Of 25 years spent in Somerset 21 were as Principal of the SFI. He also worked with the NAAS after World War 2 for which he was awarded the OBE.

The quest for improved crop quality and better marketing skills throughout both agriculture & horticulture continued to take priority.

1960. The contrary weather was again a feature of this season with Spring/early summer drought succeeded by an exceptionally wet July-October period. Although hay-making was very successful, other farm operations including cereal harvesting suffered badly and the Horticultural department also experienced many production and harvesting headaches.

The main feature of this year was the outcome of the de la Warr Committee Report which aimed at a comprehensive overhaul & modernisation of the delivery of Agri./Horti. Education. In short, if Cannington with its old buildings, out of date facilities and inadequate student numbers could not rapidly respond and accept the inevitability of a new custom built Institute, accommodating 4 times the current student numbers, then Cannington's days as a leading centre for rural education in the West were numbered. Mr W.W.Ballardie took on the enormous task of accepting the challenge and soon a policy was refined and agreed with the Ministry of Education who wanted work on the new Institute to commence immediately and to be completed by circa 1964/5.

1961. The main item to record is the retirement of Miss Monie, Head Dairying Instructress, after 35 years in service. Another influential and popular staff member, Mr Bryan Thomas (Agri. Instructor) also departed to become Vice Principal at Askham Bryan Institute, Yorkshire, after 9 years service at Cannington.

There is speculation about the general effect on British agriculture and horticulture if and when Britain joins the European Common Market. The Horticultural Department gave a sigh of relief following the release of the long awaited Lampard Vachel Report which confirmed that horticultural training at Cannington would continue on condition that student numbers were significantly increased. With this objective in view efforts are being redoubled to attract students from neighbouring counties in addition to Hampshire from now on.

1962/3. This year started off with an unprecedented hard winter which continued into late March, having almost paralysed the country's transport and communications system. Land based activities were made proportionately more difficult at the same time.

The SFI reeled from two further blows - the sad death of Miss Monie such a short time after her retirement and the sudden illness of the Principal, Mr Ballardie, who was in hospital for many weeks followed by a lengthy convalescence.

The OSA magazine failed to appear in 1962 mainly due to the termination of the East Hull Press contract to print it.

No doubt the ongoing disruptions caused by construction of Phase 1 of the New Institute buildings, the mounting activity of the Hinckley Point construction scheme in adverse weather, coupled with the continuing uncertainties surrounding the future educational role of the Institute, all contributed to the unusual shortfall in achieving pre-planned targets.

The SFI started to participate in the MAFF Charollais breed testing trial, which signalled the future direction in which livestock farmers in Britain were moving - another example of the way in which Cannington demonstrated its willingness to be in the forefront of development in British Agriculture or to challenge entrenched traditional views.

1964/5. This year featured the retirement due to ill health of Mr Ballardie, the Principal, and the appointment of Mr Marval to the post. The Institute was being transformed into its new identity with major new buildings to accommodate extra student numbers, while the farm and horticultural units were undergoing major reorganisation to cater for the expanded number of courses on offer, as required under the new National Education and Training policies.

The OSA magazine became reduced in quality to a rough printed A4 size publication as a result of significantly increased printing costs and lack of financial backing for the publication.

1965/6. The retirement of Stan Acland after 43 years service to students taking the Agricultural course, attracted many heartfelt tributes to this very special countryman.

In contrast to the previous year, this year's weather was decidedly unkind to agriculture in Somerset, with much spoilt hay and a difficult cereal harvest due to a poor summer. The Institute's Horticultural Department went through a traumatic period with the promised new developments being put on hold. However, the new Decorative Horti. Courses were going well as the traditional cut flower production was replace by Nursery Stock.

Bill Heywood, the Stan Acland of the Horticultural Department, reached his fortieth year of unbroken service to the Institute and to the hundreds of students who had passed through his able hands.

1966/7. Mr Marval felt the need for a less arduous life and Mr Phil Keen DFC BSc from Wye College was appointed Principal in his place. The Institute was still challenged by the enormous upheaval of expansion, modernisation and establishment of new training courses. The once key Dairying course was demoted to Day Release status due to lack of student support - an unthinkable change a few years previously. The stress of change for all staff was eased by the enthusiasm and leadership of the new Principal.

For the first time Farm Management had been added to the curriculum, as had Industrial Dairying as a block course, and other associated training subjects.

Likewise the Horticultural Department with its three new glasshouses and ancillary equipment, had expanded into two principle sections dealing with Parks & Grounds Maintenance, Landscape and Commercial Horticulture.

There was much debate on changing the name of the Institute to "College" in line with other former County Institutes. Once again there was strong local opposition to these policy decisions from "above" but the outcome still remained to be decided.

The completion of the draining of part of Rodway Marsh and subsequent drilling of Winter Wheat on it took place in the past year.

Foot & Mouth restrictions were in place over the 1967 Winter period, which delayed OSA winter meeting and AGM until April 1968.

1968/9. The reclamation of Rodway Marsh continues with some 60 acres drained, with 30 acres to complete next season. The removal of hedges and ditches on Court Farm has necessitated redistribution of fields. All this development coincides with the construction of a second dairy on Rodway Farm and refurbishment of the existing dairy, so that intensification of livestock and milk production can be achieved via paddock grazing systems.

Commercial Horticulture and Amenity Horticulture continued to expand as did the poultry section with new egg laying and rearing units. However, piggery development and new stock housing plans are shelved due to restrictions placed on capital expenditure.

It was announced that Stage 2 of the Institute building development had been officially approved with a start date in 1969. This will create a new office block and bedroom accommodation for up to 100 students.

There was speculation that OND (Ordinary National Diploma) courses may be undertaken by Farm Institutes.

1969/70. The Principal, Mr Keen, reported a record total of full time students at the Institute, 80 divided equally between Agri. and Horti. This total included 12 females. The average age of students was 20½ years, 60% of whom had 2 or more years of previous experience prior to arriving at the Institute. 33% were sons or daughters of farmers or growers and 50% originated from outside Somerset, which reflected the National and Regional nature of some of the courses.

Stimulated by the finest summer for a decade, planned development work and building construction on the farm and elsewhere continued apace, with more land purchased and drained, the top fruit plantations modified and planting intensified. Amenity Horticulture and other courses expanded. The Institute was aiming to accommodate up to 140 students and preparing to introduce Agricultural Diploma Courses for the first time. Over the year some 12,000 guests visited the Institute, including 1,000 at the Spring Bulb Show, 7,000 at the 'Open Day' (over 3 days of events) while 2,000 unexpectedly almost swamped the Institute at the Autumn Gardeners Open Day.

A notable event took place during the 'Open Day', when former Principals including W.D.Hay, W.J.England., W.W.Ballardie and A.J.Marval met for lunch with Chairman M.A.Jeanes, former Chairmen Capt. D.M.Wills and G.C.Woodhouse - and also the Institute Governors - surely a unique gathering of agricultural might! (Photo: page 99 - Ed.).

Spare a thought for the Institute staff, battling to adopt new courses, new crops, new systems and coping with extra work loads and student numbers. Then to add insult - they had to face decimalisation also! How many hectares did they say Court Farm was?

1972/3. As the years pass on so do well loved and respected Cannington Staff. A.J.Marval retired in 1971 together with Miss Hobbs, followed in 1972 by stalwarts Bill Heywood and Albert Webber. Then Mr Maitland retired in 1973 - marking an end of an era of service to Horticulture in Somerset. The Institute continues to adopt and transform new systems and courses. Its expansion was matched by Cannington village itself, which had 70 houses built over the past 18 months,

OND courses in Amenity Horticulture, Agriculture, Food Technology (Quality Control) and shorter courses covering Agricultural Marketing, Amenity Agriculture and Applied Agriculture were being established at Cannington, together with reintroduction of Building Construction Training. The Institute gardens were opened in May under the National Gardens Scheme with 500 visitors recorded.

Appendix

Miss K.D. Maddever OBE, ADAS Regional Dairy Husbandry Officer for SW England retired in 1971, and as the World Ploughing Championships were being held in Somerset at the same time Mr Henry Plumb, NFU President, took time out to visit Cannington to make a presentation to her to mark 40 years of outstanding service to Somerset dairy farmers. Some 250 NFU officials attended.

1973/4. Both Cannington and its OSA suffered a grievous loss at the death of Capt. D.M. Wills CBE, JP, Chairman of the Governors, past President and Patron for many years.

The Institute graduated to the title of College. In full: Somerset College of Agriculture & Horticulture. The old Cannington Court, in keeping with the new status, underwent a 'makeover' with new fire prevention and safety systems installed.

The farm suffered 2 years of Brucellosis and the loss of over 50 cows with the abandonment of the Accreditation Scheme.

To keep up with external trends, the College decided to adopt a five day working week, but to balance a shortfall of working hours the half-term breaks were abandoned. Academic progress was satisfactory. Residential student numbers reached 129.

The Cannington Student's bar licence was not renewed (for reasons not reported). So for a month students had no bar!

1977. The OSA magazine changed radically in form, with a fresh title: "The Cannngton Echo". The College continues to digest all its new training responsibilities and achieve the standards external authorities now impose on such Educational Institutions. The OSA was teetering on the edge of collapse as the inflationary situation escalated and members concentrated on financial survival.

1978. Due to revamping of the OSA organisation, its finances improved and now it was becoming proactive and self-supporting once more.

The College had 150 full time students and 500 on Day Release courses.

The creation of the administrative county of Avon siphoned off 30% of Somerset's population, a factor which the Principal and others were examining carefully in case of adverse effects on Somerset student recruitment for the future.

The death of Mr B.A.Galloway, Head of the Dairy and Food Technology Department, was reported. He was only in his mid forties. This gifted and much respected family man soon made his mark on arriving at Cannington - at the College, among the students, in the village and in the county generally. He had succeeded no less a personage than Miss Monie.

1978/80. The Principal, Mr Keen, reported a year of consolidation on the farm, with planned developments having to be financed out of profits and thus taking longer than expected to complete.

The Commercial and Amenity Horticultural Departments were adversely affected by the severe winter frosts which killed off some crops. The OSA May Ball, held in the old college (Cannington Manor) proved an outstanding success, attracting in excess of 100 pre 1940 students. Organised by Pat Carr with the able assistance of Noreen (Rum) Selway, a distinguished list of guests were present, among whom were Mr & Mrs Keen, Miss K.D.Maddever, Miss E.M. Hobbs, Mr & Mrs D. Lovell, G.Jarret, Nan Eaves and Stan Acland BEM.

Sadly Stan Acland's death came on Boxing Day in 1979. A legend and an era passed from view and no more would countless Cannington students be called "Johnny" or "Mary" depending on their sex. This ploy served Stan well throughout his distinguished career since he did not need to memorise new student names each year, nor cause offence to any old student whose name was beyond his recall.

Early preparations for suitably marking the SFI's Diamond Jubilee in 1981 were under discussion.

The Recent Years: 1980-2004
Compiled by Caroline Woolley from COSA Magazines

Each year includes a mix of highlights gleaned from the Principal's Report together with Editorial comment and here and there a word from the Chairman. Also mentioned will be notable occurrences from Magazine articles and dates to remember.

Attempting to pre'cis almost 30 years of magazine contributions will inevitably result in some vital piece of information being omitted. Sometimes, too, the year recorded may be wrong. Apologies, dear reader, if this has been the case.

Heralding the 1980s was the **Diamond Jubilee** of the opening of the Somerset Farm Institute in 1921. George Jarrett (Editor of the Magazine at that time) pointed out that when the Institute was founded no one imagined it would reach College status and he hoped that the young people of the day would be as happy as he had been and would carry on the proud traditions of the Farm Institute.

1980. Stan Acland BEM, died on December 26th 1980. Members of the Old Students Association were pall bearers at his funeral on 2nd January 1981. There are many references to Stan throughout this Chronicle, so suffice it to say that an era had come to an end!

'Goff' Berridge retired from the Machinery Department in December 1980, having been at the College for 29 years. Ex-Students of those years will remember someone of original and creative mind and who, over the years, helped keep dozens of student cars legally on the road!

1981. Alan Brownsey, Chairman, reported that a dinner was to be held on September 4th 1981 to commemorate the **Diamond Jubilee**. He also commented that the economy was failing and that massive unemployment and rising fuel costs were not helped by the appalling harvest weather of that year.

There is an interesting article in the 1981 magazine about the Farm Based Recreation Information Centre at Cannington which looked at the burgeoning Tourist Industry and provided a Centre for farmers wishing to establish tourist and recreational enterprises. This had been the brainchild of Principal Phil Keen more than ten years earlier.

1982. This year saw the 50th Anniversary of the Young Farmers' Movement.

A report of the Diamond Jubilee Dinner, which 182 guests attended - including even some 1921 students - quoted a favourite adage of the guest speaker, Ralph Whitlock's "Here's to this ole house. May the roof of it never fall in, And those who walk in never fall out"

A main article in the Magazine was about the Milk Marketing Board, contributed by a local Board member, Denley Brown (p.100, Ed.). Little did we know at the time that this Institution would be dismantled in favour of 'free enterprise'!!

This was the year which, on the Downs, saw the opening of the new training centre for West Country Blacksmiths. The new generation of 'Smiths' fashion wrought iron into accessories for the home. Comfortable shoes for the 'toiler of the soil' as working horses were once known, are now made by 'Farriers'. This centre was the creation of one Frank Day - 'That man is a legend in his own lifetime' was only one of the accolades given about Frank on his 'retirement' in 1980. Frank had, during his working life advised blacksmiths the length and breadth of Britain. The work he did after his retirement was always 'without charge'.

1983. Editor since 1947, George Jarrett died on February 6th in Clevedon at the home he shared with his sister Connie. By this time he had been elevated to Patron and a few words were collected from him in early January. His memories were such happy ones and he would not have missed his time at Somerset Farm Institute in 1934/35 for anything.

The Principal reported that new educational challenges resulted in the appointment of 7 new staff and establishing many new courses including the introduction of Rural Skills and Food Technology. Cannington Creamery on the Minehead road was opened and the College was involved with the new range of Lymeswold cheese initiated by the Milk Marketing Board.

1984. The Magazine reported that ex-Principal Jack England had died in September 1983 in Kenya where he had gone in 1951 as Principal of the Egerton College of Agriculture at Nakuru. Jack England started his working life with SFI as Warden following his time as a student. He then became Vice-Principal and subsequently Principal and was an integral part of the 'Stute' throughout the war years.

This was the year that Miss Evelyn Hobbs MBE passed away. She had served as College Matron from 1947 until 1971. The Gilbert and Sullivan productions were all the more decorative through Miss

Hobbs' ministrations to the wardrobe department. A Thanksgiving for her Life was held at Cannington Church on May 16th 1984.

In this year the Magazine featured an account of the Young Farmers Movement and Cannington's contribution to it through WDHay and Miss Maddever (p.101). Early clubs in the Long Sutton area had been initiated through the "Rural Community Council" in order to 'improve the production of rabbits' (Presumably these were domestic rabbits - wild rabbits notoriously needed no encouragement to multiply in those days before myxamatosis - Ed).

1985. The Principal reported, in a 10 year update that the new Food Hall was under construction - it was subsequently named the 'Galloway' Building to commemorate Brian Galloway who had arrived at SFI in 1961 and who sadly passed away a few years before 1985. He mentioned, too, the Youth Training Scheme (YTS) an extension to the Day Release Scheme that had enabled those young people that preferred to remain 'at home' to work, to take part in agricultural training and to work towards certification with City and Guilds examinations without the need to attend the College full time.

The engineering department was by this time able to function independently of the agricultural department and had introduced several new courses and the advent of the Jack Humphrey building dedicated to the County co-ordinator of the National Association of Agricultural Workers (NAAW) which doubled the practical working space of the department. The Centre was officially opened by the Rt. Hon. Tom King MP for Bridgwater and Minister of Employment on 26th January 1985.

In his address to the annual gathering of student prize winners, Dr. JD Leaver (Farm Director at Crichton Royal Farm, West of Scotland Agricultural College in Dumfries) spoke of the new era in which agriculture was moving. He mentioned that two hundred and fifty years earlier 95% of the country's labour force was engaged in the production of food for the other 5%, and that in 1984 3% were involved in agriculture supporting the other 97% and their families!! He also added that the good news was that Agriculture and Horticulture would continue to be important as an industry in that we ll have to eat and to take pleasure in the countryside!

During this year Stuart Brookfield, Head of Horticulture, retired having joined the College in 1952. He was presented with a crystal decanter and a large cheque - some of which he used , for his wife and himself, on a joint lifetime membership of the National Trust.

1985 was a very busy year at the College. The OSA was finally able to see the culmination of 4 years effort to create a small covert of trees at the entrance to the Downs. Many were the luminaries that attended the ceremony, led by Victor Bonham-Carter from Exmoor who planted a tree in memory of his cousin Basil Bonham-Carter and all ex-students who fell during the conflict.

Mentioned earlier, the much loved 'Goff' Berridge died during the Christmas break in 1985.

As Cannington was an important centre in the Womens Land Army wartime training programme, during 1985 a Reunion was held to commemorate the 40 years since the WLA was disbanded.

1986. The Principal reflected that the budget was now approaching £3 million and that the initial suspicion about milk quotas was abating, but nevertheless new approaches to management were surely to follow the new challenges that this system will throw up. He also noted that conservationists were being listened to by agriculturalists all with a common aim to preserve the best of the past.

A familiar sight in the centre of the village of Cannington was finally removed despite continued efforts to conserve it. Known as the 'Willow Tree' but actually a Holly Oak, it became rotted in its trunk. (Benny Goodman suggests it was really a 'Holme Oak', which seems most likely - Ed.). So much a part of the Cannington atmosphere was this tree that it has been segmented and villagers were allowed substantial parts of it to carve into mementos. The major part of the tree has been utilised around the College.

David House (1948/49) described his year as NFU County Chairman and the business of trying to run a farm at the same time.

1987. The Principal wrote that his lasting memory was of the 1985/86 winter, particularly February, which kept the ground locked in unrelenting frost until after the Spring Bulb Show. Margaret Daly, the then MEP for the area opened the Brian Galloway building, the new Dairy and Food Technology building mentioned earlier.

Miss Nina Heywood, Cannington's longest serving in-house staff member retired this year after 39 years as both Matron and Assistant Matron.

This was also the first year that the proposed Cannington by-pass was discussed with several routes considered, one of which would have segmented the Downs in half and much thought was given to students on tractors dodging the traffic!

Land that the College owned at Tone Vale was exchanged for land at Putnell, opposite the Grain Store. Pigs had returned to Rodway and there was an anticipated merging of the then two dairy herds into one.

Many students were taking advantage of study tours to other parts of Europe and likewise their counterparts were visiting Cannington.

The weather caused further havoc in March when the whole of the facade on the right hand side of Cannington Court collapsed onto the roof behind. (p.103). Amazingly no-one was hurt.

1988. Mr Keen retired this year after 21 years as Principal and his place was taken by David Chapman.

The farm bought a small herd of Aberdeen Angus suckler cows and proceeded to gain local fame by showing these at various local agricultural events. Ashford farm was purchased with the idea that an Organic Unit could be created within this small holding. The new flock of sheep produced lambs at a percentage of over 200%!

The new glasshouse at Crockers continued to produce flowers for the floristry department.

1989. It was an enormous shock to learn that the new Principal, David Chapman, died in post during this year. As Heads of Department were already experiencing greater responsibilities through extra courses being developed, it was not too onerous a task to continue the day to day running of the College. However, the very able Cy Bartlett took up the reins as acting Principal until a new appointment could be made. David's vision for the College was to be kept in view. Courses in Land Use and Recreation were added to the stable of subjects on offer. Cannington Court was fully restored after the gales of 1987.

There arose the Education Reform Act giving managerial and financial responsibility to Colleges. To be implemented by 1993.

The Royal Horticultural Society established links with Cannington in their programme for Rosemoor in North Devon with the College hosting practical demonstrations and short courses for R.H.S. members.

This was also the year that the National Trust established a Youth Training Scheme and selected Cannington for off-the-job training.

The College was host to the Organic Way conference held on 11th October 1989. This was very supportive to the new organic venture at Ashford Farm.

The Hinckley Point Enquiry was held at Clifford Hall and a huge financial investment was made by the Central Electricity Generating Board to bring the Hall up to the standard expected by Government officials.

1990/91. Nan Eaves in her first Editorial remarked that as Somerset Farm Institute and Somerset College for Agriculture and Horticulture seemed here to stay, then it was time to have a new - and lasting - name for the Association. "Cannington Old Students Association" seemed to be the most appropriate and was duly adopted. She also mentions that contributions of news etc., for the 60s, 70s, and 80s were very thin on the ground.

Barry Gimbert joined the staff at Cannington as its new Principal in January 1990 and was very conscious of being the fourth such in two years! He mentions that the new equestrian centre at Porters field with two stable blocks and an outdoor school was currently in its first year.

'Duke' Hussey, the then Chairman of the BBC, took over as President of the Royal Bath and West Society at this time and there is a photograph of him with our 'first lady of cheese' - and erstwhile President of COSA, Miss K.D. Maddever.

An innovative measure - Food Tech. West was inspired by two Food Technology staff and attracted well over 100 visitors and 60 exhibitors.

Cannington is now recognised as a centre for Green-keeper training in the South West and a plant centre is opening in the Spring of 1990.

The cows at Rodway were low in their production as a result of two very dry summers and Arthur Bolton took over the Engineering Department from John Hudson who retired in 1989.

Computer facilities continued to grow as did the Home Study and Management courses.

As you see, the College at this time was growing apace. Maybe this is one of the reasons why the cohesive approach enjoyed by so many in the early days was just not going to happen while the College continued to diversify. Lots of little courses and folk not knowing who else was a student and only meeting at the odd disco.. Progress cannot be halted but it does cost dear!

Bill Heywood, Horticultural foreman from 1930 to 1972 died in Taunton on 22nd August 1990. Having been made foreman at the tender age of 18 his quiet authoritarian approach to his craft made him an inspirational man and many hundreds if not thousands of students have benefited from his knowledge and humour. He knew everything about all the fruit trees that he grew and lived his understanding of the ways of plants.

'AJ' Marvel died during 1991, having retired from the College in 1972 as Vice-Principal - a role he preferred! Wonderful man - quiet and unassuming. 'Too nice to be a Principal'!

Appendix

W.W.Ballardie also died in 1991, Principal during the '50s and '60s. It was he who purchased Rodway Farm and installed an irrigation system and a reservoir to aid cow management. He also masterminded day release classes for young people the length and breadth of Somerset.

1992. The role of Matron disappeared this year and in her place was appointed a Student Services Manager, a grand title for one who had a team of wardens to assist. With a larger number of young students on campus the student support team were revamped to address the issues that so young an intake would create.

The College obtained 'Kite Marks' to British Standard BS5750 to indicate excellence with the added bonus that in pursuing this 'rubber stamp' the management of the College improved its own performance. Cannington was the first College of Agriculture and Horticulture to obtain this quality assurance in England.

More news about the 'incorporation' of the College. From the First of April 1993 the College is to be independent of the Somerset County Council and will be responsible for its own Budgets and Finance, land, buildings and assets, drawing down Funding from the new Further Education Funding Council (FEFC). A very exciting new era for Further Education.

The Machinery Department have been instrumental in the setting up of the new Somerset Machinery Association - set up to provide a focus for the industry in Somerset.

Both the Countryside and the Horse Care departments have expanded, creating problems for staff space.

Crockers no longer grows vegetables and so the farm shop has closed. However, the new Plant Sales centre based beside the walled garden is flourishing. Floristry is growing as is Arboriculture. The Food Technology Department continues to liaise with a college in Normandy.

There is now a nine hole professional golf course on the Downs where Downs South and Wadland used to be! The course will be ready for play by July 1993.

Sadly the Somerset Young Farmers, so long sharing occupancy of Cannington Court with the College, have found new premises in the old school at Westonzoyland. Their new premises were officially opened on 6th November by Lord Plumb, MEP. Several old students attended.

1993. 'Incorporation' took place on First April 1993 and the College is now totally responsible for all that it does!

This year there is a report from the Yeovil Centre, where for eighteen years students have attended mostly for day-release studies (p.76 - Ed.). This year some full-time courses are to be introduced. Frank Facey has moved back to Cannington to join the Engineering Department and Neville Charles has retired as Head of Centre.

The Floristry Department is now running a National Diploma in Floristry.

The Tropical Greenhouse in the Cannington Gardens was declared unsafe this year and eventually all the greenhouses were removed and many of the plants therein found their way to the evolving Eden Project near St. Austell in Cornwall. The glass-houses will be replaced one day.

1994. The Principal commented that the College's new paymasters since Incorporation - the Further Education Funding Council - are hard taskmasters and are continually asking for computer returns, statistics, strategic plans and the like.

The number of full-time students has now risen to 520.

The Cannington by-pass became a reality this year, work having started at last.

Departmental reports concentrate on 'X' numbers of students following 'Y' numbers of courses, which makes rather 'dry' reading. However, it was noted that the early days of satellite mapping were first introduced to the Engineering Department, aided by Massey Ferguson, at one of the Somerset Machinery Association meetings.

With the opening of the Golf Course Ron Macrow joined the staff as Golf Manager/Professional. Ron returned to England from New Zealand after five years with their National Golf Foundation.

Cy Bartlett, Vice-Principal, who was seconded to BEC for a couple of years, wrote a long article about the work of this organisation over the past ten years. It had been set up to advance and promote the quality and availability of work-related education and training for people in, or preparing for, employment, and for those planning to progress in further or higher education.

Phil Keen, retired Principal, reminisced on his experiences in a poignant piece covering 60 years of Agriculture in four pages!

1995. It was soon after Phil Keen completed his short autobiography for the COSA magazine for 1994 that he passed away in July 1995. A packed Stogursey church was to give thanks for his very full life and all that he gave. It was Phil Keen who guided Somerset Farm Institute to College status and oversaw it grow in provision from around sixty students to over several hundred, all following a wide range of courses and disciplines. All achieved with an ever smiling face and unfailing courtesy and this reflected the kind and thoughtful nature with which he was blessed.

A rather 'tough' Audit resulted in the suspension of the Principal and the staff were having to accept a major gear change. This was the first major 'hiccup' since the College became an independent body.

Chairman of the Governors - John Alvis - kindly wrote a reassuring piece about the culture shock of meeting the new Government targets and the effect it was having on the character and ethos of the College in trying to keep tradition and change working forward positively (p.78 - Ed.).

Head of the Senior Management team, Lynn Dudley, gave the Principal's report this year and told how Clifford Hall had been purchased for the College almost a year earlier. The new Golf Club has a membership of 126 - and rising - and the new Animal Care courses at Bristol Zoo and Cricket St. Thomas now included 'exotics'.

During the autumn the College won a prestigious award for the partnership with the National Trust in jointly running the 'Careership Scheme'.

One of the engineering students patented a tractor hitch that was taken up by a major manufacturer to fit as standard to all its range of British tractors.

1996. Richard Hinxman was appointed Principal as from January 1st.

Many staff changes continued to take place as the variety of courses continued to be ever more inventive. To keep up with the changes all departmental reports stressed the new courses being undertaken and the members of staff who were leaving or who had recently joined -.

Richard Swan reminisced on his days at Cannington from the big freeze in 1947/8 until his departure in 1951. He had a busy time then as he was very heavily involved in all the Gilbert and Sullivan productions and the end of term productions as well.

1997. This was the year of the BSE crisis and cattle farmers throughout the land, especially those concentrating on beef, were worried about their future.

The year of the 75th Anniversary started on 27th September 1996 (this was the actual date of the first intake of students in 1921) with an Anniversary Service in the Church at which most student years were represented by COSA members. The Lord Lieutenant of Somerset - Sir John Wills - headed the proceedings, which were overseen by the Bishop of Taunton, Richard Lewis. Lord and Lady Clifford, erstwhile owners of Cannington Court, were also in attendance. (Editor's Note: 1921 Local newspaper reports of the Cannington Opening stated that because of building delays the first term would be a short one, and would not commence until 24th October - page 4).

It was decided to commemorate this Anniversary milestone by creating a Spinney of trees and shrubs adjacent to the lower part of the golf course, across the moor past where St. Brides used to be. Ex-students and staff were invited to contribute towards the cost of a tree. The opening ceremony for this will be in a few years time when the Spinney is established.

A pre-1950s ex-student lunch was held as part of the 75th Anniversary celebrations and 162 people attended! The 1951/70 lunch was attended by over 100 and Miss Heywood was heard to remark in shocked tones that she knew everyone! For the 1970s onwards lunch, a smaller contingent was present.

The Principal reported that students numbers continued to rise and their needs were being catered for despite a further cut back in available funding from the FEFC.

As you know, the River Parrett borders College land and a 'Parrett Trail' has now been established and there will be guide books outlining points of interest from its source in Dorset to its mouth down the 'road' from Combwich.

The Golf Course now has a Clubhouse much to the relief of those players who are caught out on a wet day!

The 1997 COSA magazine devoted itself to reminiscences of Old Student sin looking back over the 75 years.

1998. Richard Hinxman remarked that his £6M Budget 'came in' on target and that there had been 15% growth in student numbers in the previous year, making a total register of 3,900 students. This figure included all full time, part-time and day release students and students at all the out centres. The College was awarded an ' Investor in People' status for quality assurance and general excellence.

This was the year that COSA reorganised its structure and decided not to follow the formal meeting procedure in that by having two coordinators and a treasurer only, other members would feel that they could make a contribution without having to commit themselves to any office holding. The Editor reported that this system worked 'surprisingly' well. She also asked for a replacement but was reassured that help would be given at busy times. It was also decided to discontinue 'Life Membership' as a membership option. The cost of producing one - yes, just one - magazine exceeds the cost of Life Membership as it was 40 years ago!

This year saw the start of Farm Reports from the Manager, Steve Bryant. The 'Cathedral Barn' was erected giving winter shelter to bulling heifers, dry cows, the ewe flock and the pedigree Angus cows and calves. Eventually a calf unit and workshop will be included in the complex.

1999. Referring to 1999 in the 2000 magazine, the Principal's report includes news that Cannington is now the National Centre for Further Education in Zoo Keeping and in Food technology, Regional Centre for Arboriculture, Blacksmithing, Golf Green Keeping, Horticulture and Rural Leisure and Recreation. And the Somerset centre for Agriculture, Countryside Management, Equine Studies and a range of other topics.

COSA reported that the magazine remained the focal point of the Association and that promoting Reunions was extremely important.

It was reported that W.B.Reynolds, first full-time Warden in the '60s had died the previous year. Also that Grace, widow of Jack England, ex-staff, had passed away.

Miss KD Maddever OBE (Patron of COSA) was honoured for her lifetime commitment to the cheese industry, when an inaugural award was made to her by the British Cheese Board.

2000. In the opening to the Year 2000 magazine the Editor reprinted the Editorial to the 1931 magazine. Seems that not one thing had changed! Mr Leeson (the Editor) talked about demands for payment from a variety of agencies (eg: inland revenue, etc.) and inspections about all and sundry by all and sundry - and requests for contributions from old students! He ended by saying that 'whilst realising that the majority of us are engaged in the wrong industry to expect a Prosperous New Year, nevertheless we live in hope'! (The magazine was published at the beginning of the year in those days).

Mr Hinxman also reported that an initiative promoted by Cannington and partnered by the British Wool Marketing Board and the National Farmers Union successfully bid for European Social Funding to underpin training for up to 250 people within the six south-west counties. These folk learnt to shear sheep or honed their existing skills, Shearing in modern parlance, according to Mr.Hinxman is 'wool harvesting'.

The Equine Section Head reported that the year had been very busy for her department and that now National Vocational Qualifications were being offered to day release students working in the horse industry in Somerset. She was also pleased to report that one of her students was now editorial assistant on the 'Pony Magazine'.

Lynn Dudley left her post as Vice-Principal in December 1999 and joined Voluntary Service Overseas in an executive position and was posted to Cambodia. Lynn worked with COSA for several years as Coordinator.

One of our COSA members (Caroline Woolley - Ed.) attended the opening of the ill fated Millennium Dome on New Year's Eve 1999. It happened that her daughter was performing an aerial ballet at 150 ft up. This performance heralded 'The Show in the Dome' which ran for the length of 2000 and was enjoyed by anything up to six million visitors!

On November 15th a Copper Beech tree was planted as a lasting memorial to the students of 1937/38 who fell during World War II. Arranged by Reg Shattock: six members of the year attended.

2001. Editor Nan Eaves wrote about the disastrous effects of the national outbreak of Foot and Mouth Disease that had broken out in the early part of the year. This following the wettest year on record and an outbreak of Swine Fever in the eastern Counties.

The Principal told us that further 'out-centres' for Cannington had been established at Court Farm near Weston-s-Mare, at Cadbury Garden Centre in Congresbury and at East Lambrook Manor in south Somerset.. 'Saga' holidays now rent the main student accommodation block during the summer recess for their members holidaying in the Quantocks and West Somerset.

Television cameras followed a full-time student during his year of student life as a 'Fly on the Wall' documentary!

The 75th Anniversary Spinney was slowly maturing and access paths, gates and bridges had been added. The official 'Opening' of the Spinney is planned for 22nd September - the 80th birthday of the College, the ceremony to be performed by David Tremlett, Chairman to the Corporation (Governors).

2002. Sadly Miss K.D. Maddever died during February this year. Following a private family funeral in Cornwall a Memorial Service was held at St. Mary's Parish Church of Cannington on April 23rd. Many of her ex-students and colleagues attended. A fuller report appears in the 2002 magazine.

The Principal wrote about the changing nature of the type of student who now attends the College. Whereas in the early days students were almost exclusively from farming or horticultural backgrounds, this is not so prevalent these days. Age is no longer a barrier either - 66% of students being over the age of twenty-five! He referred back to the devastating 'on' effects of the outbreak of FMD in 2001 creating logistical problems for students whose homes were in restricted areas and who therefore could not attend College once they had gone home. The College farm was just outside a 'contiguous zone', and thus was not directly affected. On the farm an outbreak of 'Blue Ear' Disease has affected sow fertility and a distressing post-weaning disease has increased mortality in the little pigs to over 30%.

There is a piece from as ex-Dartmoor Prison inmate who through grit and determination was able to join the 1978/79 NCH course and as a result put his life back together. He had had to wait a couple of years in order to satisfy the Prison Authorities and those awarding him Grant aid, but he spent a totally happy time at the College and gained his Certificate at Distinction level.

2003. The Principal reported that there were now links with Bournemouth University and that the College now offers Foundation Degrees in ten subject areas and fourteen Certificates in Higher Education in land-based subjects. There were no reports from the farm this year or from the various departments.

Nan Eaves, the COSA Magazine Editor, mused on the emergence of Wind Farms, which seem to be causing much discussion. She pointed out that at one time the land must have been dotted with windmills (the old-fashioned sort) and also electricity pylons have been around for a long time.

Mr Jack Humphrey MBE (after whom the new engineering block was named) left this life in November 2002 at the age of 94. He had come to Somerset as District Officer of the National Union of Agricultural Workers and stayed.

This was the year that it became known that Cannington College was to be merged with Bridgwater College - the neighbouring Further Education College - with Fiona McMillan OBE at the helm. Ms McMillan had been asked by the College Corporation to join the College staff and work towards the planned merger which, if approved, will take place from 1st September 2004.

2004. In her letter to the Association Ms. McMillan assured COSA membership that they play a valuable role in the College and she was looking forward to meeting members at the earliest opportunity. She was also hoping that the College Open Day would be reinstated after an absence of three years.

Suggestions for a Web page were also made in order that a wider section of ex-students could be reached. It remains to be seen how realistic this will be, given that most of the membership are not computer literate!

There was a long collaboration with Somerset Young Farmers at this time to see what the College could offer in the way of courses which would match up with what the young farmers wanted in the way of learning. In the event it was not a good match! The Young Farmers wanted courses that lasted 3 hours and the College could only fund those that lasted 30 hours!

Again, no reports from the various departments.

2005. The magazine Editor, Nan Eaves, remarked on the unusual weather conditions that prevailed during the preceding year, culminating with the dreadful tsunami in the Far East. We had had the deluge at Boscastle and some northern towns had had 9-10 inches of rain in a few hours. Global warming is on its way?

Stuart Brookfield, Patron, remarked on how he looked forward to the new Glasshouse being built to replace the ones taken down so long ago. Very difficult for horti. students to study when there is nowhere for them to practise!

Fiona McMillan, now Principal of Cannington Centre for Land Based Studies, confirmed that Tom Williams had been appointed Head of Centre with four Section Leaders and Programme managers within each Section. Focus in horticulture is to be on the Heritage Walled Garden with a new glasshouse. The Animal Care Section will have a new building to be placed on the Downs. At Rodway the Pig Unit is to be improved and the Dairy Herd increased. A strong look at the needs of the Food industry will enhance existing student programmes an the Food Technology Section.

Gordon Fraser, erstwhile Chairman of Corporation commented: "We should all rejoice in Somerset and further afield in that it will continue to have a dynamic, land-based educational provision where it has always been - Cannington".

2006. It was noted that the final OFSTED monitoring visit after a long and difficult period for Cannington was that the "quality of teaching and learning has much improved".

Our Editor, Nan Eaves, remarked that she found it difficult to comprehend how such a practical industry as ours can be taught without the 'hands-on' experience that is gained through a complete year's cycle of weather experience - there not being a need for a year's practical experience before taking a course. In addition, because of so many restrictions placed through the 'Health and Safety Executive' a student when at College is further unable to gain the practical experience and 'feel' that our industry requires. It would be interesting to see how a College teaches sheep dog training without a dog or sheep!

In Conclusion. The Magazine throughout the years has continued to report information about old students, exchanges of views, finding folk thought to be lost and generally keeping the merry-go-round going round! The subject matter of articles is very varied - Cannington spawned a creative pond!

There are still ghosts of Gilbert and Sullivan performances in Clifford Hall; you can just about see Miss Hobbs and her 'ciggie' in the old dining room and maybe the breath of a lad disappearing homewards from the girls 'horseboxes'!

Somerset Farm Institute, Somerset College of Agriculture and Horticulture, Cannington College

College Staff & the Officers of the Old Students Association

Principals

T. Limond.   September 1921 to December 1921

J. Mackie M.A., BSc. 1922-1924

W.D.Hay OBE, BSc. 1924-1944

W.J.England NDA, NDD, 1944-1951

W.W.Ballardie BSc, NDD, 1951 - 1964

A.J.Marval MA, Dip.Rural Econ. (Oxon). NDA, NDD 1964 - 1967

P.H.Keen DFC, BSc. 1967 - 1988

D. Chapman 1988 - 1989

B. Gimbert BSc, NCA 1989 - 1995

R. Hinxman BSc, NDA. 1996-2003

Matrons

Miss H. Heywood	Miss M. Wilson
Mrs Brookes	Miss E.M. Hobbs MBE
Miss J. Wenham	Miss N. Heywood (see page 67)
Mrs Abrahams	Ms. Hazel Gould
Miss V. Stride	

Bursars

Mr M. Mallett : (until 1960s)

Mr I. Pilkington : (1960s onwards)

Caretakers

Mr G. Croaker   1921 - 1946

Mr I. Harmer

Mr. Tony Davey

Patrons of COSA

Capt. D.M. Wills	1928
Miss K.D.Maddever OBE	1969
Mr. Stuart Brookfield	2001

Presidents of COSA

Capt. D.M.Wills	1928
Miss K.D.Maddever OBE	1968
Mr. Ivor Crane	1990

COSA Chairmen

Miss M. Mackie	1928	Mrs J.Madge	1965
Mr I. J.Palmer	1931	Mr. D.M.Lawson	1966
Mr. Reg. Shattock	1946	Mrs K. Rogers	1967
Nesta Hawkins	1955	Mr. Ivor Crane	1972
Mrs. Nan Eaves	1957	Mr. Alan Brownsea	1978
D.J.Gunningham	1961	Mr. Roger Lane	1989
M. Vearncombe	1963		

(This may not be a complete list)

From 1998 there was no Chairman. The Association elected to be run as a group with two Coordinators appointed to oversee the gathering of Magazine material, to arrange the AGM and generally promote the Association. A Treasurer was appointed and together with the President and Patron the legal aspects of running the Association were covered.

NOTE ON THE NAME INDEX

As readers will have noticed, in the early days at Cannington students were addressed by their surname only, while all staff were graced with Miss or Mr. attached to their surnames.

In recent years, however, all staff and students have been recorded also by their first names, and sometimes even only by their first names. Moreover, to add to the confusion, perhaps there was a period when both systems were used,.

While the later egalitarian or "democratic" system no doubt pleased sensitive teen-agers, it makes for confusion in compiling an index.

Furthermore, in much of the material available, names have been recorded with some abandon: e.g: Haywood and Hayward; Deremond and Deyermond, and so on.

All the various forms of each surname have therefore been included in the index.

Name Index

Abrahams, Mrs, 192
Acland, Stan, 46, 97, 112, 176, 181, 182, 184, 185
Adams, Maurice, 136
Adams, 157
Adams, A.C. 170
Addison, 157
Addison, John, 173, 176, 179
Adlam, Janet, 59
Adlam, 158
Affran, Albert, 154
AH, 74
Aitken. A.W., 5, 14, 114, 130
Aldan, 156
Allen, 157
Allen, Paul, 173
Allery, Miss, 158
Allsup. E., Miss
Alvis, John, 78, 189
Anderson, C., 64
Angela, 73
Appleby, Gay, 148
Arnold, 156
Ash, 156
Ashley, Roy, Mr., 60
Atkins, Jim, 148
Atkinson, Jenny, 145
Attrill, 158
Aucott, 157
Austin, E.A.,vi, 42
Avery, 158
Ayres, Tim, 154
Baber, Kenneth, 108
Badcock, J.C., 42
Badman, C.R.J., 34
Baker, Ginger, 22
Baker, 157
Baker, S.A., 170
Baker, Chris, 178
Bakewell, ix
Baldwin, Bob, 147
Ball, Mr., 30, 157
Ballardie,W.W., 57, 99, 145. 147, 148, 154, 180, 181, 182, 183, 187, 192
Ballerdie, Robin, 74, 75
Baring, Lady, 17, 22
Barnes, Jill, 46
Barnes, David, 136
Barr, Miss, 179
Barry, 76
Bartholomew, 156
Bartlett, 45
Bartlett, Ruth, 145
Bartlett, R.G., 171
Bartlett, Cy., 176, 187, 188
Bartram, Richard, 154
Baskerville, W.G., 34
Bastable, 34
Bateman, Sue, 73
Bates, ix

Bates, Liz,. 46
Bates, R., 63
Bates, John, 176
Bayliss, George, 154
Beasley, Toby, 173
Beauchamp, John, 148
Beck, Ron, 141
Bell, Michael, 53, 141
Bell, Bob. 111
Bell, Miss, 147, 148
Bell, Geoff, 154
Bell, June, 175
Bennet, Mr., 59
Benson, Angie, 64
Berkley, Mr., 61, 62
Berridge, Goff, 115, 176, 185, 186
Berry Mr. 5, 29
Besant, 148
Betts, Claire, (Kellond), 148
Betty, 113
Bigge, Helen, 75
Bigwood, R., 170
Billingsley, John, ix
Billington, 130
Binnie, 156
Bird, R.C., 40
Bird, Ted, 154
B.J.B., 74
Blacker, Philip, 20
Blacker, W.H.G., 36
Boffey, Daniel, 80
Boller, M.,
Bolton, Arthur, 187
Bolwell, Miss, 157
Bonham-Carter, Victor, 186
Bonham-Carter, Basil, 186
Booth, Ken, 141
Booth, I.W., 170
Bootle-Wilbraham, 156
Bosker, 37
Botterell, 156
Bourke, 158
Boutflour, Robt., 106
Bowden, R., 20
Bowden, Derek, 178
Bowditch, 130
Bowering, Mrs., 30
Bowley, 36
Box, 37
Boyce, 157
Boyt, Jim, 147
Bracey, Alan, 94
Bragg, Gordon, 148
Braithwaite, 37
Brake, Nick, 59
Breckenridge, S.P.,170
Brewer, B.C., iv
Brice, Tony, 74
Briscoe, Paul, 154
Brittain, Miss, 12, 19, 30
Bromfield, 156

Brookes, Mrs, 192
Brooke-Wilkinson, H.,14
Brookes. S., Mrs. vi
Brookfield, 54, 61, 65, 82, 147, 148, 154, 179, 180, 181, 186, 191, 193
Brooks, Geoff, 136
Brooks, Clive, 154
Broom, Mr., 6, 621
Browen, Denley, 185
Brown, A.H.M., 34
Brown, Denley, 100
Brown, Sheila, 136
Brown, Monica, 136
Brown, Phil, 147
Brown, Hugh, 154
Brownsey, Alan, 104, 185
Bryan, John, 141
Bryant, Steve, 74, 189
Buffrey, Bill, 52
Buffrey, Bob, 141
Bulford, Mr J.B., 145, 147, 148, 175, 176, 180
Bulleid, 157
Bunchie, 14
Bunting, 158
Burchett, 158
Burden, Tim, 154
Burdett, 156
Burge, Tom, 14, 39, 114
Burgoine, Nick, 173
Burnham, 157
Burrell, Ron, 145
Burrough, H., 24
Burt, Mrs., 46, 54
Burton, Maria, 75
Busby, 156
Bush, Bunny, 14
Bush, Miss, 156
Butler, Gladys, 16
Butler, N., 63
Butler, Jean, 147
Butler, Peter, 154
Butler, 157
Butt, Miss, 156
Bynoth, 157
Bythell, 157
Cameron, B., 14
Campion, P., 61, 62
Candy, 157
Cann. J.H., vi, 1, 7
Cannall, Alan, 178
Capel, Mrs., 30
Capel, 61
Capcl, David, 73, 74, 116, 171, 178
Carlisle, Brian, 147
Carlisle, Mike, 154
Carnell, P., 170
Carp, Paul, 74
Carr, (Taylor), Pat, 148
Carver, 156
Caterer, Roy, 148

195

Place Index

Snowdrop Books

Queen Charlton Perambulation by GAJLoxton (Published 1999) ISBN 0 9537458 0 5

Somerset village history, 120 pages A4 paperback, comprehensive, many primary sources, 17 drawings, 47 photographs, 8 maps, 6 documents, 300 surnames indexed. (Queen Charlton was part of Keynsham Abbey estates before the Reformation, and then part of the Popham estates for 200 years).

Ston Easton Perambulation by GAJLoxton (Published 2000) ISBN 0 9537458 1 3

Somerset village history, 185 pages A4 paperback, comprehensive, mainly primary sources, 38 drawings, 12 photographs, 22 maps, 36 documents, 400 surnames indexed. Because of its mainly primary sources, especially the Hippisley Papers (DD/HI at Somerset Record Office) this is the most comprehensive of Snowdrop village histories.

Emborough Perambulation by GAJLoxton (Published 2002) ISBN 09537458 2 1

Somerset village history, 114 pages A4 paperback, comprehensive, mainly primary sources, 17 drawings, 16 photographs, 19 maps, 30 documents, 500 surnames indexed. Emborough was part of the Hippisley estate for 400 years.

Farming the Hungry Fifties by GAJLoxton (Published 2004) ISBN 0 9537458 3 X

1950s hands-on farm-management. 139 pages A4 paperback, 28 drawings, 31 photographs, 2 maps. Account by the farm manager covering ten years of the management of an 850 acre Somerset mixed heavy land farm near Frome, (including 1956 and 1957 NIAB Wheat Trials, a 1957 NAAS Farm Walk and a 1958 F&M Disease outbreak), with flashbacks to earlier farming and wartime aircrew memories of the author.

Forthcoming

Broughton (Hants) Concise Perambulation by GAJLoxton

Hampshire village history source. A4 Paperback. This work complements existing Broughton histories with names, facts and figures. It includes copies of manor rolls, the 1790 pre and post enclosure maps and awards, Land Tax lists and Tithe map and awards. More than 200 surnames indexed. By the founding tutor of the 1970s Broughton Local History Evening Class.

Hardington Perambulation   by GAJLoxton

Somerset village history. Brief history of a small (1000 acre) heavy land manor near Frome. A4 Paperback Few primary sources. Some maps, photographs and drawings.